Astronomy and Space Science

interactive SCIENCE

PEARSON

Boston, Massachusetts
Chandler, Arizona
Glenview, Illinois
Upper Saddle River, New Jersey

AUTHORS

You're an author!

As you write in this science book, your answers and personal discoveries will be recorded for you to keep, making this book unique to you. That is why you are one of the primary authors of this book.

✏️ **In the space below, print your name, school, town, and state. Then write a short autobiography that includes your interests and accomplishments.**

YOUR NAME

SCHOOL

TOWN, STATE

AUTOBIOGRAPHY

_____

_____

_____

_____

_____

_____

_____

Your Photo

Acknowledgments appear on pages 177–178, which constitute an extension of this copyright page.

ISBN-13: 978-0-13-368487-2
ISBN-10: 0-13-368487-3

18 17

●●● Astronomy and Space Science

interactive SCIENCE

ON THE COVER
A Big Repair Job
How do you repair a telescope that's floating in space? Send an astronaut! This astronaut helped repair the Hubble Space Telescope, or HST, in May 2009. He's shown here outside the space shuttle *Atlantis*, which brought the repair crew to the HST. The astronauts repaired, replaced, and adjusted the HST's instruments.

Program Authors

DON BUCKLEY, M.Sc.
Information and Communications Technology Director, The School at Columbia University, New York, New York
Mr. Buckley has been at the forefront of K–12 educational technology for nearly two decades. A founder of New York City Independent School Technologists (NYCIST) and long-time chair of New York Association of Independent Schools' annual IT conference, he has taught students on two continents and created multimedia and Internet-based instructional systems for schools worldwide.

ZIPPORAH MILLER, M.A.Ed.
Associate Executive Director for Professional Programs and Conferences, National Science Teachers Association, Arlington, Virginia
Associate executive director for professional programs and conferences at NSTA, Ms. Zipporah Miller is a former K–12 science supervisor and STEM coordinator for the Prince George's County Public School District in Maryland. She is a science education consultant who has overseen curriculum development and staff training for more than 150 district science coordinators.

MICHAEL J. PADILLA, Ph.D.
Associate Dean and Director, Eugene P. Moore School of Education, Clemson University, Clemson, South Carolina
A former middle school teacher and a leader in middle school science education, Dr. Michael Padilla has served as president of the National Science Teachers Association and as a writer of the National Science Education Standards. He is professor of science education at Clemson University. As lead author of the *Science Explorer* series, Dr. Padilla has inspired the team in developing a program that promotes student inquiry and meets the needs of today's students.

KATHRYN THORNTON, Ph.D.
Professor and Associate Dean, School of Engineering and Applied Science, University of Virginia, Charlottesville, Virginia
Selected by NASA in May 1984, Dr. Kathryn Thornton is a veteran of four space flights. She has logged over 975 hours in space, including more than 21 hours of extravehicular activity. As an author on the *Scott Foresman Science* series, Dr. Thornton's enthusiasm for science has inspired teachers around the globe.

MICHAEL E. WYSESSION, Ph.D.
Associate Professor of Earth and Planetary Science, Washington University, St. Louis, Missouri
An author on more than 50 scientific publications, Dr. Wysession was awarded the prestigious Packard Foundation Fellowship and Presidential Faculty Fellowship for his research in geophysics. Dr. Wysession is an expert on Earth's inner structure and has mapped various regions of Earth using seismic tomography. He is known internationally for his work in geoscience education and outreach.

Instructional Design Author

GRANT WIGGINS, Ed.D.
President, Authentic Education, Hopewell, New Jersey
Dr. Wiggins is a co-author with Jay McTighe of *Understanding by Design, 2nd Edition* (ASCD 2005). His approach to instructional design provides teachers with a disciplined way of thinking about curriculum design, assessment, and instruction that moves teaching from covering content to ensuring understanding.
UNDERSTANDING BY DESIGN® and UbD™ are trademarks of ASCD, and are used under license.

Planet Diary Author

JACK HANKIN
Science/Mathematics Teacher, The Hilldale School, Daly City, California Founder, Planet Diary Web site
Mr. Hankin is the creator and writer of Planet Diary, a science current events Web site. He is passionate about bringing science news and environmental awareness into classrooms and offers numerous Planet Diary workshops at NSTA and other events to train middle and high school teachers.

ELL Consultant

JIM CUMMINS, Ph.D.
Professor and Canada Research Chair, Curriculum, Teaching and Learning department at the University of Toronto
Dr. Cummins focuses on literacy development in multilingual schools and the role of technology in promoting student learning across the curriculum. *Interactive Science* incorporates essential research-based principles for integrating language with the teaching of academic content based on his instructional framework.

Reading Consultant

HARVEY DANIELS, Ph.D.
Professor of Secondary Education, University of New Mexico, Albuquerque, New Mexico
Dr. Daniels is an international consultant to schools, districts, and educational agencies. He has authored or coauthored 13 books on language, literacy, and education. His most recent works are *Comprehension and Collaboration: Inquiry Circles in Action* and *Subjects Matter: Every Teacher's Guide to Content-Area Reading.*

Contributing Writers

Edward Aguado, Ph.D.
Professor, Department of Geography
San Diego State University
San Diego, California

Elizabeth Coolidge-Stolz, M.D.
Medical Writer
North Reading, Massachusetts

Donald L. Cronkite, Ph.D.
Professor of Biology
Hope College
Holland, Michigan

Jan Jenner, Ph.D.
Science Writer
Talladega, Alabama

Linda Cronin Jones, Ph.D.
Associate Professor of Science and Environmental Education
University of Florida
Gainesville, Florida

T. Griffith Jones, Ph.D.
Clinical Associate Professor of Science Education
College of Education
University of Florida
Gainesville, Florida

Andrew C. Kemp, Ph.D.
Teacher
Jefferson County Public Schools
Louisville, Kentucky

Matthew Stoneking, Ph.D.
Associate Professor of Physics
Lawrence University
Appleton, Wisconsin

R. Bruce Ward, Ed.D.
Senior Research Associate
Science Education Department
Harvard-Smithsonian Center for Astrophysics
Cambridge, Massachusetts

Content Reviewers

Paul D. Beale, Ph.D.
Department of Physics
University of Colorado at Boulder
Boulder, Colorado

Jeff R. Bodart, Ph.D.
Professor of Physical Sciences
Chipola College
Marianna, Florida

Joy Branlund, Ph.D.
Department of Earth Science
Southwestern Illinois College
Granite City, Illinois

Marguerite Brickman, Ph.D.
Division of Biological Sciences
University of Georgia
Athens, Georgia

Bonnie J. Brunkhorst, Ph.D.
Science Education and Geological Sciences
California State University
San Bernardino, California

Michael Castellani, Ph.D.
Department of Chemistry
Marshall University
Huntington, West Virginia

Charles C. Curtis, Ph.D.
Research Associate Professor of Physics
University of Arizona
Tucson, Arizona

Diane I. Doser, Ph.D.
Department of Geological Sciences
University of Texas
El Paso, Texas

Rick Duhrkopf, Ph.D.
Department of Biology
Baylor University
Waco, Texas

Alice K. Hankla, Ph.D.
The Galloway School
Atlanta, Georgia

Mark Henriksen, Ph.D.
Physics Department
University of Maryland
Baltimore, Maryland

Chad Hershock, Ph.D.
Center for Research on Learning and Teaching
University of Michigan
Ann Arbor, Michigan

Jeremiah N. Jarrett, Ph.D.
Department of Biology
Central Connecticut State University
New Britain, Connecticut

Scott L. Kight, Ph.D.
Department of Biology
Montclair State University
Montclair, New Jersey

Jennifer O. Liang, Ph.D.
Department of Biology
University of Minnesota–Duluth
Duluth, Minnesota

Candace Lutzow-Felling, Ph.D.
Director of Education
The State Arboretum of Virginia
University of Virginia
Boyce, Virginia

Cortney V. Martin, Ph.D.
Virginia Polytechnic Institute
Blacksburg, Virginia

Joseph F. McCullough, Ph.D.
Physics Program Chair
Cabrillo College
Aptos, California

Heather Mernitz, Ph.D.
Department of Physical Science
Alverno College
Milwaukee, Wisconsin

Sadredin C. Moosavi, Ph.D.
Department of Earth and Environmental Sciences
Tulane University
New Orleans, Louisiana

David L. Reid, Ph.D.
Department of Biology
Blackburn College
Carlinville, Illinois

Scott M. Rochette, Ph.D.
Department of the Earth Sciences
SUNY College at Brockport
Brockport, New York

Karyn L. Rogers, Ph.D.
Department of Geological Sciences
University of Missouri
Columbia, Missouri

Laurence Rosenhein, Ph.D.
Department of Chemistry
Indiana State University
Terre Haute, Indiana

Sara Seager, Ph.D.
Department of Planetary Sciences and Physics
Massachusetts Institute of Technology
Cambridge, Massachusetts

Tom Shoberg, Ph.D.
Missouri University of Science and Technology
Rolla, Missouri

Patricia Simmons, Ph.D.
North Carolina State University
Raleigh, North Carolina

William H. Steinecker, Ph.D.
Research Scholar
Miami University
Oxford, Ohio

Paul R. Stoddard, Ph.D.
Department of Geology and Environmental Geosciences
Northern Illinois University
DeKalb, Illinois

John R. Villarreal, Ph.D.
Department of Chemistry
The University of Texas–Pan American
Edinburg, Texas

John R. Wagner, Ph.D.
Department of Geology
Clemson University
Clemson, South Carolina

Jerry Waldvogel, Ph.D.
Department of Biological Sciences
Clemson University
Clemson, South Carolina

Donna L. Witter, Ph.D.
Department of Geology
Kent State University
Kent, Ohio

Edward J. Zalisko, Ph.D.
Department of Biology
Blackburn College
Carlinville, Illinois

Museum of Science.

Special thanks to the Museum of Science, Boston, Massachusetts, and Ioannis Miaoulis, the Museum's president and director, for serving as content advisors for the technology and design strand in this program.

Earth, Moon, and Sun

 **Enter the Lab zone
for hands-on inquiry.**

Chapter Lab Investigation:
• Directed Inquiry: Reasons for the Seasons
• Open Inquiry: Reasons for the Seasons

Inquiry Warm-Ups: • Earth's Sky • What
Causes Day and Night? • What Factors
Affect Gravity? • How Does the Moon Move?
• When Is High Tide? • Why Do Craters Look
Different From Each Other?

Quick Labs: • Observing the Night Sky
• Watching the Sky • Sun Shadows • What's
Doing the Pulling? • Around and Around We
Go • Moon Phases • Eclipses • Modeling the
Moon's Pull of Gravity • Moonwatching

my science online

Go to MyScienceOnline.com to
interact with this chapter's content.
Keyword: Earth, Moon, and Sun

> **UNTAMED SCIENCE**
• Phased by the Moon!

> **PLANET DIARY**
• Earth, Moon, and Sun

> **INTERACTIVE ART**
•Constellations •Seasons and Earth's
Revolution •Solar and Lunar Eclipses

> **ART IN MOTION**
• Cause of Tides

> **VIRTUAL LAB**
• What Affects Gravity?

CHAPTER 2

Exploring Space

Lab zone® Enter the Lab zone for hands-on inquiry.

Chapter Lab Investigation:
• Directed Inquiry: Space Spinoffs
• Open Inquiry: Space Spinoffs

Inquiry Warm-Ups: • What Force Moves a Balloon? • Where on the Moon Did the Astronauts Land? • Using Space Science

Quick Labs: • History of Rockets • Be a Rocket Scientist • Modeling Multistage Rockets • Humans in Space • Which Tool Would You Use in Space? • Remote Control • What Do You Need to Survive in Space? • Useful Satellites

my science online.com

Go to MyScienceOnline.com to interact with this chapter's content.
Keyword: Exploring Space

> UNTAMED SCIENCE
• A Little Outer Space Here on Earth

> PLANET DIARY
• Exploring Space

> INTERACTIVE ART
• Multistage Rocket • Build an Orbiter • Space Spinoffs

> VIRTUAL LAB
• Get a Rocket Into Orbit

CONTENTS

Lab zone® Enter the Lab zone for hands-on inquiry.

Chapter Lab Investigation:
• Directed Inquiry: Speeding Around the Sun
• Open Inquiry: Speeding Around the Sun

Inquiry Warm-Ups: • What Is at the Center? • How Big Is Earth? • How Can You Safely Observe the Sun? • Ring Around the Sun • How Big Are the Planets? • Collecting Micrometeorites

Quick Labs: • Going Around in Circles • A Loopy Ellipse • Clumping Planets • Layers of the Sun • Viewing Sunspots • Characteristics of the Inner Planets • Greenhouse Effect • Density Mystery • Make a Model of Saturn • Changing Orbits

my science online.com

Go to MyScienceOnline.com to interact with this chapter's content.
Keyword: The Solar System

> **UNTAMED SCIENCE**
• 100 Meters to Neptune

> **PLANET DIARY**
• The Solar System

> **INTERACTIVE ART**
• Objects of the Solar System • Anatomy of the Sun

> **ART IN MOTION**
• Formation of the Solar System

> **VIRTUAL LAB**
• Why Isn't Pluto a Planet?

Stars, Galaxies, and the Universe

CHAPTER 4

Lab zone Enter the Lab zone for hands-on inquiry.

Chapter Lab Investigation:
• Directed Inquiry: Design and Build a Telescope
• Open Inquiry: Design and Build a Telescope

Inquiry Warm-Ups: • How Does Distance Affect an Image? • Stringing Along • How Stars Differ • What Determines How Long Stars Live? • Why Does the Milky Way Look Hazy? • How Does the Universe Expand?

Quick Labs: • Observing a Continuous Spectrum • How Far Is That Star? • Measuring the Universe • Star Bright • Interpreting the H-R Diagram • Life Cycle of Stars • Death of a Star • Planets Around Other Stars • A Spiral Galaxy • Future of the Universe

my science online.com

Go to MyScienceOnline.com to interact with this chapter's content. Keyword: Stars, Galaxies, and the Universe

PLANET DIARY
• Stars, Galaxies, and the Universe

INTERACTIVE ART
• Universe at Different Scales • Lives of Stars • Refracting and Reflecting Telescopes

ART IN MOTION
• Expanding Universe

REAL-WORLD INQUIRY
• How Can Light Help You Find Life?

interactive SCIENCE

This is your book. You can write in it!

HOW CAN WIND KEEP YOUR LIGHTS ON?

THE BIG ? **What are some of Earth's energy sources?**

This man is repairing a wind turbine at a wind farm in Texas. Most wind turbines are at least 30 meters off the ground where the winds are fast. Wind speed and blade length help determine the best way to capture the wind and turn it into power. **Develop Hypotheses** Why do you think people are working to increase the amount of power we get from wind?

Wind energy collected by the turbine does not cause air pollution.

> UNTAMED SCIENCE Watch the **Untamed Science** video to learn more about energy resources.

174 Energy Resources

THE BIG ?

Get Engaged!

At the start of each chapter, you will see two questions: an Engaging Question and the Big Question. Each chapter's Big Question will help you start thinking about the Big Ideas of Science. Look for the Big Q symbol throughout the chapter!

Untamed Science™

Follow the Untamed Science video crew as they travel the globe exploring the Big Ideas of Science.

Interact with your textbook.   Interact with inquiry.   Interact online.

Build Reading, Inquiry, and Vocabulary Skills

In every lesson you will learn new ꙮ Reading and ▲ Inquiry skills. These skills will help you read and think like a scientist. Vocabulary skills will help you communicate effectively and uncover the meaning of words.

Go Online!

Look for the MyScienceOnline.com technology options. At MyScienceOnline.com you can immerse yourself in amazing virtual environments, get extra practice, and even blog about current events in science.

Explore the Key Concepts.

Each lesson begins with a series of Key Concept questions. The interactivities in each lesson will help you understand these concepts and Unlock the Big Question.

MY PLANET DIARY

At the start of each lesson, My Planet Diary will introduce you to amazing events, significant people, and important discoveries in science or help you to overcome common misconceptions about science concepts.

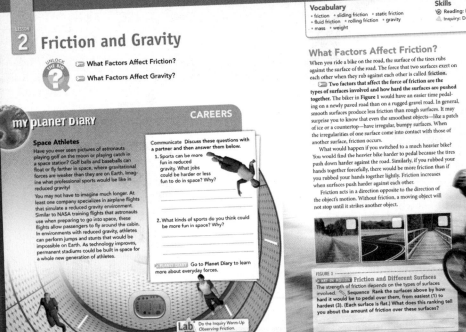

Explain what you know.

Look for the pencil. When you see it, it's time to interact with your book and demonstrate what you have learned.

apply it!

Elaborate further with the Apply It activities. This is your opportunity to take what you've learned and apply those skills to new situations.

Lab Zone

Look for the Lab zone triangle. This means it's time to do a hands-on inquiry lab. In every lesson, you'll have the opportunity to do a hands-on inquiry activity that will help reinforce your understanding of the lesson topic.

...ertile area becomes depleted ...become a desert. The ...eas that previously were ...t uh fih KAY shun). ...te. For example, a **drought** ...alls in an area. During ...r, the exposed soil easily ...y cattle and sheep and ...se desertification, too. ...People cannot grow crops ...n has occurred. As a result, ...Desertification is severe in ...there are moving to the ...rt themselves on the land.

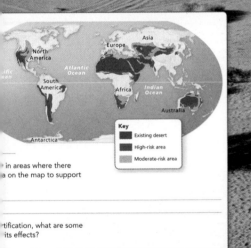

...in areas where there ...a on the map to support

...tification, what are some ...its effects?

Land Reclamation Fortunately, it is possible to replace land damaged by erosion or mining. The process of restoring an area of land to a more productive state is called **land reclamation.** In addition to restoring land for agriculture, land reclamation can restore habitats for wildlife. Many different types of land reclamation projects are currently underway all over the world. But it is generally more difficult and expensive to restore damaged land and soil than it is to protect those resources in the first place. In some cases, the land may not return to its original state.

FIGURE 4 ....
Land Reclamation
These pictures show land before and after it was mined.

✎ **Communicate** Below the pictures, write a story about what happened to the land.

Assess Your Understanding

1a. Review Subsoil has (less/more) plant and animal matter than topsoil.

b. Explain What can happen to soil if plants are removed?

c. Apply Concepts ... that could prev... land reclam...

Lab zone — Do the Quick Lab Modeling So...

got **it?**

○ I get it! Now I know that soil management is important becau...

○ I need extra help with
Go to MY SCIENCE COACH online for help with this subject.

got it?

Evaluate Your Progress.

After answering the Got It question, think about how you're doing. Did you get it or do you need a little help? Remember, MY SCIENCE COACH is there for you if you need extra help.

Explore the Big Question.

At one point in the chapter, you'll have the opportunity to take all that you've learned to further explore the Big Question.

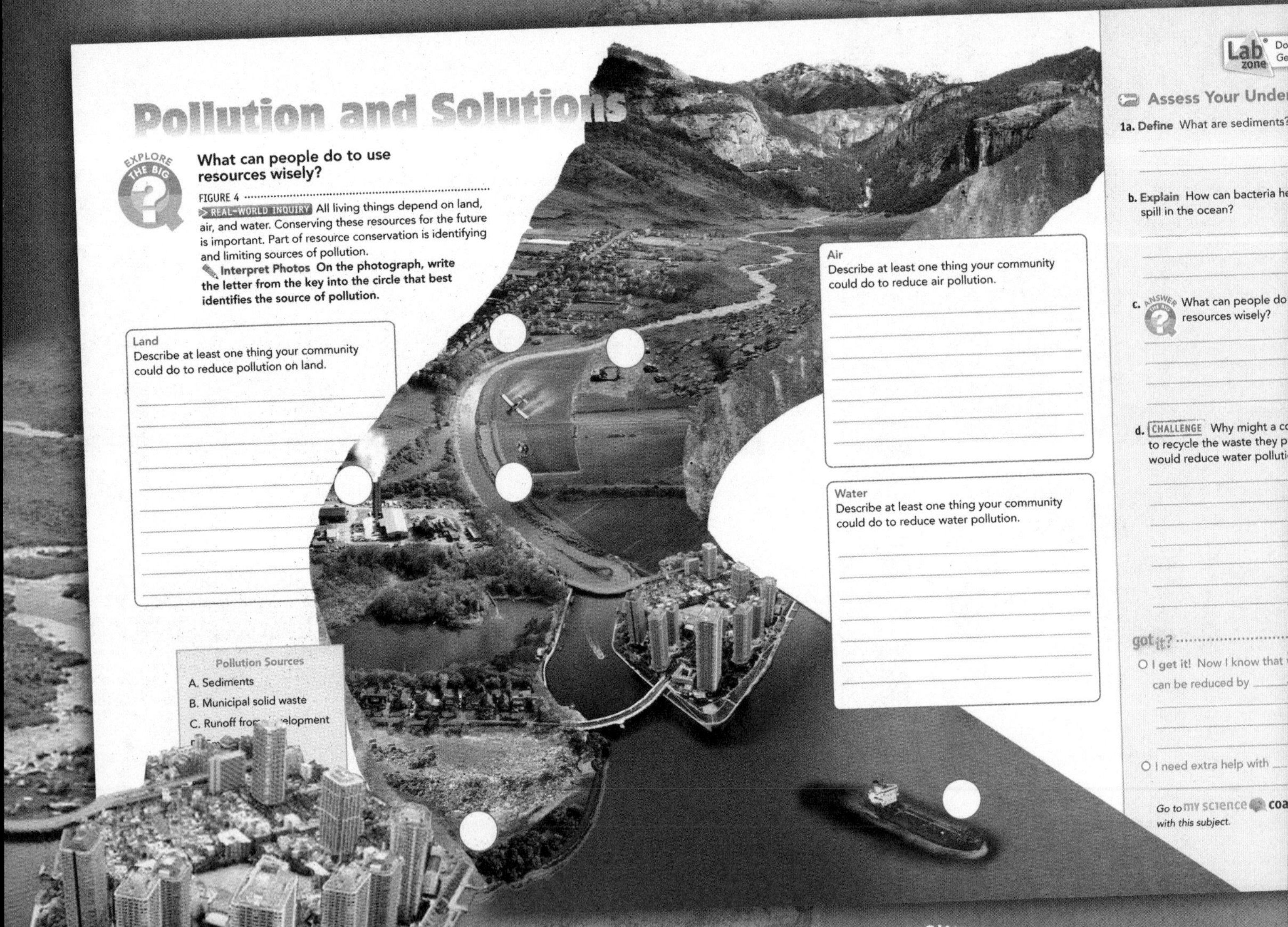

Pollution and Solutions

What can people do to use resources wisely?

FIGURE 4

> REAL-WORLD INQUIRY All living things depend on land, air, and water. Conserving these resources for the future is important. Part of resource conservation is identifying and limiting sources of pollution.

Interpret Photos On the photograph, write the letter from the key into the circle that best identifies the source of pollution.

Land
Describe at least one thing your community could do to reduce pollution on land.

Air
Describe at least one thing your community could do to reduce air pollution.

Water
Describe at least one thing your community could do to reduce water pollution.

Pollution Sources

A. Sediments

B. Municipal solid waste

C. Runoff from development

Lab Do
zone Ge

🔖 **Assess Your Under**

1a. Define What are sediments?

b. Explain How can bacteria he
spill in the ocean?

c. ANSWER What can people do
resources wisely?

d. CHALLENGE Why might a co
to recycle the waste they p
would reduce water polluti

got it?

○ I get it! Now I know that
can be reduced by _____

○ I need extra help with ____

Go to MY SCIENCE 🔖 coa
with this subject.

Answer the Big Question.

Now it's time to show what you know and answer the Big Question.

Review What You've Learned.

Use the Chapter Study Guide to review the
Big Question and prepare for the test.

Practice Taking Tests.

Apply the Big Question and take
a practice test in standardized
test format.

INTERACT... WITH YOUR TEXTBOOK...

Go to **MyScienceOnline.com** and immerse yourself in amazing virtual environments.

> THE BIG QUESTION

Each online chapter starts with a Big Question. Your mission is to unlock the meaning of this Big Question as each science lesson unfolds.

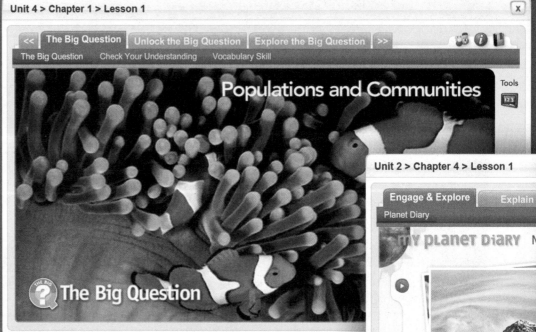

Unit 4 > Chapter 1 > Lesson 1

The Big Question | Unlock the Big Question | Explore the Big Question | >>
The Big Question   Check Your Understanding   Vocabulary Skill

Populations and Communities

Tools

The Big Question

Unit 2 > Chapter 4 > Lesson 1

Engage & Explore | Explain
Planet Diary

my planet Diary

> VOCAB FLASH CARDS

Practice chapter vocabulary with interactive flash cards. Each card has an image, definitions in English and Spanish, and space for your own notes.

Unit 4 > Chapter 1 > Lesson 1

The Big Question | Unlock the Big Question | Explore the Big Question | >>
The Big Question   Untamed Science   Check Your Understanding   Vocabulary Skill   Vocabulary Flashcards

Vocabulary Flashcards   Tools

Card List   Create-a-Card   10 Cards Left   Test Me
Lesson Cards   My Cards

Birth Rate
Carrying Capacity   Science Vocabulary
Commensalism
Community   Term: **Community**
Competition
Death Rate   Definition: All the different populations that live
Ecology   together in a particular area.
Ecosystem
Emigration
Habitat   View Spanish
Host
Immigration   Add Notes
Limiting Factor
                                           Card 5 of

Unit 6 > Chapter 1 > Lesson

Engage & Explore | Ex
Apply It   Directed Virtual Lab

Color in Light

Unit 6 > Chapter 1 > Lesson 1

Engage & Explore | Explain | Elaborate | Evaluate
Apply It   Do the Math   Art in Motion   Interactive Art   Real World Inquiry

The Nebraska Plains

▶ Bald Eagle
   Information   Media

Haliaeetus leucocephalus
Bald Eagles are 80-95 cm tall with a wingspan of 180-230 cm. These birds are born with all brown feathers but grow white feathers on their head, neck, and tail.

Layers List   ▲ Show

Next
22 of 22
Back

> INTERACTIVE ART

At MyScienceOnline.com, many of the beautiful visuals in your book become interactive so you can extend your learning.

interactive SCIENCE

GO ONLINE

my science online.com ▸ Populations and Communities ▸ PLANET DIARY ▸ LAB ZONE ▸ VIRTUAL LAB

C + 🌐 http://www.myscienceonline.com/

▸ PLANET DIARY

My Planet Diary online is the place to find more information and activities related to the topic in the lesson.

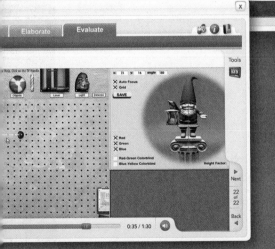

Elaborate | Evaluate

Everest   Tools

Still Growing! Mount Everest in the Himalayas is the highest mountain on Earth. Climbers who reach the peak stand 8,850 meters above sea level. You might think that mountains never change. But forces inside Earth push Mount Everest at least several millimeters higher each year. Over time, Earth's forces slowly but constantly lift, stretch, bend, and break Earth's crust in dramatic ways!

Planet Diary Go to Planet Diary to learn more about forces in the Earth's crust.

Next

22 of 22

Back

Find Your Chapter

1 Go to www.myscienceonline.com.

2 Log in with username and password.

3 Click on your program and select your chapter.

Keyword Search

1 Go to www.myscienceonline.com.

2 Log in with username and password.

3 Click on your program and select Search.

4 Enter the keyword (from your book) in the search box.

Other Content Available Online

▸ **UNTAMED SCIENCE** Follow these young scientists through their amazing online video blogs as they travel the globe in search of answers to the Big Questions of Science.

▸ **MY SCIENCE COACH** Need extra help? My Science Coach is your personal online study partner. My Science Coach is a chance for you to get more practice on key science concepts. There you can choose from a variety of tools that will help guide you through each science lesson.

▸ **MY READING WEB** Need extra reading help on a particular science topic? At My Reading Web you will find a choice of reading selections targeted to your specific reading level.

▸ VIRTUAL LAB

Get more practice with realistic virtual labs. Manipulate the variables on-screen and test your hypothesis.

? BIG IDEAS OF SCIENCE

Have you ever worked on a jigsaw puzzle? Usually a puzzle has a theme that leads you to group the pieces by what they have in common. But until you put all the pieces together you can't solve the puzzle. Studying science is similar to solving a puzzle. The big ideas of science are like puzzle themes. To understand big ideas, scientists ask questions. The answers to those questions are like pieces of a puzzle. Each chapter in this book asks a big question to help you think about a big idea of science. By answering the big questions, you will get closer to understanding the big idea.

✎ **Before you read each chapter, write about what you know and what more you'd like to know.**

BIGIDEA
Earth is part of a system of objects that orbit the sun.

What do you already know about Earth and the other objects in the solar system? ✎ **What more would you like to know?**

_____
_____
_____
_____

Big Questions

❓ How do Earth, the moon, and the sun interact? Chapter 1

❓ Why are objects in the solar system different from each other? Chapter 3

✎ **After reading the chapters, write what you have learned about the Big Idea.**

_____
_____
_____
_____
_____
_____

Jupiter, its moons, and Earth are all parts of the solar system. Each of them is held in its orbit by gravity.

Science, technology, and society affect each other.

Astronauts have developed new tools that can be used in space. Some of these tools also make life easier on Earth.

What do you already know about how society and technology affect each other? ✎ **What more would you like to know?**

_____

_____

_____

_____

Big Question

❓ How does exploring space benefit people on Earth? Chapter 2

✎ **After reading the chapter, write what you have learned about the Big Idea.**

_____

_____

_____

The universe is very old, very large, and constantly changing.

This galaxy, visible near the Big Dipper, is so far away that light from it takes 12 million years to reach Earth!

What do you already know about the universe? ✎ **What more would you like to know?**

_____

_____

_____

_____

Big Question

❓ How do astronomers learn about distant objects in the universe? Chapter 4

✎ **After reading the chapter, write what you have learned about the Big Idea.**

_____

_____

_____

WHAT'S HAPPENING TO THE MOON?

How do Earth, the moon, and the sun interact?

This photograph shows a series of images of the moon taken over the course of an evening. Why do you think the moon looks different in each image?
⊿Develop Hypotheses **Explain what you think happened during the period of time shown in the photograph.**

_____

_____

_____

_____

_____

_____

_____

> UNTAMED SCIENCE Watch the **Untamed Science** video to learn more about the moon.

Earth, Moon, and Sun

Getting Started

Check Your Understanding

1. **Background** Read the paragraph below and then answer the question.

Santiago is studying a globe. He sees that Earth has North and South poles. The globe **rotates** around a line through its center between the two poles. Another line called the **equator** divides Earth into two halves, the **Northern Hemisphere** and the **Southern Hemisphere.**

To **rotate** is to spin in place around a central line, or axis.

The **equator** is the imaginary line that divides Earth into two halves, the **Northern Hemisphere** and the **Southern Hemisphere.**

• Where is the equator found?

_____

_____

> **MY READING WEB** If you had trouble answering the question above, visit **My Reading Web** and type in **Earth, Moon, and Sun.**

Vocabulary Skill

Identify Multiple Meanings Words you use every day may have different meanings in science. Look at the different meanings of the words below.

Word	Everyday Meaning	Scientific Meaning
weight	*n.* a heavy object used for exercise **Example:** The athlete lifted *weights* to build strength.	*n.* a measure of the force of gravity on an object **Example:** The object's *weight* was 10 newtons.
force	*v.* to use power to make someone do something **Example:** She had to *force* herself to get up early.	*n.* a push or pull exerted on an object **Example:** You exert *force* when you open and close a door.

2. **Quick Check** Circle the sentence below that uses the scientific meaning of *force*.

• The *force* of gravity holds objects in their orbits.

• Her parents are trying to *force* her to get a job.

solstice

inertia

phase

solar eclipse

Chapter Preview

LESSON 1
- satellite • planet • meteor
- comet • star • constellation
- ⟳ Identify the Main Idea
- △ Predict

LESSON 2
- axis • rotation • revolution
- orbit • calendar • solstice
- equinox
- ⟳ Sequence
- △ Infer

LESSON 3
- force • gravity
- law of universal gravitation
- mass • weight • inertia
- Newton's first law of motion
- ⟳ Ask Questions
- △ Draw Conclusions

LESSON 4
- phase • eclipse • solar eclipse
- umbra • penumbra
- lunar eclipse
- ⟳ Relate Text and Visuals
- △ Make Models

LESSON 5
- tide • spring tide • neap tide
- ⟳ Relate Cause and Effect
- △ Observe

LESSON 6
- maria • crater • meteoroid
- ⟳ Compare and Contrast
- △ Develop Hypotheses

> VOCAB FLASH CARDS For extra help with vocabulary, visit **Vocab Flash Cards** and type in *Earth, Moon, and Sun.*

The Sky From Earth

UNLOCK THE BIG ?

🔑 **What Can You See in the Night Sky?**

🔑 **How Do Objects in the Sky Appear to Move?**

my pLaneT DiaRY

BIOGRAPHY

Communicate Discuss Aryabhata's discoveries with a partner. Then answer the questions below.

1. What did Aryabhata infer about the motion of Earth?

_____

_____

_____

Watching the Stars

When you look up at the night sky, what questions do you ask yourself? Do you wonder why the stars seem to move, or why the moon shines? Aryabhata (ar yah BAH tah) was an early Indian astronomer who thought about these questions. He was born in India in A.D. 476.

Many historians think that Aryabhata realized that the stars appear to move from east to west because Earth rotates from west to east. He also wrote that the moon and the planets shine because they reflect light from the sun. And he made all these inferences using just his eyes and his mind. The first telescopes wouldn't come along for more than a thousand years!

2. What questions do you think about when you look at stars, the moon, or the planets?

_____

_____

_____

▶ PLANET DIARY Go to **Planet Diary** to learn more about the night sky.

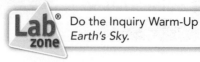

Lab zone® Do the Inquiry Warm-Up *Earth's Sky.*

Vocabulary
- satellite • planet • meteor
- comet • star • constellation

Skills
↩ Reading: Identify the Main Idea
⚠ Inquiry: Predict

What Can You See in the Night Sky?

Depending on how dark the sky is where you are, you might see 2,000 or 3,000 stars using just your eyes. 🔑 On a clear night, you may see stars, the moon, planets, meteors, and comets.

Moon About half of every month, Earth's moon outshines everything else in the night sky. The moon is Earth's only natural satellite. A **satellite** is a body that orbits a planet.

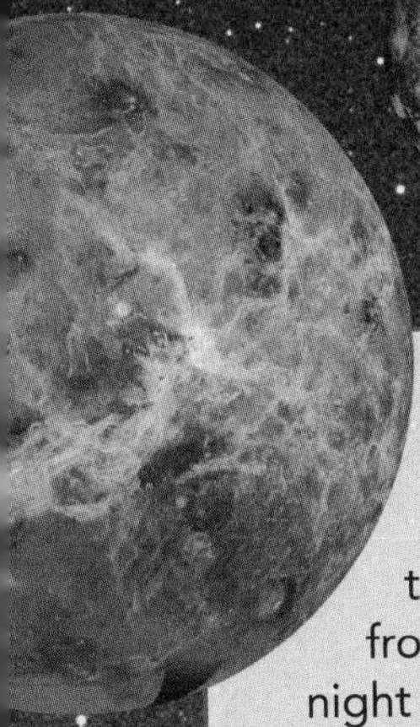

Planets You may see objects that move from night to night against the background stars. These are planets. A **planet** is an object that orbits the sun, is large enough to have become rounded by its own gravity, and has cleared the area of its orbit. There are eight planets in the solar system. Five are visible from Earth without a telescope: Mercury, Venus, Mars, Jupiter, and Saturn.

Meteors and Comets Have you ever seen a "shooting star"? These sudden bright streaks are called **meteors.** A meteor is the streak of light produced when a small object burns up entering Earth's atmosphere. You can see a meteor on almost any night. Comets are rarer. A **comet** is a cold mixture of dust and ice that gives up a long trail of light as it approaches the sun.

Stars Stars appear as tiny points of light. However, scientists infer that a **star** is a giant ball of hot gas, mainly composed of hydrogen and helium. As seen from Earth, the positions of stars relative to each other do not seem to change.

FIGURE 1 ·····························
These photos show examples of stars, planets, and other objects.

✏ **Observe** What can you observe about the objects shown on this page? Include at least two different objects.

_____

_____

_____

_____

_____

5

Constellations

For thousands of years humans have seen patterns in groups of stars and given names to them. 🔑 **A constellation is a pattern or group of stars that people imagined to represent a figure, animal, or object.** Astronomers also use the word *constellation* for an area of the sky and all the objects in that area.

Different cultures have identified different constellations. In Western culture, there are 88 constellations. Most constellation names used today come from the ancient Greeks, who probably took them from the Egyptians and Mesopotamians.

Some constellations' names come from Latin. The constellation Leo, for example, is named from the Latin word meaning "lion." Some constellations are named for people or animals in Greek myths. You may have read some of these myths in school. Do the names *Pegasus* or *Perseus* sound familiar? They are mythological characters and also constellations.

FIGURE 2 ....

> INTERACTIVE ART How to Use a Star Chart
To use a star chart at night, follow these steps.

1. Choose the chart that fits your location and season. This is a summer chart for the Northern Hemisphere. (There are charts for the other seasons in the Appendix.)

2. Hold the chart upright in front of you. Turn the chart so the label at the bottom matches the direction you face. (*Hint:* If you are looking at the Big Dipper, you are looking north.)

3. Hold the chart at eye level. Compare the figures on the bottom half of the chart to the sky in front of you.

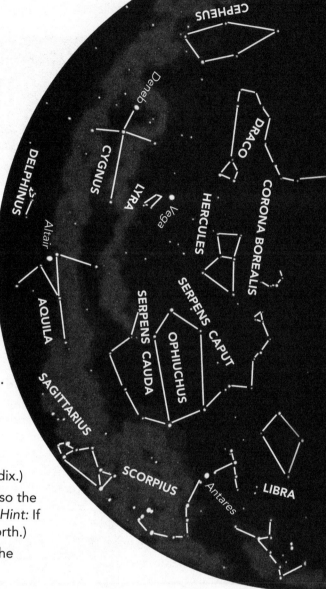

Eastern Horizon

Southern Horizon

apply it!

❶ Interpret Diagrams Find these constellations in **Figure 2**. Then write each constellation's name by its picture.

❷ CHALLENGE Choose another constellation from **Figure 2**. What does it represent? Do research to find out.

_____

_____

_____

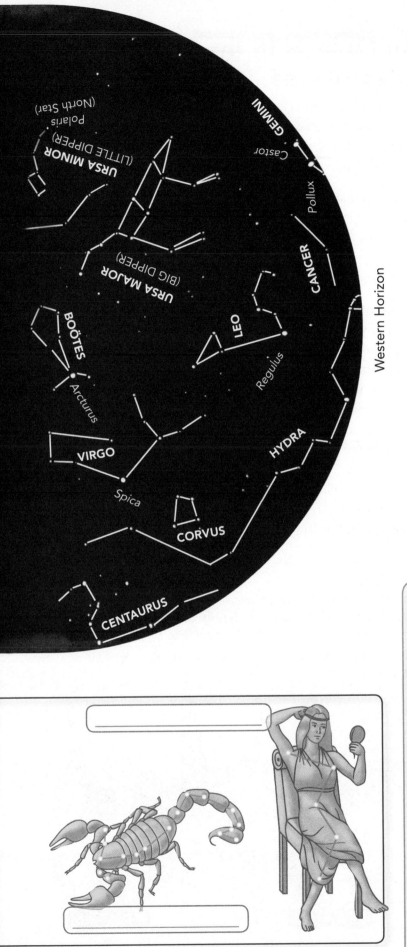

Northern Horizon

Western Horizon

Polaris (North Star)

URSA MINOR (LITTLE DIPPER)

GEMINI

Castor

Pollux

URSA MAJOR (BIG DIPPER)

CANCER

BOÖTES

LEO

Arcturus

Regulus

VIRGO

HYDRA

Spica

CORVUS

CENTAURUS

Finding Constellations

A star chart, like the one shown in **Figure 2,** can help you find constellations in the night sky. Read the instructions for how to use the chart. It may seem a little strange at first, but with some practice, these charts are easy to use. Here is one tip to help you get started.

You can probably recognize the Big Dipper. This group of stars is actually not a constellation itself. It is part of the constellation Ursa Major, or the Great Bear. The two stars at the end of the dipper's "bowl" are called the Pointers.

Picture an imaginary line between those two stars. If you continue it away from the "bowl," the first fairly bright star you'll reach is called Polaris (po LA ris). Polaris is commonly called the North Star. It is located close to the sky's North Pole.

In the Appendix, you can find star charts for all four seasons. Take one outside on a clear night and see what you can find!

Lab zone® Do the Quick Lab *Observing the Night Sky.*

Assess Your Understanding

got it? ....

O **I get it!** Now I know that objects visible in the night sky include _____

_____

_____

_____

O **I need extra help with** _____

_____

_____

Go to MY SCIENCE ⬤ COACH *online for help with this subject.*

How Do Objects in the Sky Appear to Move?

Stars, planets, and other objects appear to move over time. They do move in space, but those actual motions and their apparent, or visible, motions may be very different. 🔑 **The apparent motion of objects in the sky depends on the motions of Earth.**

Star Motions Stars generally appear to move from east to west through the night. As Aryabhata thought, this apparent motion is actually caused by Earth turning from west to east. The sun's apparent motion during the day is also caused by Earth's motion. **Figure 3** shows how this kind of apparent motion occurs.

Seasonal Changes Constellations and star patterns remain the same year after year, but which ones you can see varies from season to season. For example, you can find Orion in the eastern sky on winter evenings. But by spring, you'll see Orion in the west, disappearing below the horizon shortly after sunset.

These seasonal changes are caused by Earth's orbit around the sun. Each night, the position of most stars shifts slightly to the west. Soon you no longer see stars once visible in the west, and other stars appear in the east.

There are a few constellations that you can see all year long. These are the ones closest to the North Star. As Earth rotates, these constellations never appear to rise or set.

✏️ **Identify the Main Idea**
Underline the main idea in the paragraph called Star Motions.

FIGURE 3 ···

Opposite Motions

The restaurant on top of Seattle's Space Needle rotates much as Earth does. The restaurant turns in one direction, which makes objects outside appear to move in the opposite direction.

▲ **Predict** Draw the mountain as it would appear at each time shown.

Motion of restaurant

6:00 P.M.   6:35 P.M.   7:20 P.M.

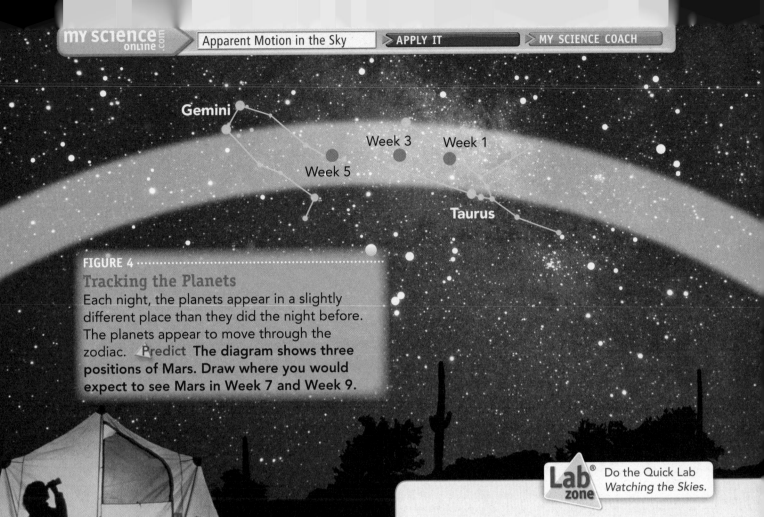

Gemini

Week 3   Week 1

Week 5

Taurus

FIGURE 4 ....

Tracking the Planets

Each night, the planets appear in a slightly different place than they did the night before. The planets appear to move through the zodiac. Predict **The diagram shows three positions of Mars. Draw where you would expect to see Mars in Week 7 and Week 9.**

Lab zone ® Do the Quick Lab *Watching the Skies.*

Planets Planets appear to move against the background of stars, as shown in **Figure 4.** Because the planets all orbit the sun in about the same plane, they appear to move through a narrow band in the sky. This band is called the zodiac. It includes constellations such as Taurus, Leo, and Virgo.

Some planets, when they are visible, can be seen all night long. Mars, Jupiter, and Saturn are all farther from the sun than Earth is. Sometimes, Earth passes between them and the sun. When this occurs, the planets are visible after sunset, once the sun's bright light no longer blocks the view.

You can see Venus and Mercury only in the evening or morning. They are closer to the sun than Earth, and so they always appear close to the sun. Venus is the brightest object in the night sky, other than the moon. Mercury appears low in the sky and is visible for a limited time around sunrise or sunset.

🔑 **Assess Your Understanding**

1a. Explain Objects in the sky appear to move from _____ to _____ because Earth turns from _____ to _____

b. Make Generalizations What determines whether a planet is visible all night long?

_____

_____

_____

_____

got it? ....

○ **I get it!** Now I know that objects in the sky appear to move _____

_____

_____

○ **I need extra help with** _____

Go to **my science COACH** *online for help with this subject.*

9

Earth in Space

UNLOCK THE BIG ?

🔑 **How Does Earth Move?**

🔑 **What Causes Seasons?**

my planet diary

The Seasons

Misconception: The seasons change because Earth's distance from the sun changes.

Fact: Seasons are the result of Earth's tilted axis.

Evidence: Earth's distance from the sun does change, but that's not why Earth has seasons. If that were the cause, people in the Northern and Southern hemispheres would have the same seasons at the same time. Instead, seasons in the Northern and Southern hemispheres are reversed. As Earth moves around the sun, sometimes the Northern Hemisphere is tilted toward the sun. At other times the Southern Hemisphere is tilted toward the sun.

January 21

where are you and what are you doing today?

MISCONCEPTION

Before you read the rest of this lesson, answer the questions below.

1. Why are summers generally warmer than winters?

_____

_____

_____

_____

2. Where on Earth is the tilt of Earth least likely to affect seasons? Why?

_____

_____

_____

_____

> **PLANET DIARY** Go to **Planet Diary** to learn more about Earth's motions.

Lab zone® Do the Inquiry Warm-Up *What Causes Day and Night?*

Vocabulary
- axis • rotation • revolution • orbit
- calendar • solstice • equinox

Skills
- Reading: Sequence
- Inquiry: Infer

How Does Earth Move?

Until a few hundred years ago, most people thought that Earth stood still and the sun, moon, and stars moved around it. But today, scientists know that Earth itself moves and that objects seem to move across the sky because of Earth's motion. **Earth moves in space in two major ways: rotation and revolution.**

Rotation The imaginary line that passes through Earth's center and the North and South poles is Earth's **axis.** The spinning of Earth on its axis is called **rotation.**

Earth's rotation causes day and night, as you can see in **Figure 1.** As Earth rotates eastward, the sun appears to move west across the sky. As Earth continues to turn to the east, the sun appears to set in the west. Sunlight can't reach the side of Earth facing away from the sun, so it is night there. It takes Earth about 24 hours to rotate once. As you know, each 24-hour cycle of day and night is called a day.

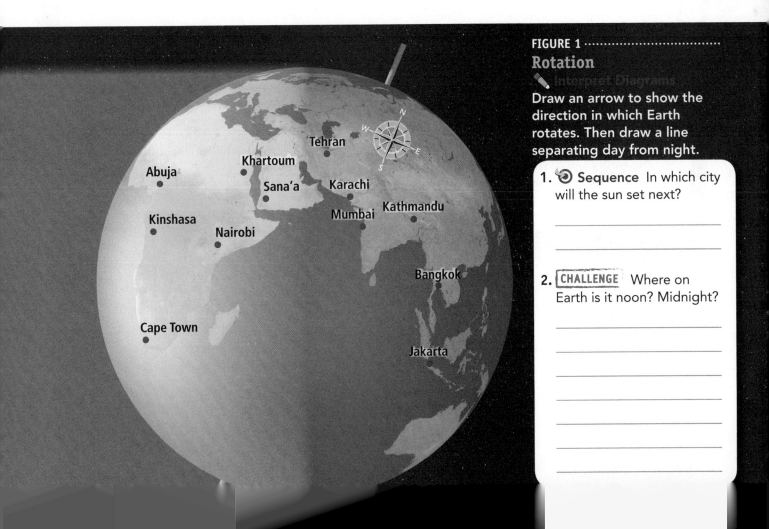

FIGURE 1
Rotation

Interpret Diagrams
Draw an arrow to show the direction in which Earth rotates. Then draw a line separating day from night.

1. **Sequence** In which city will the sun set next?

_____

_____

2. CHALLENGE Where on Earth is it noon? Midnight?

_____

_____

_____

_____

_____

_____

Revolution In addition to rotating, Earth travels around the sun. **Revolution** is the movement of one object around another. One revolution of Earth around the sun is called a year. Earth's path, or **orbit,** is a slightly elongated circle, or ellipse. Earth's orbit brings the planet closest to the sun in January.

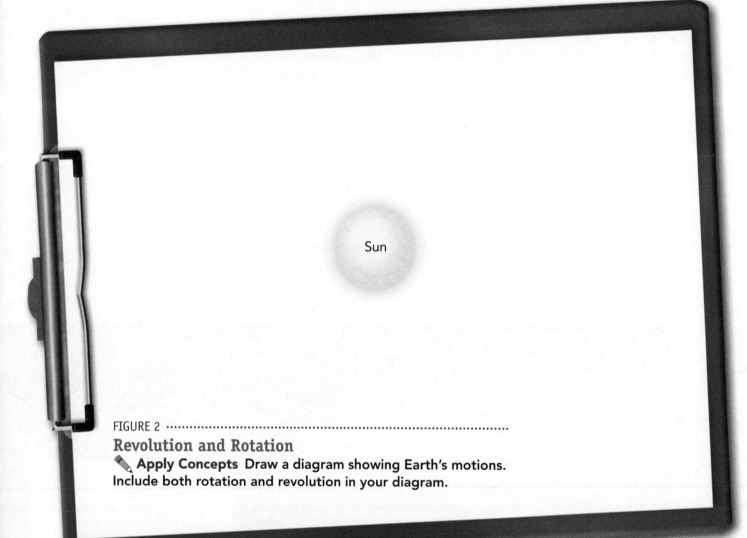

Sun

FIGURE 2 ···
Revolution and Rotation
✎ **Apply Concepts** Draw a diagram showing Earth's motions. Include both rotation and revolution in your diagram.

✎
⟳ **Sequence** Which calendar discussed in this section was developed most recently?

Calendars
People of many cultures have divided time based on the motions of Earth and the moon. They have used the motions to establish calendars. A **calendar** is a system of organizing time that defines the beginning, length, and divisions of a year.

The most common calendar today is divided into years, months, and days. One year equals the time it takes Earth to complete one orbit. One day equals the time it takes Earth to turn once on its axis. People also divide the year into months based on the moon's cycle. The time from one full moon to another is about 29 days, though modern months do not match the moon's cycle exactly.

The History of the Calendar

Egyptian

The ancient Egyptians created one of the first calendars. Based on star motions, they calculated that the year was about 365 days long. They divided the year into 12 months of 30 days each, with an extra 5 days at the end.

Roman

The Romans borrowed the Egyptian calendar. But Earth's orbit actually takes about 365¼ days. The Romans adjusted the Egyptian calendar by adding one day every four years. You know this fourth year as "leap year," when February is given 29 days instead of its usual 28. Using leap years helps to ensure that annual events, such as the beginning of summer, occur on the same date each year.

Gregorian

The Roman calendar was off by a little more than 11 minutes a year. Over the centuries, these minutes added up. By the 1500s, the beginning of spring was about ten days too early. To straighten things out, Pope Gregory XIII dropped ten days from the year 1582. He also made some other minor changes to the Roman system to form the calendar that we use today.

 Do the Quick Lab *Sun Shadows.*

🔑 Assess Your Understanding

1a. Identify What are the two major motions of Earth as it travels through space?

_____

b. Explain Which motion causes day and night?

_____

c. Infer Why do people use Earth's motions to determine units of time?

_____

_____

_____

got it?

○ **I get it!** Now I know that Earth moves by _____

○ **I need extra help with** _____

Go to **MY SCIENCE COACH** online for help with this subject.

13

What Causes Seasons?

Many places that are far from Earth's equator and its poles have four distinct seasons: winter, spring, summer, and autumn. But there are differences in temperature from place to place. For instance, it is generally warmer near the equator than near the poles. Why?

How Sunlight Hits Earth **Figure 3** shows how sunlight strikes Earth's surface. Notice that, near the equator, sunlight hits Earth's surface from almost overhead. Near the poles, sunlight arrives at a steep angle. As a result, it is spread out over a greater area. That's why it is warmer near the equator than near the poles.

Earth's Tilted Axis If Earth's axis were straight up and down relative to its orbit, temperatures in an area would remain fairly constant year-round. There would be no seasons. 🔑 **Earth has seasons because its axis is tilted as it revolves around the sun.**

Notice in **Figure 4** that Earth's axis is always tilted at an angle of 23.5° from the vertical. The North Pole always points in the same direction. As Earth revolves around the sun, the north end of its axis is tilted away from the sun for part of the year and toward the sun for part of the year. Summer and winter are caused by Earth's tilt as it revolves around the sun.

FIGURE 3 ······

Sunlight on Earth
The diagram shows how Earth's tilted axis affects the strength of sunlight in different places.

△ **Infer** Draw a circle around the area where sunlight is most direct. Mark an X on the places that sunlight reaches, but where it is less direct.

Near the equator, sunlight does not spread very far. The sun's energy is concentrated in a smaller area.

Near the poles, the same amount of sunlight spreads over a greater area.

June In June, the north end of Earth's axis is tilted toward the sun. In the Northern Hemisphere, the noon sun is high in the sky and there are more hours of daylight than darkness. The sun's rays are concentrated. It is summer in the Northern Hemisphere.

At the same time south of the equator, the sun's energy is spread over a larger area. The sun is low in the sky and days are shorter than nights. It is winter in the Southern Hemisphere.

December In December, people in the Southern Hemisphere receive the most direct sunlight, so it is summer. At the same time, the sun's rays in the Northern Hemisphere are more slanted and there are fewer hours of daylight. So it is winter in the Northern Hemisphere.

March

June

December

September

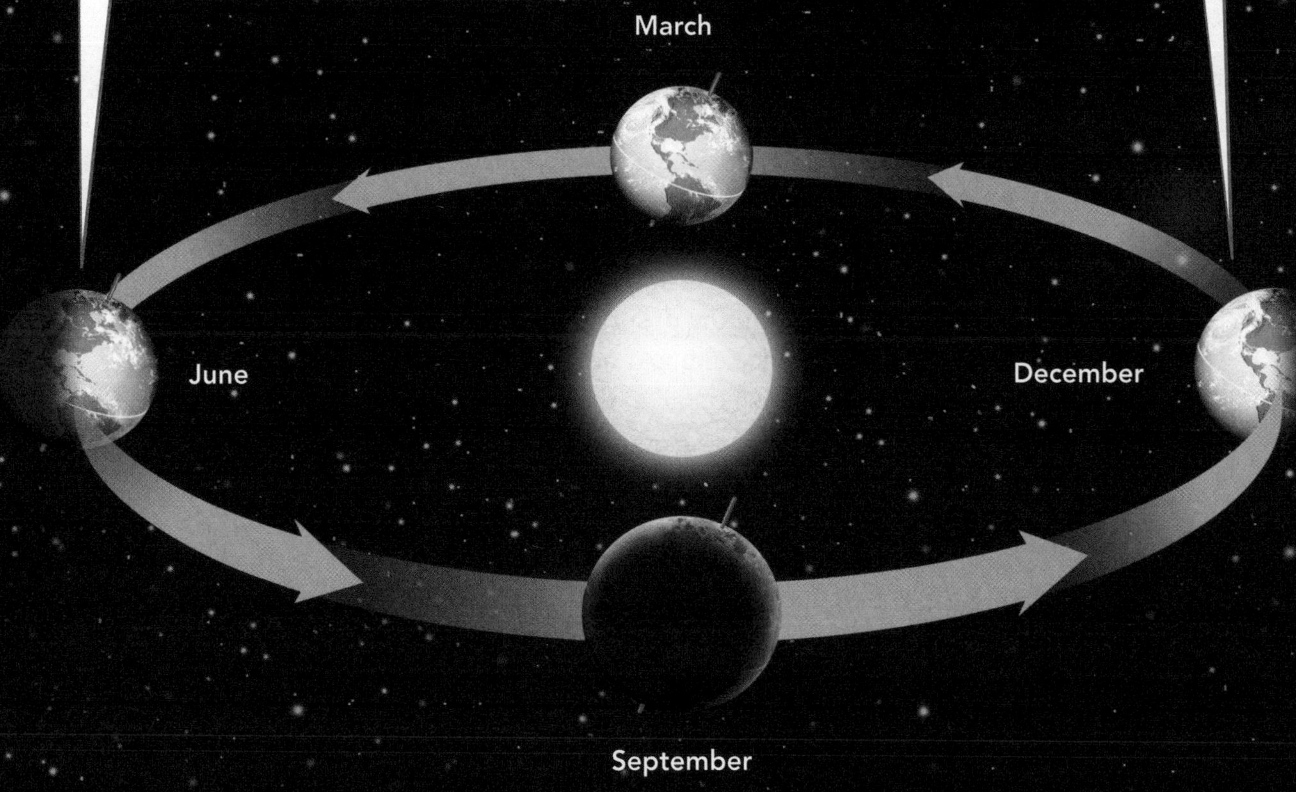

FIGURE 4 ······························
> INTERACTIVE ART **Seasons**
The diagram shows how Earth moves during the year. It is not drawn to scale.

✎ **Make Generalizations**
Describe the weather and sunlight in the Northern and Southern hemispheres in March and September.

_____
_____
_____
_____
_____
_____
_____
_____
_____
_____

Solstices

The sun appears farthest north of the equator once each year and farthest south once each year. Each of these days is known as a **solstice** (SOHL stis). The day when the sun appears farthest north is the summer solstice in the Northern Hemisphere and the winter solstice in the Southern Hemisphere. This solstice occurs around June 21 each year. It is the longest day of the year in the Northern Hemisphere and the shortest day in the Southern Hemisphere. As you can see in **Figure 5,** the sun rises to the northeast and sets to the northwest.

Similarly, around December 21, the sun appears farthest south. This is the winter solstice in the Northern Hemisphere and the summer solstice in the Southern Hemisphere. The sun rises to the southeast and sets to the southwest.

Equinoxes

Halfway between the solstices, neither hemisphere is tilted toward the sun. The noon sun is directly overhead at the equator, rises due east, and sets due west. Each of these days is known as an **equinox,** which means "equal night." During an equinox, day and night are each about 12 hours long everywhere. The vernal (spring) equinox occurs around March 21 and marks the beginning of spring in the Northern Hemisphere. The fall, or autumnal, equinox occurs around September 22. It marks the beginning of fall in the Northern Hemisphere.

FIGURE 5 ·······························

Solstices and Equinoxes

The diagrams show the apparent path of the sun at the solstices and equinoxes in the Northern Hemisphere. The sun rises and sets farthest north at the June solstice and farthest south at the December solstice.

✏️ **Apply Concepts** Draw the sun's path at the equinoxes and the December solstice for the Southern Hemisphere.

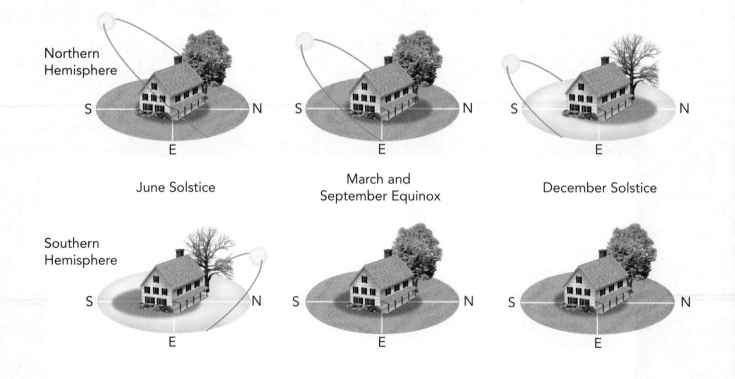

Northern Hemisphere

June Solstice

March and September Equinox

December Solstice

Southern Hemisphere

do the math! Sample Problem

Calculating Percents

The table shows the number of hours of sunlight in three cities at different times of year. What percentage of a 24-hour day has sunlight in Guadalajara on January 1?

STEP 1 Divide the number of hours of sunlight by the total number of hours.

$$\frac{\text{Hours of sunlight}}{\text{Total hours}} = \frac{10.90 \text{ hours}}{24 \text{ hours}} = 0.45$$

STEP 2 Multiply by 100 to find the percent.

$$0.45 \times 100 = 45\%$$

In Guadalajara, 45% of a 24-hour day has sunlight on January 1.

City	Approximate Latitude	Hours of Daylight			
		January 1	April 1	July 1	October 1
Helsinki, Finland	60°N	5.98	13.33	18.80	11.45
Philadelphia, United States	40°N	9.38	12.68	14.95	11.77
Guadalajara, Mexico	20°N	10.90	12.37	13.37	11.95

1 Calculate What percentage of a day has sunlight in Helsinki on July 1?

2 Calculate What is the difference in the percentage of the day that has sunlight in Helsinki and in Philadelphia on January 1?

3 Infer What percentage of the day would you expect to have sunlight at the equator in January? In June?

 Do the Lab Investigation *Reasons for the Seasons.*

🔑 Assess Your Understanding

2a. Define The noon sun is directly overhead at the equator during (a solstice/an equinox).

b. Relate Cause and Effect What causes the seasons? _____

_____

_____

c. Predict How would the seasons be different if Earth were not tilted on its axis? Explain.

_____

_____

_____

_____

_____

got it? ....

○ **I get it!** Now I know that Earth's seasons are caused by _____

_____

○ **I need extra help with** _____

Go to **MY SCIENCE COACH** *online for help with this subject.*

Gravity and Motion

UNLOCK THE BIG Q?

🔑 **What Determines Gravity?**

🔑 **What Keeps Objects in Orbit?**

my planet diary

Gravity Assists

You might think that gravity only brings objects down. But gravity can also speed things up and send them flying! If a space probe comes close to a planet, the planet's gravity changes the probe's path. Engineers plan space missions to take advantage of these "gravity assists." A gravity assist can shorten the probe's interplanetary trip by many years. The diagram shows how the probe *Voyager 2* used gravity assists to visit all four outer planets!

Path of spacecraft

Lab zone Do the Inquiry Warm-Up *What Factors Affect Gravity?*

TECHNOLOGY

Use what you know about gravity to answer this question.

How does a planet's gravity change the path of a space probe?

_____

_____

_____

> **PLANET DIARY** Go to **Planet Diary** to learn more about gravity.

What Determines Gravity?

Earth revolves around the sun in a nearly circular orbit. The moon orbits Earth in the same way. But what keeps Earth and the moon in orbit? Why don't they just fly off into space?

The first person to answer these questions was the English scientist Isaac Newton. In the 1600s, Newton realized that there must be a force acting between Earth and the moon that kept the moon in orbit. A **force** is a push or a pull.

Vocabulary

- force • gravity • law of universal gravitation
- mass • weight • inertia • Newton's first law of motion

Skills

↪ Reading: Ask Questions

△ Inquiry: Draw Conclusions

Gravity

Newton hypothesized that the force that pulls an apple to the ground also pulls the moon toward Earth, keeping it in orbit. This force, called **gravity,** attracts all objects toward each other. Newton's **law of universal gravitation** states that every object in the universe attracts every other object. 🗝 **The strength of the force of gravity between two objects depends on two factors: the masses of the objects and the distance between them.**

Gravity, Mass, and Weight

The strength of gravity depends in part on the masses of each of the objects. **Mass** is the amount of matter in an object. Because Earth is so massive, it exerts a much greater force on you than this book does.

The measure of the force of gravity on an object is called **weight.** Mass doesn't change, but an object's weight can change depending on its location. On the moon, you would weigh about one sixth as much as on Earth. This is because the moon has less mass than Earth, so the pull of the moon's gravity on you would also be less.

Gravity and Distance

Gravity is also affected by the distance between two objects. The force of gravity decreases rapidly as distance increases. If the distance between two objects doubles, the force of gravity decreases to one fourth of its original value.

FIGURE 1 ....

> VIRTUAL LAB **Gravity, Mass, and Distance**

✏ **Compare and Contrast** Draw arrows showing the force of gravity in the second and third pictures.

The longer the arrow, the greater the force.

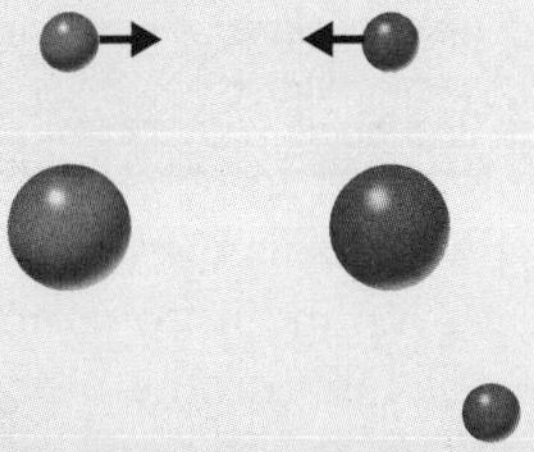

did you know?

You could say we owe our understanding of gravity to disease! In 1665, Isaac Newton was a student. Then a disease called plague shut down the university for 18 months. Newton had to go home. While he was there, he thought of the ideas that led to his theory. (But it may not be true that he got the idea when an apple fell from a tree.)

Lab zone® Do the Quick Lab *What's Doing the Pulling?*

🗝 Assess Your Understanding

got it? ....

○ **I get it!** Now I know that the force of gravity depends on _____

_____

○ **I need extra help with** _____

Go to my science ⑤ **COACH** *online for help with this subject.*

What Keeps Objects in Orbit?

If the sun and Earth are constantly pulling on one another because of gravity, why doesn't Earth fall into the sun? Similarly, why doesn't the moon crash into Earth? The fact that such collisions have not occurred shows that there must be another factor at work. That factor is called inertia.

Inertia The tendency of an object to resist a change in motion is **inertia.** You feel the effects of inertia every day. When you are riding in a car and it stops suddenly, you keep moving forward. If you didn't have a seat belt on, your inertia could cause you to bump into the car's windshield or the seat in front of you. The more mass an object has, the greater its inertia. An object with greater inertia is more difficult to start or stop.

Isaac Newton stated his ideas about inertia as a scientific law. **Newton's first law of motion** says that an object at rest will stay at rest and an object in motion will stay in motion with a constant speed and direction unless acted on by a force.

Orbital Motion Why do Earth and the moon remain in orbit? ▰ **Newton concluded that inertia and gravity combine to keep Earth in orbit around the sun and the moon in orbit around Earth.** You can see how this occurs in **Figure 2.**

✏️ **Ask Questions** Before you read the paragraphs under Inertia, write a question you would like to have answered. Look for the answer as you read.

_____

_____

_____

_____

_____

FIGURE 2 ···
Orbital Motion
✏️ **Predict** How would the moon move if Earth's mass increased?

_____

_____

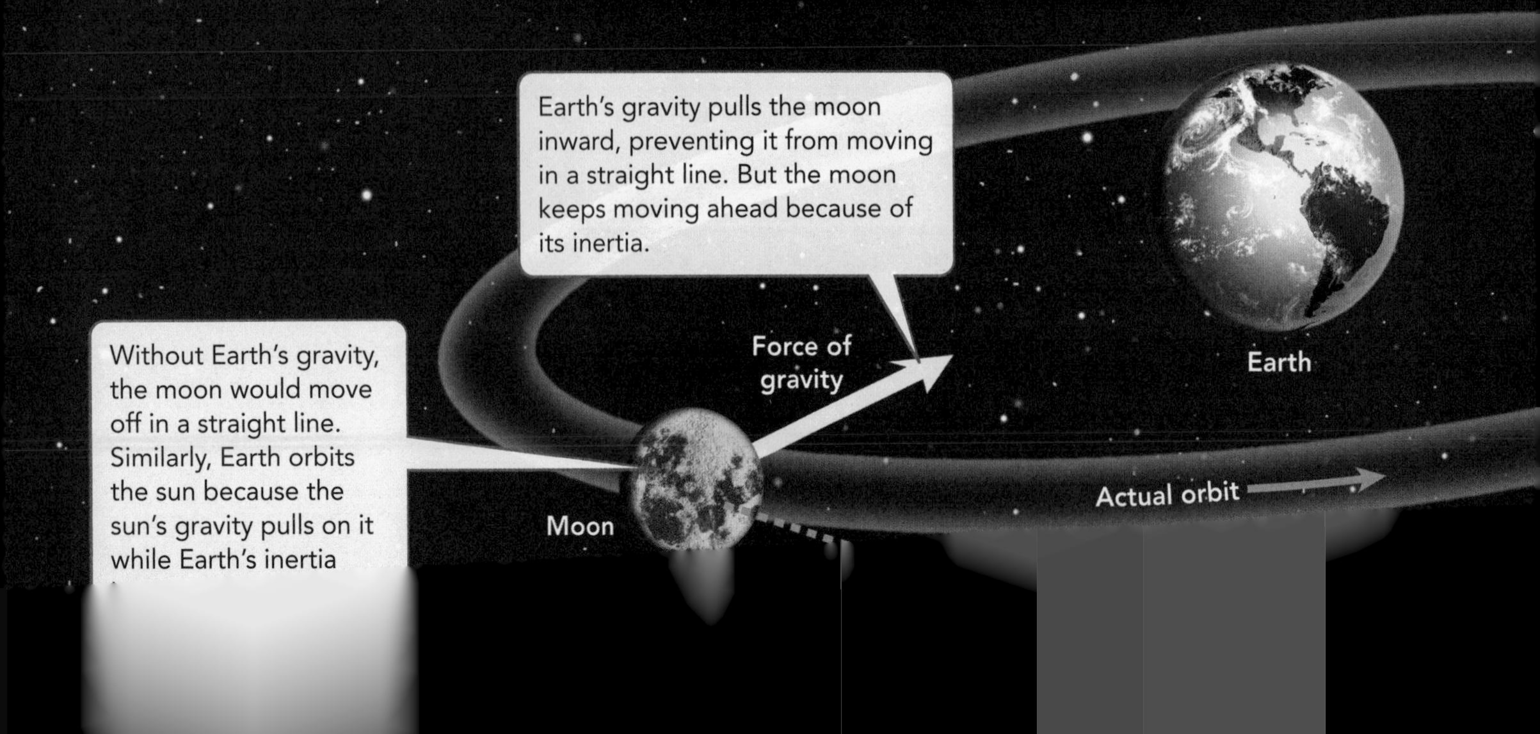

Earth's gravity pulls the moon inward, preventing it from moving in a straight line. But the moon keeps moving ahead because of its inertia.

Without Earth's gravity, the moon would move off in a straight line. Similarly, Earth orbits the sun because the sun's gravity pulls on it while Earth's inertia

Force of gravity

Earth

Actual orbit

Moon

do the math! Analyzing Data

Gravity Versus Distance

As a rocket leaves a planet's surface, the force of gravity between the rocket and the planet changes. Use the graph to answer the questions below.

❶ Read Graphs The variables being graphed

are _____

and _____

❷ Read Graphs What is the force of gravity on the rocket at the planet's surface?

_____

❸ Read Graphs What is the force of gravity on the rocket at two units (twice the planet's radius from its center)?

_____

❹ Make Generalizations In general, how does the force of gravity on the rocket change as its distance from the planet increases?

_____

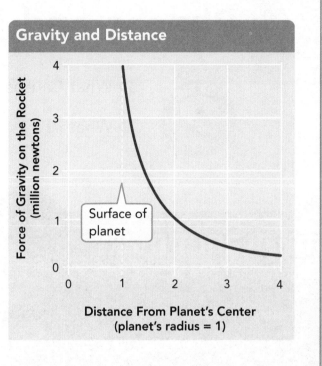

Gravity and Distance

Force of Gravity on the Rocket (million newtons)

Surface of planet

Distance From Planet's Center (planet's radius = 1)

 Do the Quick Lab *Around and Around We Go.*

🔑 Assess Your Understanding

1a. Identify What two factors keep a planet in orbit around the sun?

_____

b. Draw Conclusions What keeps Earth from falling into the sun?

_____

c. CHALLENGE How would a planet move if the sun suddenly disappeared? Explain.

_____

_____

_____

got it?

○ **I get it!** Now I know that objects are kept in orbit by _____

○ **I need extra help with** _____

Go to MY SCIENCE ⓢ COACH online for help with this subject.

Phases and Eclipses

UNLOCK
THE BIG
?

🗝 **What Causes the Moon's Phases?**

🗝 **What Are Eclipses?**

my planet Diary

BLOG

Posted by: Nicole

Location: Bernhard's Bay, New York

One night, my mom, dad, and I were coming home from eating dinner. When we got out of the car, we saw that the moon was turning red. We looked at the moon for a while. Then our neighbor called and said that it was a lunar eclipse. It was an amazing sight.

Think about your own experiences as you answer the question below.

What is the most interesting or unusual event you have ever seen in the sky?

_____
_____
_____
_____
_____

Do the Inquiry Warm-Up
How Does the Moon Move?

▶ PLANET DIARY Go to **Planet Diary** to learn more about eclipses.

What Causes the Moon's Phases?

Have you ever been kept awake by bright moonlight? The light streaming through your window actually comes from the sun! The moon does not shine with its own light. Instead, it reflects light from the sun. When the moon is full, this light may be bright enough to read by! But at other times, the moon is just a thin crescent in the sky. The different shapes of the moon you see from Earth are called **phases.** Phases are caused by the motions of the moon around Earth.

Vocabulary

- phase   - eclipse   - solar eclipse
- umbra   - penumbra   - lunar eclipse

Skills

↺ **Reading:** Relate Text and Visuals

△ **Inquiry:** Make Models

Motions of the Moon When you look up at the moon, you may see what looks like a face. What you are really seeing is a pattern of light-colored and dark-colored areas on the moon's surface that just happens to look like a face. Oddly, this pattern never seems to move. The same side of the moon, the "near side," always faces Earth. The "far side" of the moon always faces away from Earth. Why? The answer has to do with the moon's motions.

Like Earth, the moon moves through space in two ways. The moon revolves around Earth and also rotates on its own axis. The moon rotates once on its axis in the same time that it takes to revolve once around Earth. Thus, a "day" on the moon is the same length as a month on Earth. For this reason, the same side of the moon always faces Earth, as you can see in **Figure 1.**

As the moon orbits Earth, the relative positions of the moon, Earth, and sun change. ⚷ **The changing relative positions of the moon, Earth, and sun cause the phases of the moon.**

Vocabulary Identify Multiple Meanings Which sentence uses the scientific meaning of *phase*?

○ The doctor told the parent that the child was just going through a phase.

○ The moon goes through a cycle of phases every month.

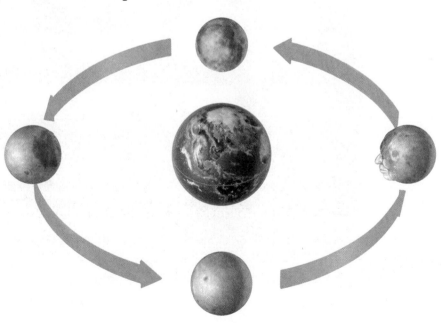

FIGURE 1 ·······················

The Moon's Motion

The diagram shows the moon's rotation and revolution. ✎ **Infer Find the face on the rightmost view of the moon. Draw the face as it would appear on each view.**

CHALLENGE How would the moon appear from Earth if the moon did not rotate?

_____

_____

Phases of the Moon

Half the moon is almost always in sunlight. But since the moon orbits Earth, you see the moon from different angles. The phase of the moon you see depends on how much of the sunlit side of the moon faces Earth.

During the new moon phase, the side of the moon facing Earth is not lit. As the moon revolves around Earth, you see more of the lit side of the moon, until you see all of the lit side. As the month continues, you see less of the lit side. You can see these changes in Figure 2. About 29.5 days after the last new moon, a new moon occurs again.

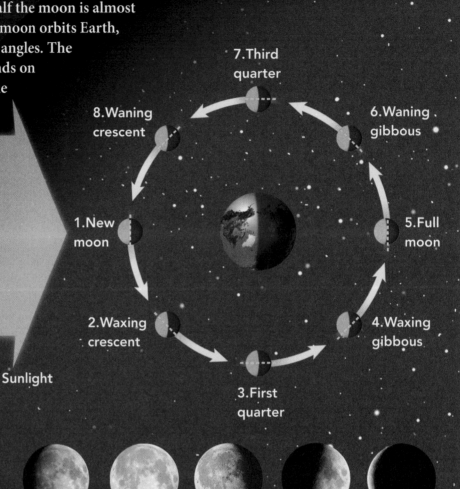

Sunlight

7. Third quarter
8. Waning crescent
6. Waning gibbous
1. New moon
5. Full moon
2. Waxing crescent
4. Waxing gibbous
3. First quarter

apply it!

△ **Make Models** Describe a way to model the moon's phases using items you might have at home.

_____
_____
_____
_____
_____
_____

FIGURE 2 ·······················

Moon Phases

As the moon revolves around Earth, the amount of the moon's surface that is lit remains the same. The part of the lit surface that can be seen from Earth changes.

✏ **Interpret Diagrams** **Match each photo to its phase shown on the diagram. Write the number of the phase.**

 Do the Quick Lab *Moon Phases.*

🔑 Assess Your Understanding

got it? ··

○ **I get it!** Now I know that moon phases are caused by _____

○ **I need extra help with** _____

Go to MY SCIENCE COACH online for help with this subject.

What Are Eclipses?

The moon's orbit around Earth is slightly tilted with respect to Earth's orbit around the sun. As a result, the moon travels above and below Earth's orbit. But on rare occasions, Earth, the moon, and the sun line up.

When an object in space comes between the sun and a third object, it casts a shadow on that object, causing an **eclipse** (ih KLIPS) to take place. There are two types of eclipses: solar eclipses and lunar eclipses. (The words *solar* and *lunar* come from the Latin words for "sun" and "moon.")

Solar Eclipses During a new moon, the moon lies between Earth and the sun. 🔑 A solar eclipse occurs when the moon passes directly between Earth and the sun, blocking sunlight from Earth. The moon's shadow then hits Earth.

Total Solar Eclipses The very darkest part of the moon's shadow is the umbra (UM bruh). You can see how the umbra strikes Earth in **Figure 3**. Within the umbra, the sun's light is completely blocked. Only people within the umbra experience a total solar eclipse. During a total solar eclipse, the sky grows as dark as night. The air gets cool and the sky becomes an eerie color. You can see the stars and the solar corona, which is the faint outer atmosphere of the sun.

Partial Solar Eclipses The moon casts another part of its shadow that is less dark than the umbra. This larger part of the shadow is called the penumbra (peh NUM bruh). In the penumbra, part of the sun is visible from Earth. During a solar eclipse, people in the penumbra see only a partial eclipse.

FIGURE 3 ·······························

Solar Eclipse
The diagram shows the moon's penumbra and umbra during an eclipse. It is not drawn to scale.

↻ **Relate Text and Visuals**
Mark an X to show where a total solar eclipse would be visible. Circle the area in which a partial solar eclipse would be visible.

Sunlight
Moon
Umbra
Penumbra
Earth

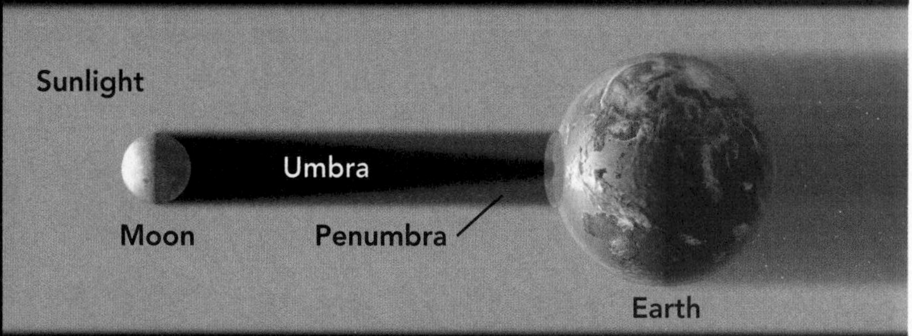

Lunar Eclipses During most months, the moon moves near Earth's shadow but not quite into it. A lunar eclipse occurs at a full moon when Earth is directly between the moon and the sun. You can see a lunar eclipse in Figure 4. 🔑 During a lunar eclipse, Earth blocks sunlight from reaching the moon. Lunar eclipses occur only when there is a full moon because the moon is closest to Earth's shadow at that time.

✏️ Relate Text and Visuals
Mark an X on the photograph above that shows a total eclipse.

Total Lunar Eclipses Like the moon's shadow in a solar eclipse, Earth's shadow has an umbra and a penumbra. When the moon is in Earth's umbra, you see a total lunar eclipse. Unlike a total solar eclipse, a total lunar eclipse can be seen anywhere on Earth that the moon is visible. So you are more likely to see a total lunar eclipse than a total solar eclipse.

Partial Lunar Eclipses For most lunar eclipses, Earth, the moon, and the sun are not quite in line, and only a partial lunar eclipse results. A partial lunar eclipse occurs when the moon passes partly into the umbra of Earth's shadow. The edge of the umbra appears blurry, and you can watch it pass across the moon for two or three hours.

FIGURE 4 ·····································
Lunar Eclipse
As the moon moves through Earth's shadow, total and partial eclipses occur. This diagram is not to scale.

✏️ Infer **Draw a circle labeled *T* to show where the moon would be during a total eclipse. Draw two circles labeled *P* to show two places the moon could be during a partial eclipse.**

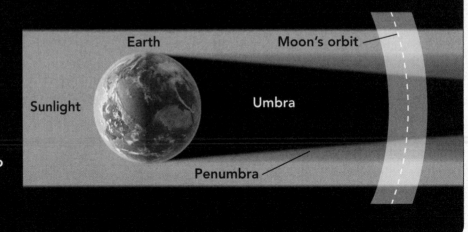

Seasons and Shadows

How do Earth, the moon, and the sun interact?

FIGURE 5 ···

INTERACTIVE ART Look at the diagram below. (The diagram is not to scale.) Identify what season it is in the Northern Hemisphere, what the phase of the moon is, and what kind of eclipse, if any, could occur.

Season
_____

Moon Phase
_____

Eclipse
_____

Use the above diagram as a model. Draw the arrangement of Earth, the moon, and the sun during a total lunar eclipse in December.

Lab ® Do the Quick Lab
zone *Eclipses.*

🔑 Assess Your Understanding

1a. Explain A (solar/lunar) eclipse occurs when the moon passes into Earth's shadow. A (solar/lunar) eclipse occurs when Earth passes into the moon's shadow.

b. ANSWER **THE BIG ?** How do Earth, the moon, and the sun interact? _____
_____
_____
_____

got it? ···

○ **I get it!** Now I know that eclipses occur when _____
_____

○ **I need extra help with** _____

Go to **MY SCIENCE** Ⓢ **COACH** *online for help with this subject.*

Tides

🔑 **What Are Tides?**

my planeт DiaRY

A River in Reverse

If you were visiting New Brunswick in Canada, you might see the Saint John River flowing into the ocean. But six hours later, you might find that the river changed direction while you were gone! How could this happen? The Saint John River really does reverse course twice a day. At low tide, it empties into the Bay of Fundy, shown below. At high tide, the Bay of Fundy's tide pushes into the river, forcing the river to run in the opposite direction. The Bay of Fundy's tides are among the highest in the world.

Use your experience to answer the questions.

1. Why does the Saint John River change direction?

_____

_____

_____

2. Have you ever seen a natural event that surprised you? Why was it surprising?

_____

_____

_____

▷ PLANET DIARY Go to **Planet Diary** to learn more about tides.

Lab **zone** Do the Inquiry Warm-Up *When Is High Tide?*

High tide

Low tide

Vocabulary
- tide
- spring tide
- neap tide

Skills
- Reading: Relate Cause and Effect
- Inquiry: Observe

What Are Tides?

The reversing Saint John River is caused by ocean **tides,** the rise and fall of ocean water that occurs every 12.5 hours or so. The water rises for about six hours, then falls for about six hours.

The Tide Cycle The force of gravity pulls the moon and Earth (including the water on Earth's surface) toward each other. **Tides are caused mainly by differences in how much gravity from the moon and the sun pulls on different parts of Earth.**

At any one time on Earth, there are two places with high tides and two places with low tides. As Earth rotates, one high tide occurs on the side of Earth that faces the moon. The second high tide occurs on the opposite side of Earth. **Figure 1** explains why.

Relate Cause and Effect As you read **Figure 1,** underline the causes of high and low tides.

FIGURE 1 ·····················

ART IN MOTION Tides

You can think of Earth as a ball surrounded by a layer of water, as shown here. The layer is really much thinner than this, but is drawn thicker so it is easier to see.

North Pole

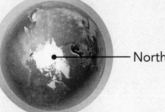

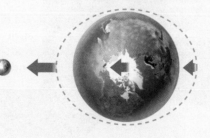

The Near Side The moon's gravity pulls a little more strongly on the water on the side closest to the moon than on Earth as a whole. This difference causes a bulge of water on the side of Earth closest to the moon. This bulge causes high tide.

Interpret Diagrams Write an *H* where high tides occur and an *L* where low tides occur.

The Far Side The moon's gravity pulls more weakly on the water on the far side of Earth than on Earth as a whole. Since Earth is pulled more strongly, the water is "left behind." Water flows toward the far side, causing high tide. Halfway between the high tides, water flows toward the high tides, causing low tide.

The Sun's Role Even though the sun is about 150 million kilometers from Earth, it is so massive that its gravity affects the tides. The sun pulls the water on Earth's surface toward it. 🔑 **Changes in the positions of Earth, the moon, and the sun affect the heights of the tides during a month.**

New Moon

The sun, the moon, and Earth are nearly in a line during a new moon. The gravity of the sun and the moon pull in the same direction. Their combined forces produce a tide with the greatest difference between consecutive low and high tides, called a **spring tide.** The term "spring tide" comes from an Old English word, *springen,* meaning "to jump."

First Quarter

During the moon's first-quarter phase, the line between Earth and the sun is at right angles to the line between Earth and the moon. The sun's pull is at right angles to the moon's pull. This arrangement produces a **neap tide**, a tide with the least difference between consecutive low and high tides. Neap tides occur twice a month.

Full Moon

At full moon, the moon and the sun are on opposite sides of Earth. Since there are high tides on both sides of Earth, a spring tide is also produced. It doesn't matter in which order the sun, Earth, and the moon line up.

Third Quarter

✏️ **Infer** Draw the position of the moon and the tide bulges at third quarter. What kind of tide occurs?

_____

The table shows high and low tides at four times in May 2008, in St. John, New Brunswick. St. John is on the Bay of Fundy.

High and Low Tides at St. John, New Brunswick

Date	High Tide (meters)	Low Tide (meters)
May 6–7	8.7	0.0
May 13–14	7.1	1.7
May 21	7.5	1.2
May 26	6.9	2.0

❶ Interpret Data Spring tides occurred at two of the times shown. Which two? How do you know?

_____

_____

_____

❷ CHALLENGE Would the tide be higher when the moon is on the same side of Earth as New Brunswick or on the opposite side? Why?

_____

_____

_____

_____

_____

Vocabulary Identify Multiple Meanings Does a spring tide always happen in the season of spring? Explain your answer.

_____

_____

_____

_____

_____

_____

 Lab zone® Do the Quick Lab *Modeling the Moon's Pull of Gravity.*

🔑 **Assess Your Understanding**

1a. Review Most coastal areas have _____ high tides and _____ low tides each day.

b. ⟳ Relate Cause and Effect What causes tides?

_____

_____

_____

c. ◢ Observe Look at the diagrams on the previous page. What is the angle formed by the sun, Earth, and the moon during a neap tide? A spring tide?

_____

_____

_____

got it? ⋯⋯⋯⋯⋯⋯⋯⋯⋯⋯⋯⋯⋯⋯⋯⋯⋯⋯⋯⋯⋯⋯⋯

○ **I get it!** Now I know that tides are _____

_____

○ **I need extra help with** _____

Go to **MY SCIENCE ⓢ COACH** online for help with this subject.

Earth's Moon

UNLOCK THE BIG

🔑 **What Is the Moon Like?**

my planet Diary

VOICES FROM HISTORY

Galileo Galilei

In 1609, the Italian astronomer Galileo Galilei turned a new tool—the telescope—toward the moon. What he saw amazed him: wide dark areas and strange spots and ridges.

I have been led to that opinion... that I feel sure that the surface of the Moon is not perfectly smooth...but that, on the contrary, it is ... just like the surface of the Earth itself, which is varied everywhere by high mountains and deep valleys.

Today, scientists know that Galileo was right. Powerful telescopes have shown the mountains and craters on the moon, and astronauts have walked and driven over the moon's surface.

✏️ **Communicate** Discuss Galileo's observations with a partner. Then answer the questions below.

1. What conclusions did Galileo draw about the moon?

    _____

    _____

2. How do you think it would feel to make an observation that no one had made before?

    _____

    _____

    _____

> PLANET DIARY Go to **Planet Diary** to learn more about Earth's moon.

Lab zone® Do the Inquiry Warm-Up *Why Do Craters Look Different From Each Other?*

Vocabulary
- maria • crater
- meteoroid

Skills
- Reading: Compare and Contrast
- Inquiry: Develop Hypotheses

What Is the Moon Like?

For thousands of years, people could see the moon, but didn't know much about it. Galileo's observations were some of the first to show details on the moon's surface. Scientists have since learned more about the moon's features. **The moon is dry and airless and has an irregular surface. Compared to Earth, the moon is small and has large variations in its surface temperature.**

Surface Features As **Figure 1** shows, the moon has many unusual structures, including maria, craters, and highlands.

Maria Dark, flat areas, called **maria** (MAH ree uh), are hardened rock formed from huge lava flows that occurred 3–4 billion years ago. The singular form of *maria* is *mare* (MAH ray).

Craters Large round pits called **craters** can be hundreds of kilometers across. These craters were caused by the impacts of **meteoroids,** chunks of rock or dust from space. Maria have relatively few craters. This means that most of the moon's craters formed from impacts early in its history, before maria formed.

Highlands Some of the light-colored features you can see on the moon's surface are highlands, or mountains. The peaks of the lunar highlands and the rims of the craters cast dark shadows. The highlands cover most of the moon's surface.

FIGURE 1 ·······················
Moon Features
This photograph shows the features of the northern part of the side of the moon that you can see from Earth.

✏ **Relate Diagrams and Photos** How is the photograph different from Galileo's drawing on the previous page?

_____

_____

_____

_____

_____

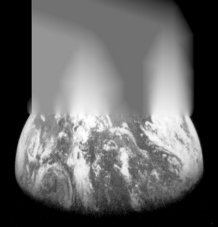

FIGURE 2 ·····································

Different Worlds
This photo of Earth, taken from orbit around the moon, clearly shows the contrast between the barren moon and water-covered Earth.

Compare and Contrast
Complete the table below to compare and contrast Earth and the moon.

Size and Density The moon is 3,476 kilometers across, a little less than the distance across the United States. This is about one fourth of Earth's diameter. However, the moon has only one eightieth as much mass as Earth. Though Earth has a very dense core, its outer layers are less dense. The moon's average density is similar to the density of Earth's outer layers. Its gravity is about one sixth of Earth's.

Temperature At the moon's equator, temperatures range from a torrid 130°C in direct sunlight to a frigid −170°C at night. Temperatures at the poles are even colder. Temperatures vary so much because the moon does not have an atmosphere. The moon's surface gravity is so weak that gases can easily escape into space.

Water For many years, people thought the moon had no water, except for small amounts of ice. In 2009, scientists using data from several space probes determined that a thin layer of water exists in the moon's soil. The total amount of water is very small, but it is found in many places on the moon's surface.

Origins of the Moon Scientists have suggested many possible theories for how the moon formed. The theory that seems to best fit the evidence is called the collision-ring theory. About 4.5 billion years ago, when Earth was very young, the solar system was full of rocky debris. Scientists theorize that a planet-sized object collided with Earth. Material from the object and Earth's outer layers was ejected into orbit around Earth, where it formed a ring. Gravity caused this material to clump together to form the moon.

	Density	Temperatures	Atmosphere	Water
Earth				
Moon				

apply it!

Within your lifetime, tourists may be able to travel to the moon. If you were taking a trip to the moon, what would you pack? Remember that the moon is dry, has almost no liquid water, and has no atmosphere.

1 Solve Problems On the packing list to the right, list five items you would need on the moon.

2 CHALLENGE List two items that you could not use on the moon. Why would they not work?

_____

_____

_____

_____

_____

_____

_____

Things to Pack

1. _____

2. _____

3. _____

4. _____

5. _____

 Do the Quick Lab
Moonwatching.

🔑 Assess Your Understanding

1a. List What are the three main surface features on the moon?

_____

b. 🔄 Compare and Contrast How does the moon's gravity compare with Earth's?

_____

c. Develop Hypotheses Write a hypothesis explaining why the moon has very little liquid water.

_____

_____

_____

got it? ....

○ **I get it!** Now I know that the characteristics of Earth's moon are _____

_____

_____

○ **I need extra help with** _____

Go to **MY SCIENCE COACH** *online for help with this subject.*

35

1 Study Guide

Interactions between Earth, the moon, and the sun cause _____, _____, _____, and _____.

LESSON 1 The Sky From Earth

🔑 On a clear night, you may see stars, the moon, planets, meteors, and comets.

🔑 A constellation is a pattern or grouping of stars imagined by people to represent figures.

🔑 The apparent motion of objects in the sky depends on the motions of Earth.

Vocabulary
- satellite • planet • meteor • comet
- star • constellation

LESSON 2 Earth in Space

🔑 Earth moves in space in two major ways: rotation and revolution.

🔑 Earth has seasons because its axis is tilted as it revolves around the sun.

Vocabulary
- axis • rotation
- revolution
- orbit • calendar
- solstice • equinox

LESSON 3 Gravity and Motion

🔑 The strength of the force of gravity between two objects depends on two factors: the masses of the objects and the distance between them.

🔑 Newton concluded that inertia and gravity combine to keep Earth in orbit around the sun and the moon in orbit around Earth.

Vocabulary
- force • gravity • law of universal gravitation
- mass • weight • inertia
- Newton's first law of motion

LESSON 4 Phases and Eclipses

🔑 The changing relative positions of the moon, Earth, and sun cause the phases of the moon.

🔑 A solar eclipse occurs when the moon passes directly between Earth and the sun, blocking sunlight from Earth. During a lunar eclipse, Earth blocks sunlight from reaching the moon.

Vocabulary
- phase • eclipse • solar eclipse • umbra
- penumbra • lunar eclipse

LESSON 5 Tides

🔑 Tides are caused by differences in how much gravity from the moon and the sun pulls on different parts of Earth.

🔑 Changes in the positions of Earth, the moon, and the sun affect the heights of the tides during a month.

Vocabulary
- tide • spring tide • neap tide

LESSON 6 Earth's Moon

🔑 The moon is dry and airless and has an irregular surface. Compared to Earth, the moon is small and has large variations in its surface temperature.

Vocabulary
- maria • crater
- meteoroid

Review and Assessment

LESSON 1 The Sky From Earth

1. Which of the following objects is found in Earth's atmosphere?

a. comet **b.** meteor

c. moon **d.** planet

2. Over time, people have given names to groups of stars, called _____

3. Predict The constellation Orion appears in the eastern sky in December. Where would you expect it to appear in March? Why?

_____

_____

_____

4. **Write About It** Suppose you were camping on a summer night. Describe what objects you might see in the sky and how the sky would change throughout the night.

LESSON 2 Earth in Space

5. What is Earth's annual motion around the sun called?

a. month **b.** revolution

c. rotation **d.** seasons

6. The _____ occurs when the sun is farthest north of the equator.

7. Infer Mars's axis is tilted at about the same angle as Earth's axis. Do you think Mars has seasons? Explain your answer.

_____

_____

_____

8. **Write About It** Write a guide for younger children explaining how Earth's motions are related to the lengths of days and years.

LESSON 3 Gravity and Motion

9. The tendency of an object to resist a change in motion is called

a. force. **b.** gravity.

c. inertia. **d.** weight.

10. An object is kept in orbit by _____ and _____

11. Relate Cause and Effect If you move two objects farther apart, how does the force of gravity between the two objects change?

_____

12. Compare and Contrast How are weight and mass different? _____

_____

_____

13. Explain Explain Newton's first law of motion in your own words. _____

_____

_____

_____

_____

_____

Use this illustration to answer Question 14.

450 N

14. math! How much would the person above weigh on the moon? _____

LESSON 4 Phases and Eclipses

15. The moon's shadow falling on Earth causes a

    a. full moon.   **b.** lunar eclipse.

    c. phase.   **d.** solar eclipse.

16. The darkest part of the moon's shadow is the

_____

17. Relate Cause and Effect Why does the moon have phases? _____

_____

_____

18. Make Generalizations Which occurs more often, a partial or a total lunar eclipse? Why?

_____

_____

_____

LESSON 5 Tides

19. About how long passes between high tides?

    a. 6 hours   **b.** 12 hours

    c. 24 hours   **d.** 48 hours

20. The least difference between high and low tides occurs during a _____

Use the diagram to answer Question 21.

21. Interpret Diagrams Does the diagram show a spring or a neap tide? How do you know?

_____

_____

LESSON 6 Earth's Moon

22. What caused the moon's craters?

    a. maria   **b.** meteoroids

    c. tides   **d.** volcanoes

23. The moon's light-colored highlands are

_____

24. Explain Why do temperatures vary so much on the moon? _____

_____

_____

_____

25. **Write About It** Suppose you were hired to design a spacesuit for use on the moon. What characteristics of the moon would be important for you to consider? Explain.

APPLY THE BIG ? How do Earth, the moon, and the sun interact?

26. Can more people see a total solar eclipse or a total lunar eclipse? Explain your answer.

_____

_____

_____

_____

_____

_____

_____

_____

_____

_____

_____

_____

Standardized Test Prep

Multiple Choice

Circle the letter of the best answer.

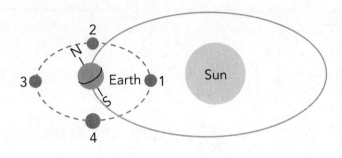

1. Which of the following can occur when the moon is at location 1?

   A only a lunar eclipse

   B only a solar eclipse

   C both a solar and a lunar eclipse

   D neither a solar nor a lunar eclipse

2. On what does the force of gravity between two objects depend?

   A mass and weight

   B speed and distance

   C weight and speed

   D mass and distance

3. What happens at a spring tide?

   A There is only one high tide each day.

   B There is only one low tide each day.

   C There is the most difference between consecutive high and low tides.

   D There is the least difference between consecutive high and low tides.

4. The dark, flat areas on the moon are called

   A craters.

   B highlands.

   C maria.

   D meteoroids.

5. Which type of object visible from Earth orbits the sun and has cleared the area of its orbit?

   A star

   B planet

   C moon

   D meteor

Constructed Response

Use the diagram below to answer the question.

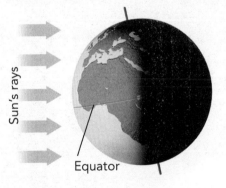

6. In the Northern Hemisphere, is it the summer solstice, winter solstice, or one of the equinoxes? Explain how you know.

KEEPING TRACK
OF
TIME

▲ This sun stone is sometimes called the Aztec calendar. It shows the 20 days in the Aztec month. The Aztec calendar was a solar calendar, with a total of 365 days in a year.

What day of the week is your birthday this year? Better check the calendar.

Calendars were invented to keep track of important events, such as planting schedules and festivals.

Early people noticed certain patterns in nature. The seasons change. The sun rises and sets. The moon changes phases. These patterns became the basis for calendars even before people understood that Earth rotates on an axis and revolves around the sun or that the moon revolves around Earth.

Calendars were lunar (based on the moon), solar (based on the sun), or lunisolar (based on a combination). But none was completely accurate—important events shifted around from one year to the next.

The Gregorian calendar, introduced in 1582, is the standard calendar in use today. It is more accurate than most calendars, but even it requires some tinkering. We add an extra day almost every four years, giving us a leap year. Century years (like 2000) are not leap years unless they are divisible by 400.

Research It There are about 40 different kinds of calendars in use today. Pick one and research it. Write an essay describing the calendar and how it is different from the Gregorian calendar. What does the calendar tell you about the society that uses it?

AFTER APOLLO: EXPLORING THE MOON

This is no ordinary footprint. It was made by an astronaut on the moon's dusty surface. Because there is no wind to weather it, it could last for a very long time.

No one has set foot on the moon since the two Apollo 17 astronauts did in 1972. But the moon has not been abandoned. Robotic spacecraft and rovers have taken over from humans.

In 2007, China and Japan sent robotic space probes to photograph and map the moon. In late 2008, India launched its moon orbiter and released a briefcase-sized probe onto the moon's surface, where it beamed back images. Next up? The National Aeronautic and Space Administration's Lunar Reconnaissance Orbiter, which will search for good landing sites and resources. Its goal is to help put humans back on the moon in the near future.

Research It Choose one of the international moon missions and prepare a timeline, from initial design to moon orbit.

The Lunar Reconnaissance Orbiter was designed to orbit approximately 50 kilometers above the moon's surface, collecting detailed information about its environment.

HOW IS THIS SWIMSUIT LIKE A SPACESUIT?

How does exploring space benefit people on Earth?

This high-tech swimsuit is made of a specially developed lightweight fabric with ultrasonically fused seams that make the suit very sleek. The swimsuit compresses the body to help the athletes go faster. △Develop Hypotheses **How might this swimsuit be similar to a spacesuit?**

_____

_____

_____

_____

_____

> UNTAMED SCIENCE Watch the **Untamed Science** video to learn more about exploring space.

Exploring Space

CHAPTER 2

Check Your Understanding

1. **Background** Read the paragraph below and then answer the question.

Bill wonders how a rocket gets off the ground. His sister Jan explains that the rocket's engines create a lot of **force.** The force causes the rocket to travel upward with great **speed.** The force helps the rocket push against **gravity** and have enough speed to rise into space.

> A **force** is a push or pull.
>
> **Speed** is the distance an object moves per unit of time.
>
> **Gravity** is the force that pulls objects toward each other.

- What force is pulling down on the rocket as it pushes off the ground?

⟩ MY READING WEB If you had trouble completing the question above, visit **My Reading Web** and type in *Exploring Space.*

Vocabulary Skill

Identify Related Word Forms You can expand your vocabulary by learning the related forms of a word. If you know that the verb *collect* means "to gather together," then you can figure out the meaning of the noun *collection* and the adjective *collective.*

Verb	Noun	Adjective
probe to examine something carefully	**probe** an unmanned space vehicle	**probing** serving to test or try
vacuum to clean with a vacuum cleaner	**vacuum** a place empty of all matter	**vacuum** partially or completely empty of all matter

2. **Quick Check** Circle the sentence below that uses the noun form of the word *probe.*
- The satellite *probes* Earth's surface thoroughly.
- The *probe* collected photographs and data for the scientists to analyze.

rocket

satellite

space probe

space spinoff

Chapter Preview

LESSON 1
- rocket
- thrust
- velocity
- orbital velocity
- escape velocity

⟳ **Relate Text and Visuals**
△ **Interpret Data**

LESSON 2
- satellite
- space shuttle
- space station
- space probe
- rover

⟳ **Ask Questions**
△ **Make Models**

LESSON 3
- vacuum
- microgravity
- space spinoff
- remote sensing
- geostationary orbit

⟳ **Identify the Main Idea**
△ **Draw Conclusions**

➤ **VOCAB FLASH CARDS** For extra help with vocabulary, visit **Vocab Flash Cards** and type in *Exploring Space.*

The Science of Rockets

🔑 **How Were Rockets Developed?**

🔑 **How Does a Rocket Work?**

🔑 **What Is the Main Advantage of a Multistage Rocket?**

MY PLANET DiARY

Jet Packs

It's been snowing all day and the roads haven't been plowed yet. No problem. Just strap on a jet pack and fly over the snow.

Does this sound like something out of a science fiction movie? Actually, manufacturers have already started making one-person jet packs. The jet packs are very expensive. They also use a lot of heavy fuel—about 10 gallons of gasoline per hour. And jet packs can carry a person for only about 30 minutes before they have to be refueled. However, 30 minutes is long enough to get many people to work—if they can find a place to land and park the jet pack once they get there.

FUN FACT

Study the picture of the person using a jet pack. Use your knowledge of science to answer the question.

What would be the advantages and disadvantages of using a jet pack for transportation?

_____

_____

_____

_____

_____

_____

▶ PLANET DIARY Go to **Planet Diary** to learn more about rockets.

Lab zone® Do the Inquiry Warm-Up
What Force Moves a Balloon?

How Were Rockets Developed?

You've probably seen rockets at fireworks displays. As the rockets moved skyward, you may have noticed a fiery gas rushing out of the back. A **rocket** is a device that expels gas in one direction to move the rocket in the opposite direction. 🔑 **Rocket technology originated in China hundreds of years ago and then gradually spread to other parts of the world.** Rockets were developed for military use as well as for fireworks.

Vocabulary

- rocket • thrust • velocity
- orbital velocity • escape velocity

Skills

🔄 Reading: Relate Text and Visuals

△ Inquiry: Interpret Data

Origins of Rockets The first rockets were made in China in the 1100s. These early "rockets" weren't rockets, but simply arrows coated with a flammable powder that were lighted and shot with bows. By about 1200, the Chinese were using gunpowder inside their rockets.

The British greatly improved rocketry in the early 1800s. British ships used rockets against American troops in the War of 1812. "The Star-Spangled Banner" contains the words "the rockets' red glare, the bombs bursting in air." These words describe a British rocket attack on Fort McHenry in Baltimore, Maryland.

Development of Modern Rockets Modern rockets were first developed by scientists in the early 1900s. One such scientist was the Russian physicist Konstantin Tsiolkovsky. He described in scientific terms how rockets work and proposed designs for advanced rockets. The American physicist Robert Goddard also designed rockets. Beginning around 1915, he built rockets to test his designs.

Scientists made major advances in rocket design during World War II. The Germans used a rocket called the V-2 to destroy both military and civilian targets. The V-2 was a large rocket that could travel about 300 kilometers. The designer of the V-2, Wernher von Braun, was brought to the United States after the war ended. Von Braun used his experience to direct the development of many rockets used in the United States space program.

FIGURE 1 ·····················

Rocket Timeline
A legend claims the Chinese official Wan-Hoo tried to fly to the moon around the year 1500 by tying rockets to his chair.

✎ **On the cards below, write a brief entry for the events that took place in the development of rockets.**

1100s

1200s

1300s

1400s

1500s

1600s

1700s

1800s

1900s

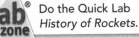

Lab zone® Do the Quick Lab *History of Rockets.*

🔑 Assess Your Understanding

got it? ·····················

○ **I get it!** Now I know that rocket technology originated _____ and gradually spread to _____

○ **I need extra help with** _____

Go to **my science** ⓢ **COACH** online for help with this subject.

How Does a Rocket Work?

A rocket can be as small as your finger or as large as a skyscraper. An essential feature of any rocket, though, is that it expels gas in one direction. 🗝 **A rocket moves forward when gases shooting out the back of the rocket push it in the opposite direction.**

A rocket works like a balloon that is propelled through the air by releasing gas. In most rockets, fuel is burned to make hot gas. The gas pushes in every direction, but it can leave the rocket only through openings at the back. This moves the rocket forward.

Action and Reaction Forces

A rocket demonstrates a basic law of physics: For every force, or action, there is an equal and opposite force, or reaction. Look at **Figure 2.** The force of the gas shooting out of the rocket is an action force. An equal force—the reaction force—pushes the rocket forward.

The reaction force that propels a rocket forward is called **thrust.** The amount of thrust depends on the mass and speed of the gases propelled out of the rocket. The greater the thrust, the greater a rocket's velocity. **Velocity** is speed in a given direction.

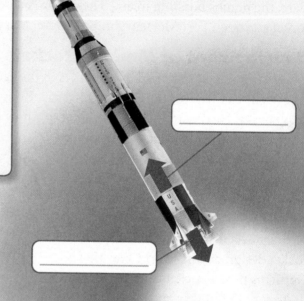

FIGURE 2 ·······························

▶ **VIRTUAL LAB** **Rocket Action and Reaction**
The force of gas propelled out the back of a rocket produces an opposing force that propels the rocket forward.

✎ **Label the action force and the reaction force in the figure, and explain how this causes the rocket to fly.**

_____

_____

_____

_____

_____

_____

_____

_____

Rocket Fuels

Three types of fuel are used to power modern rockets.

Solid-fuel rocket:
- Oxygen is mixed with the fuel (a dry explosive chemical).
- The rocket can be triggered from a distance by an igniter.
- Once the fuel is ignited, it burns until all of it is gone.

Liquid-fuel rocket:
- Oxygen and the fuel are in liquid form, stored separately.
- When the rocket fires, the fuel and oxygen are pumped into the same chamber and ignited.
- The burning of fuel can be controlled.

Ion rocket:
- This type expels charged gas particles out of the engine.
- Ion rockets are very fuel-efficient.

Orbital and Escape Velocity

In order to lift off the ground, a rocket must have more upward thrust than the downward force of gravity. Once a rocket is off the ground, it must reach a certain velocity in order to go into orbit. **Orbital velocity** is the velocity a rocket must achieve to establish an orbit around Earth. If the rocket has an even greater velocity, it can fly off into space. **Escape velocity** is the velocity a rocket must reach to fly beyond a planet's gravitational pull. The escape velocity a rocket needs to leave Earth is about 40,200 km per hour. That's more than 11 kilometers every second!

do the math!

Rocket Altitude

A rocket's altitude is how high it rises above the ground. Use the graph to answer the questions about a model rocket with a parachute packed inside, such as the one in the photo above.

1 Interpret Data What was the altitude after 2 seconds?

_____

2 **CHALLENGE** Did the rocket rise or fall faster? How do you know?

_____

_____

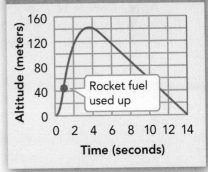

Rocket Altitude

Altitude (meters) vs. Time (seconds)

Rocket fuel used up

Lab® zone Do the Quick Lab
Be a Rocket Scientist.

🔑 Assess Your Understanding

1a. Explain What is thrust?

_____

_____

b. Interpret Diagrams Use **Figure 2** to explain how a rocket moves forward.

_____

_____

_____

_____

_____

_____

_____

got it?

○ **I get it!** Now I know that a rocket moves forward when _____

_____

_____

_____

_____

○ **I need extra help with** _____

_____

_____

Go to MY SCIENCE ⓢ COACH online for help with this subject.

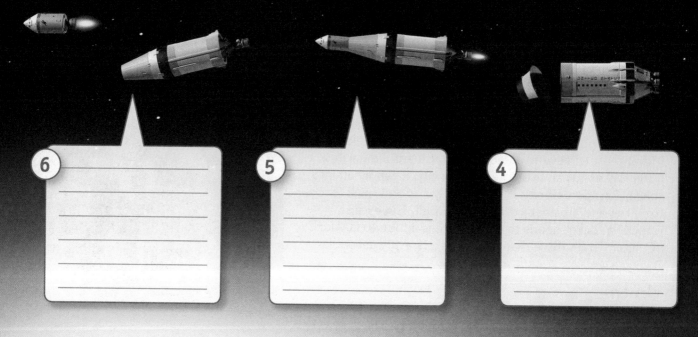

6 _____
_____
_____
_____
_____

5 _____
_____
_____
_____
_____

4 _____
_____
_____
_____
_____

FIGURE 3 ··

A Multistage Rocket

✎ **Apply Concepts** Explain what happens in the steps of the multistage rocket in the spaces provided. Which part of the rocket reaches the final destination?

_____

_____

What Is the Main Advantage of a Multistage Rocket?

A rocket can carry only so much fuel. As the fuel in a rocket burns, its fuel chambers begin to empty. Even though much of the rocket is empty, the whole rocket must still be pushed upward by the remaining fuel. But what if the empty part of the rocket could be thrown off? Then the remaining fuel wouldn't have to push a partially empty rocket. This is the idea behind multistage rockets.

Konstantin Tsiolkovsky proposed multistage rockets in 1924. 🔑 **The main advantage of a multistage rocket is that the total weight of the rocket is greatly reduced as the rocket rises.**

In a multistage rocket, smaller rockets, or stages, are placed one on top of the other and then fired in succession. **Figure 3** shows how a multistage rocket works. As each stage of the rocket uses up its fuel, the empty fuel container falls away. The next stage then ignites and continues powering the rocket toward its destination. At the end, there is just a single stage left, the very top of the rocket.

Multistage rockets were used in the 1960s to send astronauts to the moon. Today, they are used to launch a variety of satellites and space probes.

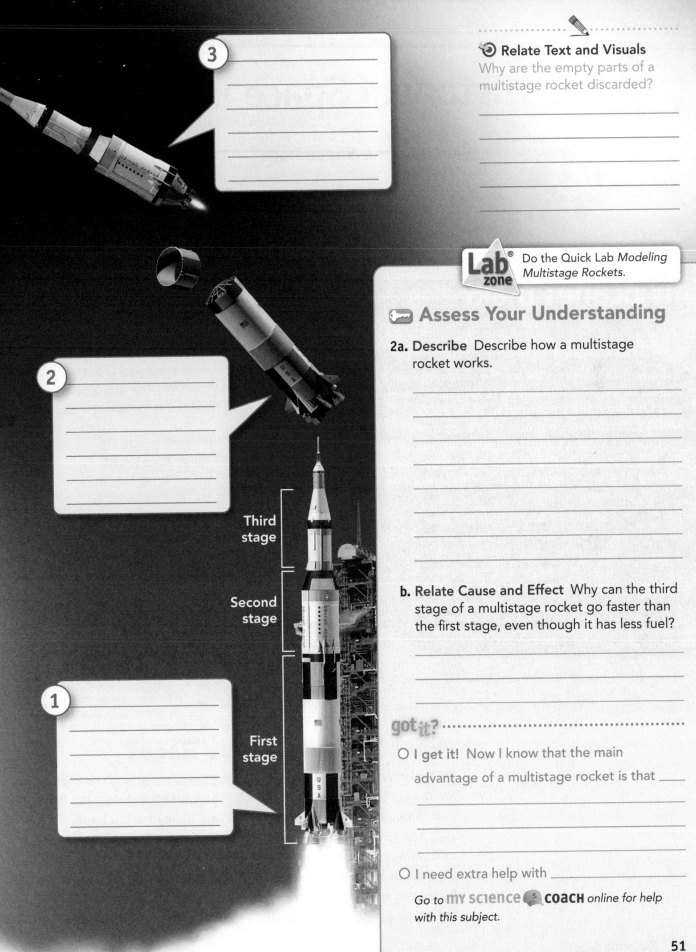

3

2

1

Third stage

Second stage

First stage

✏️ ⊙ **Relate Text and Visuals**
Why are the empty parts of a multistage rocket discarded?

_____

_____

_____

_____

_____

Lab zone ® Do the Quick Lab *Modeling Multistage Rockets.*

🔑 **Assess Your Understanding**

2a. Describe Describe how a multistage rocket works.

_____

_____

_____

_____

_____

_____

_____

_____

b. Relate Cause and Effect Why can the third stage of a multistage rocket go faster than the first stage, even though it has less fuel?

_____

_____

_____

got it? ....

○ **I get it!** Now I know that the main advantage of a multistage rocket is that ____

_____

_____

○ **I need extra help with** _____

Go to **my science** ⓢ **coach** *online for help with this subject.*

51

The History of Space Exploration

UNLOCK THE BIG ?

🔑 **What Was the Space Race?**

🔑 **How Are Space Shuttles and Space Stations Used?**

🔑 **How Are Space Probes Used?**

MY PLANET DIARY

DISCOVERY

The *Cassini* Space Probe

Scientists believe that for life to emerge on a planet or moon, there needs to be liquid water and just the right amount of heat. In 2005, NASA's *Cassini* space probe sent back evidence that one of Saturn's moons, Enceladus, might fit the bill. *Cassini* photographed geysers spewing plumes of water hundreds of kilometers above the moon's surface.

Scientists found that the best explanation for these geysers was liquid water below the surface. So it's possible that there is both enough water and heat within Enceladus to support life.

Communicate Use what you know about life on Earth to answer the question below. Then discuss your answer with a partner.

Why do scientists think that conditions for life might exist within Enceladus?

_____

_____

_____

▷ PLANET DIARY Go to **Planet Diary** to learn more about space probes.

Lab zone® Do the Inquiry Warm-Up *Where on the Moon Did the Astronauts Land?*

What Was the Space Race?

In the 1950s, the Soviet Union was the greatest rival to the United States in politics and military power. The tensions between the two countries were so high that they were said to be in a "cold war." 🔑 **The space race was the rivalry between the United States and the Soviet Union to explore space. It began in 1957, when the Soviets launched the satellite *Sputnik I* into orbit. The United States responded by speeding up its own space program, which led to the Apollo moon missions in the 1960s and the early 1970s.**

Vocabulary
- satellite • space shuttle
- space station • space probe
- rover

Skills
↻ Reading: Ask Questions
△ Inquiry: Make Models

The First Artificial Satellites

A **satellite** is an object that revolves around another object in space. The moon is a natural satellite of Earth. A spacecraft orbiting Earth is an artificial satellite. *Sputnik I* was the first artificial satellite. This success by the Soviets caused great alarm in the United States.

The United States responded in early 1958 by launching its own satellite, *Explorer 1,* into orbit. Over the next few years, the United States and the Soviet Union launched many more satellites.

Later in 1958, the United States created a government agency in charge of its space program called the National Aeronautics and Space Administration (NASA). NASA brought together the talents of many scientists and engineers. They solved the difficult technical problems of space flight.

Humans in Space

In 1961, the Soviets launched the first human into space. Yuri Gagarin flew one orbit around Earth aboard *Vostok 1.* Less than a month later, Alan Shepard became the first American in space, but did not orbit Earth. His spacecraft, *Freedom 7,* was part of the Mercury space program.

The first American to orbit Earth was John Glenn. He was launched into space aboard the space capsule *Friendship 7* in 1962. The tiny capsule orbited Earth three times.

FIGURE 1 ···

Space Race Timeline

✎ **Relate Text and Visuals** Write the name and historic first of each spacecraft with its picture.

Name: _____
First: _____
_____

Name: _____
First: _____
_____

1962

1961

1961

Name: _____
First: _____
_____

1957

1958

Name: _____
First: _____
_____

Name: _____
First: _____

The Apollo Program

"I believe that this nation should commit itself to achieving the goal, before the decade is out, of landing a man on the moon and returning him safely to Earth." With these words from a May 1961 speech, President John F. Kennedy launched a program of space exploration and scientific research. 🔑 **The American effort to land astronauts on the moon and return them to Earth was named the Apollo program.** **Figure 2** shows some major events of Apollo.

FIGURE 2 ···

Major Events in Moon Exploration

Apollo astronaut Buzz Aldrin described the landscape of the moon as "magnificent desolation."

✎ **Make Generalizations Look at the pictures of the moon's surface. Why is Aldrin's phrase appropriate?**

_____

_____

_____

_____

_____

_____

❶ Exploring the Moon

Between 1959 and 1972, the United States and the Soviet Union sent many unpiloted spacecraft to explore the moon. When a U.S. spacecraft called *Surveyor* landed on the moon, it didn't sink into the surface. This proved that the moon had a solid, rocky surface. Next, scientists searched for a suitable place to land humans on the moon.

❷ The Moon Landings

In July 1969, three American astronauts circled the moon aboard *Apollo 11*. Once in orbit, Neil Armstrong and Buzz Aldrin entered a tiny spacecraft called *Eagle*. On July 20, the *Eagle* descended toward a flat area on the moon's surface called the Sea of Tranquility. When Armstrong radioed that the *Eagle* had landed, cheers rang out at the NASA Space Center in Houston, Texas. A few hours later, Armstrong and Aldrin left the *Eagle* to walk on the surface of the moon.

3 Moon Rocks and Moonquakes

The astronauts collected 382 kilograms of lunar samples, commonly called "moon rocks," for analysis. Scientists such as Andrea B. Mosie and astronaut Jack Schmitt studied these rocks. They learned that the minerals that make up moon rocks are the same minerals that are found on Earth. However, in some moon rocks these minerals combine to form kinds of rocks that are not found on Earth.

One way Apollo astronauts explored the structure of the moon was to study the many moonquakes that occur there. Instruments they left behind, called seismometers, identified more than 7,000 moonquakes. By measuring these waves, scientists found that the moon may have a small core of molten rock or metal at its center.

4 On the Moon's Surface

Everything that the *Apollo 11* astronauts found was new and exciting. For about two hours, Armstrong and Aldrin explored the moon's surface, collecting samples to take back to Earth. They also planted an American flag.

Over the next three years, five more Apollo missions landed on the moon. In these later missions, astronauts were able to stay on the moon for days instead of hours. Some astronauts even used a lunar rover, or buggy, to explore larger areas of the moon.

Summarize After reading through the story of the Apollo program, list three discoveries that scientists made about the moon.

_____

_____

_____

_____

_____

_____

_____

_____

_____

FIGURE 3

Lunar Base

A possible future base on the moon is shown in this artist's conception.

✏️ **Describe** Explain how living on the moon would be similar to going camping.

_____

_____

_____

_____

_____

Missions Beyond the Moon The Apollo missions were a tremendous achievement. They yielded fascinating information and memorable images. Yet, the cost of those missions was high. There were few immediate benefits beyond the knowledge gained about the moon and Earth's formation. NASA moved on to other projects. For many years after, the moon was largely ignored.

In the first decade of the 21st century, interest in the moon revived for a brief period of time. In 2003, the European Space Agency launched an unpiloted spacecraft to orbit the moon. Its main purpose was to collect data for a lunar map. Such a map could be used in the future to select the best location for a possible lunar base. Figure 3 shows what a lunar base might look like.

Today, the United States is looking beyond the moon. In 2010, the country announced plans to launch a crewed spacecraft to Mars by the mid-2030's. The first missions would follow in the footsteps of the Apollo program that sent humans to the moon. A crewed mission would orbit Mars and then return. Only later would the United States attempt to land astronauts on Mars.

Lab zone ® Do the Quick Lab *Humans in Space.*

🔑 Assess Your Understanding

1a. Identify What was the Apollo program?

_____

_____

b. Draw Conclusions Was the Apollo program successful in meeting President Kennedy's challenge?

_____

_____

_____

got it?

○ **I get it!** Now I know that the space race began when the Soviets launched _____ _____ and continued with the American program called _____

○ **I need extra help with** _____

_____

Go to **MY SCIENCE** ⓢ **COACH** *online for help with this subject.*

How Are Space Shuttles and Space Stations Used?

After the great success of the moon landings, the question for space exploration was, "What comes next?" Scientists and public officials decided that one goal should be to build space shuttles and space stations where astronauts can live and work.

Space Shuttles Before 1981, spacecraft could be used only once. In contrast, a space shuttle is like an airplane—it can fly, land, and then fly again. A **space shuttle** is a spacecraft that can carry a crew into space, return to Earth, and then be reused for the same purpose. Because it can be reused, NASA doesn't have to build a new spacecraft for each mission. 🔑 **NASA has used space shuttles to perform many important tasks. These include taking satellites into orbit, repairing damaged satellites, and carrying astronauts and equipment to and from space stations.**

During a shuttle mission, astronauts live in a pressurized crew cabin at the front of the shuttle. There, they can wear regular clothes and breathe without an oxygen tank. Behind the crew cabin is a large, open area called the payload bay. A shuttle payload bay might carry a satellite to be released into orbit. It could also carry a laboratory in which astronauts can perform experiments. **Figure 4** shows the main parts of the space shuttle.

Vocabulary Identify Related Word Forms In science, the word *pressure* means "force per a given area." Why does the word *pressurized* mean that a crew cabin is filled with air?

_____

_____

_____

_____

FIGURE 4 ·····························

A Space Shuttle

A space shuttle has a crew cabin, a payload bay, and rockets.

✎ **Interpret Diagrams** On the diagram, label the main parts of the space shuttle and explain their use.

_____

_____

_____

_____

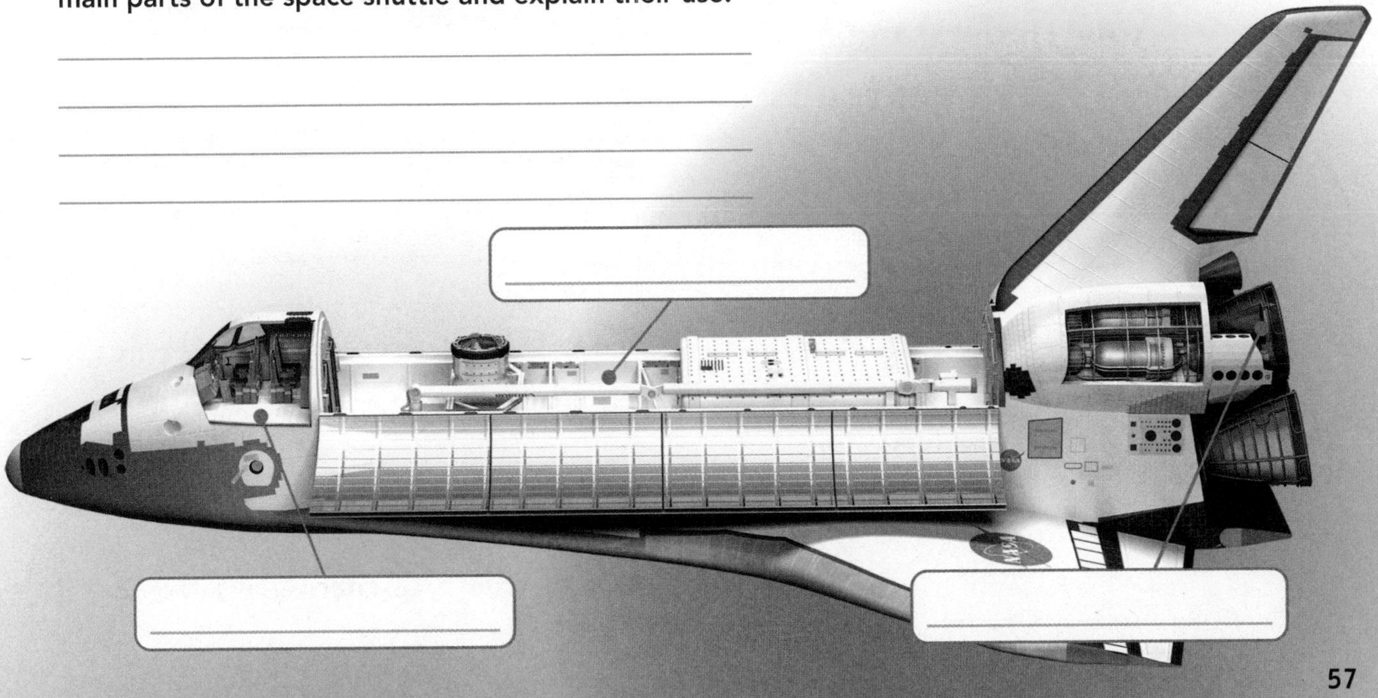

Space Stations

Have you ever wondered what it would be like to live in space? A **space station** is a large artificial satellite on which people can live and work for long periods. A **space station provides a place where long-term observations and experiments can be carried out in space.** In the 1970s and 1980s, both the United States and the Soviet Union placed space stations in orbit. The Soviet space station *Mir* stayed in orbit for 15 years before it fell to Earth in 2001. Astronauts from many countries spent time aboard *Mir*.

In the 1990s, the United States and 15 other countries began constructing the International Space Station (ISS). The first module, or section, of the station was placed into orbit in 1998. Since then, many other modules have been added. On board, astronauts from many countries are carrying out experiments in various fields of science. They are also learning more about how humans adapt to space.

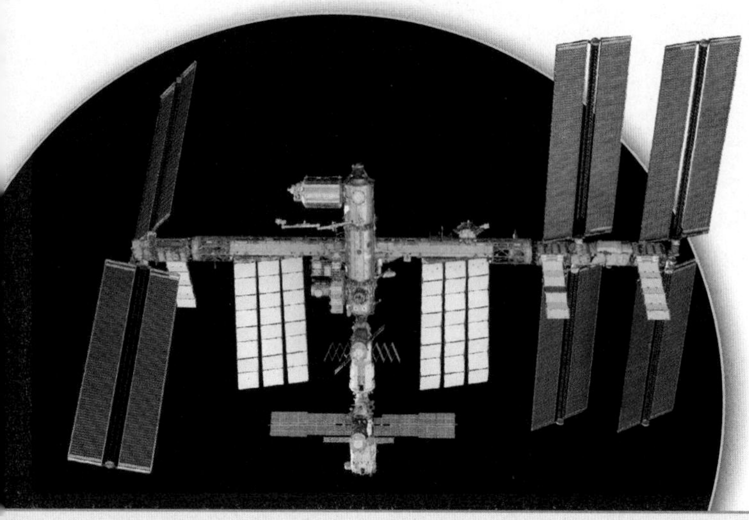

The main source of power for the International Space Station is its eight large arrays of solar panels, as shown in **Figure 5.** Together, the solar panels contain more than 250,000 solar cells, each capable of converting sunlight into electricity. At full power, the solar panels produce enough electricity to power about 55 houses on Earth. The ISS carries large batteries to provide power when it is in Earth's shadow.

FIGURE 5 ·····················

International Space Station

✎ CHALLENGE State one advantage of building a space station in orbit instead of sending it up all in one piece.

_____

_____

_____

_____

_____

_____

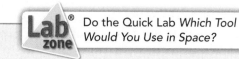

Lab zone ® Do the Quick Lab *Which Tool Would You Use in Space?*

☞ Assess Your Understanding

2a. Describe What is a space shuttle? What is a space station?

_____

_____

_____

_____

b. Compare and Contrast What is the main difference between space shuttles and space stations?

_____

_____

got it?

○ **I get it!** Now I know that space shuttles are used to _____

_____

_____

and a space station is used to _____

_____

_____

_____

○ **I need extra help with** _____

Go to MY SCIENCE ⓢ COACH *online for help with this subject.*

How Are Space Probes Used?

Since space exploration began in the 1950s, only 24 people have traveled as far as the moon. No one has traveled farther. Yet, during this period, space scientists have gathered a great deal of information about other parts of the solar system. This data was collected by space probes. A **space probe** is a spacecraft that carries scientific instruments that can collect data, but has no human crew.

Each space probe is designed for a specific mission. Some are designed to land on a certain planet, as shown in **Figure 6**. Others are designed to fly by and collect data about more than one planet. **A space probe collects data about the solar system and sends the information back to Earth.**

Each space probe has a power system to produce electricity and a communication system to send and receive signals. Probes also carry scientific instruments to collect data and perform experiments. Some probes, called orbiters, are equipped to photograph and analyze the atmosphere of a planet. Other probes, called landers, are equipped to land on a planet and analyze the materials on its surface. Some have small robots called **rovers** that move around on the surface. A rover typically has instruments that collect and analyze soil and rock samples.

🔄 **Ask Questions** What is one question about another planet you would want information from a space probe to answer?

_____

_____

_____

FIGURE 6 ....

› INTERACTIVE ART Space Probe Mission
The postcards show the steps of a space probe mission.

✎ **Write captions to tell the story of the space probe.**

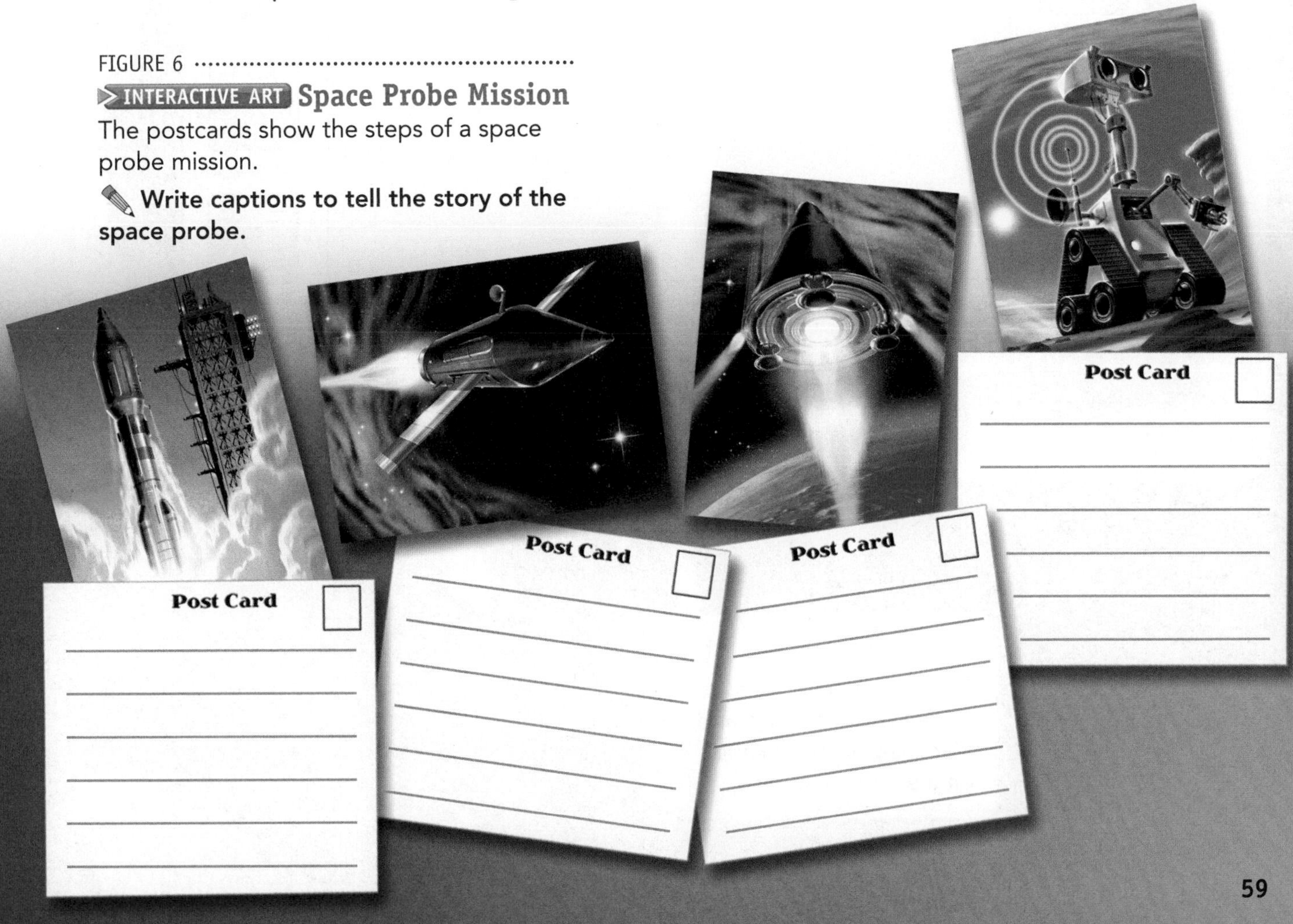

Post Card

Post Card

Post Card

Post Card

apply it!

Space probes such as the ones pictured here have now visited or passed near all of the planets. They have also explored many moons, asteroids, and comets.

❶ **Make Models** Choose a type of probe, either orbiter or lander, and draw your probe in the space provided below. List by number the tools required by each type of probe.

Lander: _____

Orbiter: _____

❷ **CHALLENGE** On the note paper, explain why you chose each item.

Design Your Own Space Probe

① Solar panel
② Wheels
③ Parachute
④ Camera
⑤ Antenna
⑥ Robotic arm
⑦ Landing pad
⑧ Mini lab

Lunar Prospector, 1998
Lunar Prospector found evidence of water ice and identified other minerals on the moon's surface.

New Horizons, 2006–2015
New Horizons is the first mission to the dwarf planet Pluto. It reached Pluto in July 2015.

_____
_____
_____
_____
_____
_____
_____
_____
_____
_____
_____
_____

Cassini, 2004
Cassini explored Saturn's moons. It launched a smaller probe, *Huygens*, which explored Titan, Saturn's largest moon.

Mars Exploration Rovers, 2004
Two rovers, *Opportunity* and *Spirit*, explored Mars's surface and found evidence of ancient water.

Lab ® Do the Quick Lab
zone *Remote Control.*

Assess Your Understanding

3a. Summarize What is a space probe?

_____
_____

b. Make Judgments What are the advantages and disadvantages of a space probe compared to a piloted spacecraft?

_____
_____
_____
_____

got it? ....

O **I get it!** Now I know that a space probe ___
_____
_____
_____

O **I need extra help with** _____

Go to **my science COACH** *online for help with this subject.*

Using Space Science on Earth

🔑 **What Are Conditions Like in Space?**

🔑 **How Has Space Technology Benefited People?**

🔑 **What Are Some Uses of Satellites Orbiting Earth?**

my planeT DiaRY

Ellen Ochoa

A couple of years after Sally Ride became the first American woman astronaut, Ellen Ochoa applied to NASA. She eventually went on missions aboard the space shuttle. Before she flew in space, however, Ochoa worked for NASA and other research organizations as an engineer. She invented three systems that use optical devices like lasers and holograms to get information from images. Her research can be applied to many different applications. They include inspecting equipment in a manufacturing plant and helping a spacecraft make a safe landing on Mars.

CAREERS

Communicate Discuss Ochoa's career with a partner. Then answer the question below.

How do you think Ochoa's inventions could be useful on Earth?

_____

_____

_____

_____

_____

_____

▶ PLANET DIARY Go to **Planet Diary** to learn more about space technology.

Lab Do the Inquiry Warm-Up
zone *Using Space Science.*

What Are Conditions Like in Space?

Astronauts who travel into space face conditions that are very different from those on Earth. 🔑 **Conditions in space that differ from those on Earth include near vacuum, extreme temperatures, and microgravity. Many types of engineers and scientists have worked together to respond to the challenges of space.**

Vocabulary

- vacuum • microgravity • space spinoff
- remote sensing • geostationary orbit

Skills

- Reading: Identify the Main Idea
- Inquiry: Draw Conclusions

Vacuum Even though you can't see the air, it fills every room in your house. But space has no air and is nearly a vacuum. A **vacuum** is a place that is empty of all matter. Except for a few stray atoms and molecules, space is mostly empty. Since there is no air in space, there is no oxygen for astronauts to breathe. To protect astronauts, spacecraft must be airtight.

Because there is no air, there is nothing to hold the sun's heat. In direct sunlight, the surface of a spacecraft heats up to high temperatures. But in shadow, temperatures fall to very low levels. Spacecraft must be well insulated to protect astronauts against the extreme temperatures outside.

Microgravity Have you ever floated in a swimming pool? Astronauts in orbit experience a similar feeling of weightlessness, or **microgravity.** Their mass is the same as it was on Earth, but on a scale their weight would register as zero. Although they are in microgravity, they are still under the influence of Earth's gravity. In fact, Earth's gravity is holding them in orbit. Astronauts in orbit feel weightless because they are falling through space with their spacecraft. They don't fall to Earth because their inertia keeps them moving forward. Recall that inertia is the tendency of an object to resist a change in motion.

Figure 1 shows astronaut Steve Frick experiencing microgravity. Engineers must create devices that are capable of working in microgravity. Drink containers must be designed so that their contents do not float off. Long periods spent in microgravity can cause health problems. Scientists are trying to discover how to reduce the effects of microgravity on people.

FIGURE 1 ·······························
Eating in Space
Astronaut Steve Frick eats a snack in orbit.

✏️ Draw Conclusions
How is eating in space different from eating on Earth?

_____

_____

_____

_____

Lab zone Do the Quick Lab *What Do You Need to Survive in Space?*

🔑 Assess Your Understanding

got it? ··

○ **I get it!** Now I know conditions in space that differ from those on Earth include _____

○ **I need extra help with** _____

Go to **my science ⑤ coach** *online for help with this subject.*

How Has Space Technology Benefited People?

The scientists and engineers who have worked on the space program have developed thousands of new materials and devices for use in space. Many of these items have proved useful on Earth as well. An item that has uses on Earth but was originally developed for use in space is called a **space spinoff.** Often such spinoffs are modified somewhat for use on Earth.

🗝 **The space program has led to the development of many thousands of products, among them consumer products, new materials, medical devices, and communications satellites.** The tables on these pages show a few familiar examples.

Consumer Products   Space spinoffs include many devices used in consumer products.

Materials	Use
Joystick controllers	Wheelchairs and video games
Scratch-resistant lenses	To make eyeglasses
Freeze-dried foods	Eaten by campers
Shock-absorbing helmets	Worn by cyclists
Shock-absorbing sneakers	Worn by runners

apply it!

Draw Conclusions Three items are shown in the top row that were developed for use in space. In the bottom row, write in the number for each item that corresponds to the space spinoff. Explain why you made each connection.

_____

_____

_____

_____

_____

_____

New Materials
A variety of materials were first developed by chemists and engineers for use in spacecraft.

Materials	Use
Composite materials	Tennis rackets and golf clubs
Memory metals	Flexible metal eyeglass frames
Clear, ceramic materials	Dental braces
Shielding materials	Houses, cars and trucks

Medical Devices
Medical science has benefited greatly from the technology of the space program.

Materials	Use
Computer-aided imaging techniques	By hospitals
Lasers	To clean clogged arteries
Pacemakers with longer-life batteries	For hearts

Lab zone Do the Lab Investigation *Space Spinoffs.*

Assess Your Understanding

1a. Define What is a space spinoff?

_____

_____

_____

b. Summarize How has medical science benefited from the space program?

_____

_____

_____

_____

_____

_____

c. Compare and Contrast Choose one space spinoff and compare how it is used in space and on Earth.

_____

_____

_____

got it? ....

○ **I get it!** Now I know that the space program has developed _____

_____

_____

○ **I need extra help with** _____

Go to my science ˢ coach *online for help with this subject.*

What Are Some Uses of Satellites Orbiting Earth?

When a World Cup soccer final is played, almost the entire world can watch! Today, hundreds of satellites are in orbit, relaying television signals from one part of the planet to another. Satellites also relay telephone signals and computer data. **Satellites are used for communications and for collecting weather data and other scientific data.**

Observation satellites are used for many purposes, including tracking weather systems, mapping Earth's surface, and observing changes in Earth's environment. Observation satellites collect data using **remote sensing,** which is the collection of information about Earth and other objects in space without being in direct contact. Modern computers take the data collected by satellites and produce images for various purposes. For example, **Figure 2** shows a scientist studying weather data. Satellite data might also be used to analyze the amount of rainfall over a wide area, or to discover where oil deposits lie underground.

Satellite orbits depend on their purpose. Most communications satellites are placed in a geostationary orbit. In a **geostationary orbit,** (jee oh STAY shuh ner ee) a satellite orbits Earth at the same rate as Earth rotates and thus stays over the same place over Earth's equator all the time.

🖉 **Identify the Main Idea**
In the paragraph at the right, underline the uses of observation satellites.

FIGURE 2 ·······································

Remote Sensing and Forest Fires
The scientist shown is studying weather data taken from a satellite by remote sensing.

🖉 [CHALLENGE] **How can remote sensing help fight forest fires?**

_____

_____

_____

_____

_____

EXPLORE THE BIG **?**

Space Spinoffs

How does exploring space benefit people on Earth?

FIGURE 3 ....

> INTERACTIVE ART The word bank below shows space spinoffs.

✎ **Demonstrate Consumer Literacy** Choose three items, and describe three ways you might use them on Earth. Label the items shown on the page.

Freeze-dried food	Solar panels	Space helmet
Communications satellites	Radio telescope	Scratch-resistant lenses
Global Positioning System (GPS)	Light-emitting diodes	Tiny fuel pumps
Gas detector	Infrared cameras	Pressurized ink

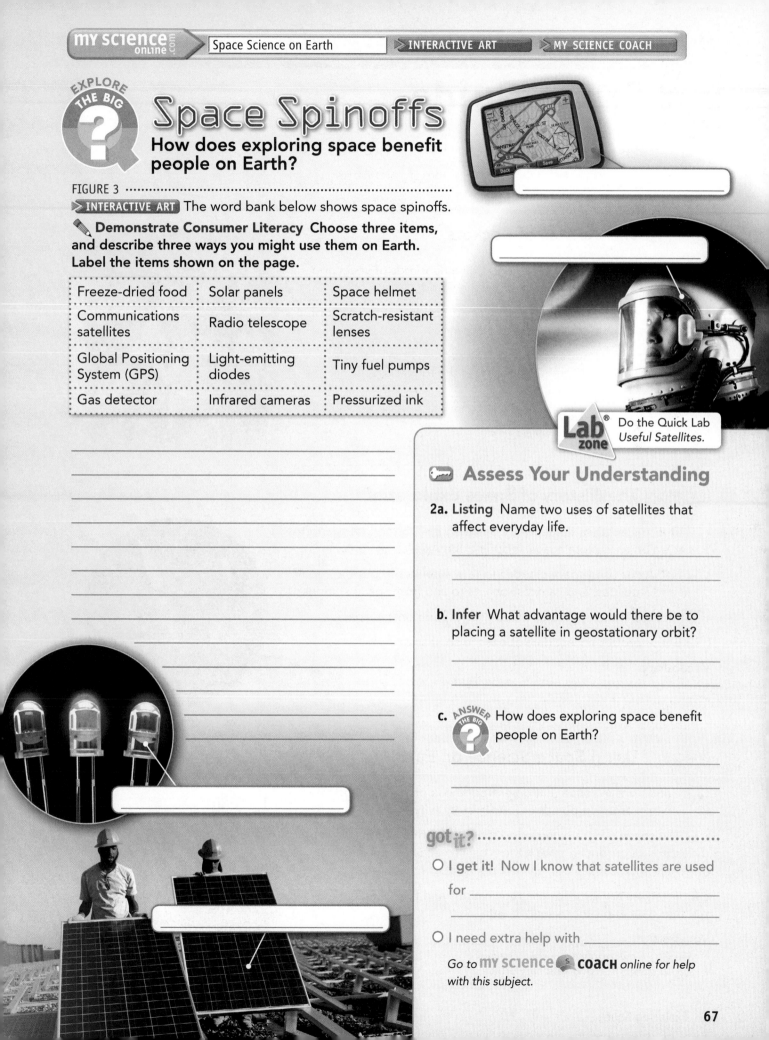

Lab® zone Do the Quick Lab *Useful Satellites.*

🔑 Assess Your Understanding

2a. Listing Name two uses of satellites that affect everyday life.

_____

_____

b. Infer What advantage would there be to placing a satellite in geostationary orbit?

_____

_____

c. ANSWER THE BIG **?** How does exploring space benefit people on Earth?

_____

_____

_____

got it? ....

O **I get it!** Now I know that satellites are used

for _____

_____

O **I need extra help with** _____

Go to my science ⓢ coach *online for help with this subject.*

Space science benefits people on Earth through _____

_____

LESSON 1 The Science of Rockets

🔑 Rocket technology originated in China hundreds of years ago and gradually spread to other parts of the world.

🔑 A rocket moves forward when gases shooting out the back of the rocket push it in the opposite direction.

🔑 The main advantage of a multistage rocket is that the total weight of the rocket is greatly reduced as the rocket rises.

Vocabulary
• rocket • thrust • velocity
• orbital velocity • escape velocity

LESSON 2 The History of Space Exploration

🔑 The space race was the rivalry between the United States and the Soviet Union to explore space, including the Apollo missions.

🔑 NASA has used space shuttles to take satellites into orbit, repair damaged satellites, and carry astronauts to and from space stations.

🔑 A space station provides a place for experiments in space.

🔑 Space probes collect data about the solar system.

Vocabulary
• satellite • space shuttle
• space station • space probe • rover

LESSON 3 Using Space Science on Earth

🔑 Conditions in space that differ from those on Earth include near vacuum, extreme temperatures, and microgravity.

🔑 The space program has led to the development of many thousands of products, among them consumer products, new materials, medical devices, and communications satellites.

🔑 Satellites are used for communications and for collecting weather data and other scientific data.

Vocabulary
• vacuum • microgravity • space spinoff
• remote sensing • geostationary orbit

Review and Assessment

LESSON 1 The Science of Rockets

1. Which term names a device that expels gas in one direction in order to move in the opposite direction?

a. space station   **b.** rover

c. space probe   **d.** rocket

2. Classify A jet airplane uses liquid fuel and oxygen from the atmosphere. The engine expels hot gases to the rear and the airplane moves forward. Is a jet a type of rocket? Explain.

_____

_____

_____

Use the illustration to answer the question below.

3. Apply Concepts The diagram shows a rocket lifting off. What does each arrow represent?

_____

_____

_____

4. math! For every force there is an equal and opposite force. Describe a line graph that shows the relationship between a rocket's reaction force and thrust.

_____

_____

LESSON 2 The History of Space Exploration

5. What is any object that revolves around another object in space?

a. rocket   **b.** vacuum

c. satellite   **d.** shuttle

6. Relate Cause and Effect After the Soviet Union launched *Sputnik I*, American educators improved math and science education. What explains this decision?

_____

_____

_____

_____

7. Make Generalizations Give one way in which the International Space Station could help with further exploration of the solar system.

_____

_____

_____

_____

8. Compare and Contrast How is a space shuttle different from a space probe?

_____

_____

_____

_____

_____

_____

_____

9. **Write About It** Suppose you are planning a Mars mission. List some major challenges the mission would face and suggest possible solutions. How will the crew's basic needs be met on the long journey?

LESSON 3 Using Space Science on Earth

10. Classify Name a space spinoff in each of the following categories: medical devices, materials, consumer products.

_____

_____

_____

_____

_____

Use the graph to answer Questions 11 and 12.

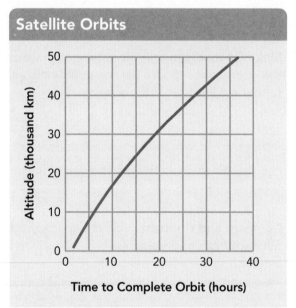

Satellite Orbits

11. Reading Graphs A geostationary satellite orbits Earth once every 24 hours. At what altitude does such a satellite orbit?

_____

_____

12. Making Generalizations What is the relationship between satellite altitude and the time needed to complete one orbit?

_____

_____

_____

APPLY THE BIG ? How does exploring space benefit people on Earth?

13. Suppose your car broke down in an unfamiliar place. Explain two ways that satellites in orbit could help you get assistance.

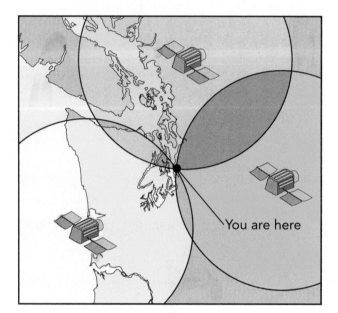

You are here

_____

_____

_____

_____

_____

_____

_____

_____

_____

_____

_____

_____

_____

Standardized Test Prep

Multiple Choice

Circle the letter of the best answer.

1. The diagram below shows a rocket and the direction of four forces.

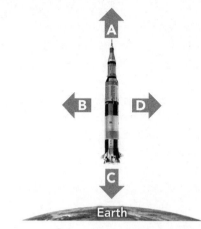

Which force represents an equal and opposite force to the thrust of the rocket?

A Force A

B Force B

C Force C

D Force D

2. Which of the following is most responsible for rockets reaching the moon?

A explosives

B single-stage rockets

C gunpowder

D multistage rockets

3. How often does a satellite in geostationary orbit revolve around Earth?

A once per hour

B once per day

C once per month

D once per year

4. Which of these did the United States accomplish first during the space race?

A sending the first human being into space

B sending the first living creature into space

C landing the first human on the moon

D launching the first satellite into space

5. What force must a rocket overcome to reach space?

A gravity

B escape velocity

C thrust

D orbital velocity

Constructed Response

Use the diagram below and your knowledge of science to help you answer Question 6. Write your answer on a separate sheet of paper.

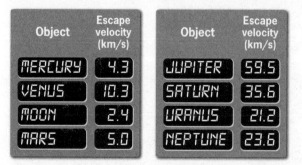

Object	Escape velocity (km/s)	Object	Escape velocity (km/s)
MERCURY	4.3	JUPITER	59.5
VENUS	10.3	SATURN	35.6
MOON	2.4	URANUS	21.2
MARS	5.0	NEPTUNE	23.6

6. The table shows the escape velocity for a rocket leaving different objects in the solar system. Explain why it might be easier to launch a rocket to Mars from the moon rather than from Earth. What would be the problem with sending astronauts to explore Jupiter?

Museum of Science | TECH & DESIGN

One Ticket to Space, Please

Soon, tourists could be lining up to visit . . . space?

Right now, highly trained astronauts who work with space agencies such as the National Aeronautics and Space Administration (NASA), the Japan Aerospace Exploration Agency, or the European Space Agency travel to space. But a small number of companies have started testing space flights that will take paying passengers the way airplanes and trains do. Passengers will be able to fly to space. Companies hope to make space travel available to many people.

So what can you look forward to as a space tourist? The aircraft will fly to the edge of the atmosphere at three times the speed of sound. Then, the aircraft will launch two rockets carrying passengers. The rockets will enter space and float for about 5 minutes. Passengers will experience total weightlessness—with enough time to do flips in zero gravity! The rockets will then return to Earth. Space tourism—it's going to be out of this world!

Write About It Create a magazine ad promoting the flights. Think about who you are targeting, where your ad should be placed, and what design will convince the most people.

Museum of Science

Living in Space:

THE EXPEDITION 18 CREW

Far above Earth, astronauts from different countries are working together to build a research facility in space.

In 1998, a Russian rocket launched the first piece of the International Space Station (ISS). Ten years later, the eighteenth crew to make the station their home arrived at the ISS.

The crew of Expedition 18 included members from the United States, Russian, and Japanese space programs. Each member of the crew had specific jobs to do in space. Flight Engineer Sandra Magnus installed a new toilet. When Magnus's stay was completed, Flight Engineer Koichi Wakata and his crew installed a system to recycle the crew's water.

The work of these astronauts represents a step toward the colonization of space. The crews who work on the ISS are learning how to address human needs in space. They are also teaching us about the effects that life in space can have on human bodies.

Research It Will a boomerang return to its thrower in zero gravity? For a fun experiment to do in his own time, Japanese astronaut Takao Doi took one to the ISS and found out. Make a hypothesis, then write a report on his results.

WHAT MIGHT SATURN'S RINGS BE MADE OF?

Why are objects in the solar system different from each other?

This photograph from the *Cassini* space probe shows Saturn and part of its magnificent system of rings. Space probes such as *Cassini* have helped scientists learn more about the objects in the solar system.

Infer What do you think Saturn's rings are made of? How might they have formed?

> **UNTAMED SCIENCE** Watch the **Untamed Science** video to learn more about the solar system.

_____

_____

_____

_____

_____

_____

The Solar System

3 Getting Started

Check Your Understanding

1. **Background** Read the paragraph below and then answer the question.

Tyrone is watching a movie. He sees astronauts explore a planet that **revolves** around a star. As the astronauts travel, they notice that the planet **rotates**. Tyrone knows that **gravity** holds the planet in orbit around the star.

> **Revolution** is the motion of one object around another.
>
> An object **rotates** when it spins around a central axis.
>
> **Gravity** is the force that attracts all objects toward each other.

• What causes day and night on a planet?

_____

_____

> **MY READING WEB** If you had trouble completing the question above, visit **My Reading Web** and type in *The Solar System.*

Vocabulary Skill

Greek Word Origins Many science words come to English from Greek. In this chapter, you will learn the term *geocentric. Geocentric* comes from the Greek word parts *ge*, meaning "Earth," and *kentron*, meaning "center."

$$\underset{\textbf{Earth}}{ge} \quad + \quad \underset{\textbf{center}}{kentron} \quad = \quad \underset{\textbf{having Earth at the center}}{geocentric}$$

Learn these Greek word parts to help you remember the vocabulary terms.

Greek Word	Meaning	Example
helios	sun	heliocentric, *adj.*
chromas	color	chromosphere, *n.*
sphaira	sphere	photosphere, *n.*

2. **Quick Check** Predict the meaning of *heliocentric.*

_____

_____

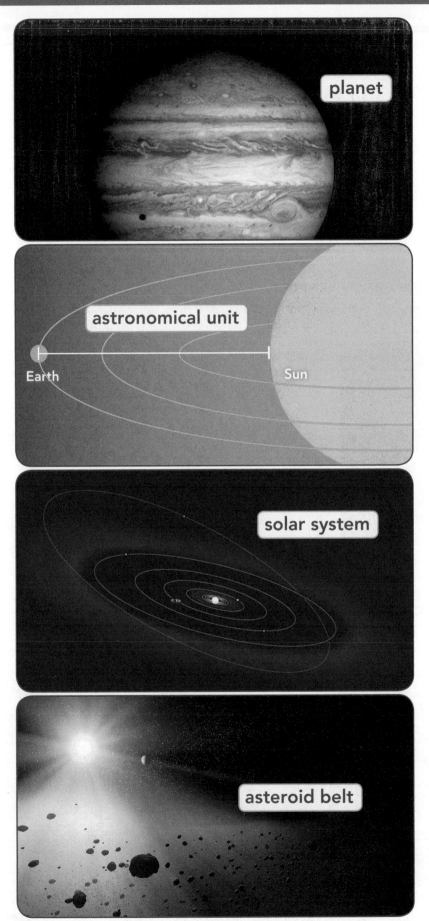

planet

astronomical unit

Earth — Sun

solar system

asteroid belt

Chapter Preview

LESSON 1
- geocentric • heliocentric
- ellipse
- Sequence
- Make Models

LESSON 2
- solar system • astronomical unit
- planet • dwarf planet
- planetesimal
- Identify Supporting Evidence
- Calculate

LESSON 3
- core • nuclear fusion
- radiation zone • convection zone
- photosphere • chromosphere
- corona • solar wind • sunspot
- prominence • solar flare
- Relate Cause and Effect
- Interpret Data

LESSON 4
- terrestrial planet
- greenhouse effect
- Compare and Contrast
- Communicate

LESSON 5
- gas giant • ring
- Outline
- Pose Questions

LESSON 6
- asteroid belt • Kuiper belt
- Oort cloud • comet
- coma • nucleus • asteroid
- meteoroid • meteor • meteorite
- Summarize
- Classify

> VOCAB FLASH CARDS For extra help
with vocabulary, visit **Vocab Flash
Cards** and type in *The Solar System.*

Models of the Solar System

UNLOCK THE BIG ?

🔑 **What Was the Geocentric Model?**

🔑 **How Did the Heliocentric Model Develop?**

my planet Diary

Picturing the Solar System

When Walter Myers was seven years old, he found a book with drawings of astronauts walking on the moons of Saturn. Ever since, he's been making space pictures himself. At first, he used pencil. Today, he works on computers. He likes using computers because he can create images that are more like photographs, such as the ones below.

As an artist, Mr. Myers can show scenes that haven't been photographed, such as ideas for future spacecraft and the views from another planet's moons. Mr. Myers especially likes creating views of what human visitors to other planets might see. His work has appeared in books, magazines, Web sites, and even on television!

Use what you have read to answer these questions.

1. What tool does Walter Myers use?

   _____

2. Why do people use art or other models to show objects in the solar system?

   _____
   _____
   _____
   _____

> PLANET DIARY   Go to **Planet Diary** to learn more about models of the solar system.

Lab zone®   Do the Inquiry Warm-Up *What Is at the Center?*

Vocabulary
- geocentric
- heliocentric
- ellipse

Skills
- Reading: Sequence
- Inquiry: Make Models

What Was the Geocentric Model?

From here on Earth, it seems as if our planet is stationary and that the sun, moon, and stars are moving around Earth. But is the sky really moving above you? Centuries ago, before there were space shuttles or even telescopes, people had no easy way to find out.

Ancient Observations
Ancient observers, including the Greeks, Chinese, and Mayans, noticed that the patterns of the stars didn't change over time. Although the stars seemed to move, they stayed in the same position relative to one another. These people also observed planets, which moved among the stars.

Many early observers thought Earth was at the center of the universe. Some Chinese observers thought Earth was under a dome of stars. Many Greek astronomers thought that Earth was inside rotating spheres nested inside each other. These spheres contained the stars and planets. Since *ge* is the Greek word for "Earth," an Earth-centered model is known as a **geocentric** (jee oh SEN trik) model. **In a geocentric model, Earth is at the center of the revolving planets and stars.**

Ptolemy's Model
About A.D. 140, the Greek astronomer Ptolemy (TAHL uh mee) further developed the geocentric model. Like the earlier Greeks, Ptolemy thought that Earth was at the center of the universe. In Ptolemy's model, however, the planets moved in small circles carried along in bigger circles.

Ptolemy's geocentric model explained the motions observed in the sky fairly accurately. As a result, the geocentric model of the universe was widely accepted for nearly 1,500 years after Ptolemy.

apply it!

Critique Scientific Explanations and Models Describe an experience from everyday life that appears to support the geocentric model.

_____
_____
_____
_____
_____
_____
_____

Do the Quick Lab
Going Around in Circles.

Assess Your Understanding

got it? ....

○ **I get it!** Now I know that the geocentric model is _____

_____

_____

○ **I need extra help with** _____

Go to MY SCIENCE COACH online for help with this subject.

How Did the Heliocentric Model Develop?

Not everybody believed in the geocentric system. An ancient Greek scientist named Aristarchus developed a sun-centered model called a heliocentric (hee lee oh SEN trik) system. *Helios* is Greek for "sun." In a heliocentric system, Earth and the other planets revolve around the sun. This model was not well received in ancient times, however, because people could not accept that Earth was not at the center of the universe.

FIGURE 1 ....

Changing Models

△ Make Models Draw each model of the solar system. Include the sun, Earth, the moon, and Jupiter. Include Jupiter's moons in Galileo's model.

CHALLENGE Why might people not have believed Galileo's discoveries?

_____

_____

1500   **1550**

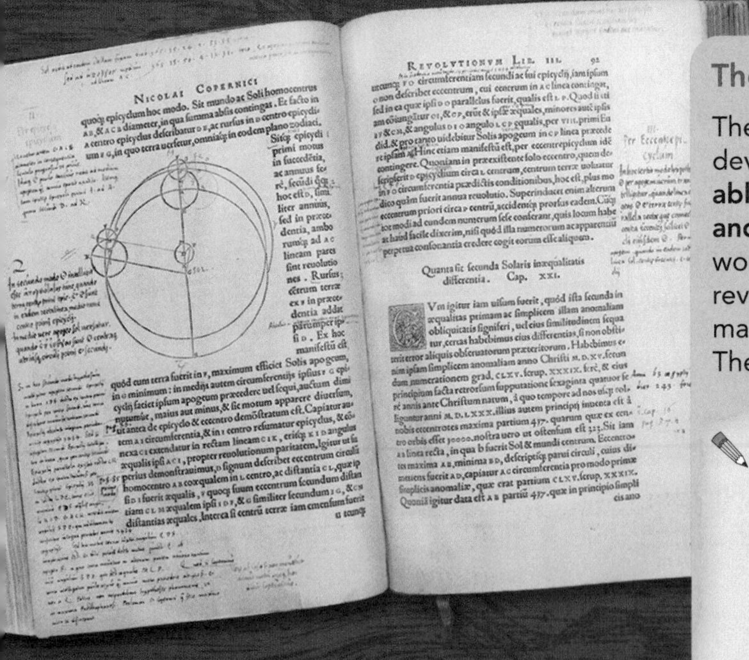

The Copernican Revolution

The Polish astronomer Nicolaus Copernicus further developed the heliocentric model. 🔑 **Copernicus was able to work out the arrangement of the known planets and how they move around the sun.** He published his work in 1543. Copernicus's theory would eventually revolutionize the science of astronomy. But at first many people were unwilling to accept his theory. They needed more evidence to be convinced.

✏️ Draw Copernicus's model.

↺ Sequence Which astronomer did his work first?
- ○ Tycho Brahe
- ○ Nicolaus Copernicus
- ○ Galileo Galilei
- ○ Johannes Kepler

Brahe and Kepler

Ptolemy and Copernicus both assumed that planets moved in perfect circles. Their models fit existing observations fairly well. But in the late 1500s, the Dutch astronomer Tycho Brahe (TEE koh BRAH uh) made much more accurate observations. Brahe's assistant, Johannes Kepler, used the observations to figure out the shape of the planets' orbits. When he used circular orbits, his calculations did not fit the observations. **After years of detailed calculations, Kepler found that the orbit of each planet is an ellipse. An ellipse is an oval shape.**

🖊 **Draw Kepler's model.**

Tycho Brahe's Observatory

○ **1600**   **1650**

Galileo's Evidence

In the 1500s and early 1600s, most people still believed in the geocentric model. **However, evidence collected by the Italian scientist Galileo Galilei gradually convinced others that the heliocentric model was correct.** In 1610, Galileo used a telescope to discover four moons around Jupiter. These moons proved that not everything in the sky revolves around Earth. Galileo also discovered that Venus goes through a series of phases similar to the moon's. But Venus would not have a full set of phases if both it and the sun circled around Earth. Therefore, Galileo reasoned, the geocentric model must be incorrect.

🖊 **Draw Galileo's model.**

Lab® Do the Quick Lab
zone *A Loopy Ellipse.*

🔑 Assess Your Understanding

1a. Review (Kepler/Copernicus) discovered that planets move in ellipses.

b. Relate Evidence and Explanation What discoveries by Galileo support the heliocentric model?

_____

_____

_____

got it?

○ **I get it!** Now I know that the heliocentric model was developed _____

_____

○ **I need extra help with** _____

Go to **MY SCIENCE** ⓢ **COACH** online for help with this subject.

81

Introducing the Solar System

UNLOCK THE BIG ?

🔑 What Makes Up the Solar System?

🔑 How Did the Solar System Form?

my planet DiaRY

Extreme Conditions

Imagine a place where the sun shines 11 times brighter than it does on Earth. How could you keep anything cool there? Engineers had to solve just that problem when designing the Mercury *MESSENGER* spacecraft. In 2008, this spacecraft began to visit Mercury, where temperatures can reach up to 370°C. Engineers designed a sunshade to protect *MESSENGER*'s instruments. It's made from ceramic fabric! The fabric, made of elements such as silicon, aluminum, and boron, is resistant to heat. It reflects most of the sun's heat away from the *MESSENGER* spacecraft, keeping all the instruments at a comfortable room temperature (about 20°C).

TECHNOLOGY

Use what you have read to answer the questions below.

1. Why did engineers need to design a sunshade for Mercury *MESSENGER*?

   _____

   _____

   _____

2. What other challenges do you think there would be for engineers designing a spacecraft to travel to Mercury?

   _____

   _____

   _____

> PLANET DIARY Go to **Planet Diary** to learn more about the solar system.

Lab zone Do the Inquiry Warm-Up *How Big Is Earth?*

Vocabulary
- solar system
- astronomical unit
- planet
- dwarf planet
- planetesimal

Skills
- ⟳ Reading: Identify Supporting Evidence
- △ Inquiry: Calculate

What Makes Up the Solar System?

Mercury is just one of many objects that make up the solar system. 🔑 **Our solar system consists of the sun, the planets, their moons, and a variety of smaller objects**. The sun is at the center of the solar system, with other objects orbiting around it. The force of gravity holds the solar system together.

Distances in the Solar System Distances within the solar system are so large that they cannot be easily measured in meters or kilometers. Instead, scientists often use a unit called the astronomical unit. One **astronomical unit** (AU) equals the average distance between Earth and the sun, about 150,000,000 kilometers. The solar system extends more than 100,000 AU from the sun.

do the math!

Converting Units

To convert from astronomical units (AU) to kilometers (km), you can multiply the number of AU by 150,000,000.

❶ **Calculate** Mars is 1.52 AU from the sun. About how many kilometers is Mars from the sun? _____

❷ **Apply Concepts** If you know an object's distance from the sun in kilometers, how can you find its distance in AU? _____

_____

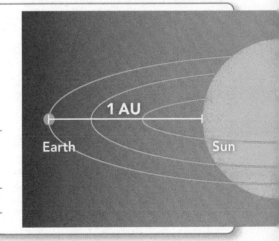

The Sun At the center of our solar system is the sun. The sun is much larger than anything else in the solar system. About 99.85 percent of the mass of the solar system is contained within the sun. Despite being more than a million times the volume of Earth, our sun is actually a very ordinary mid-sized star. Using telescopes, we see stars that have volumes a thousand times greater than the sun's! This turns out to be a very good thing for us. Large stars burn out and die quickly, but our sun will last for five billion more years.

⟳ **Identify Supporting Evidence** Underline a sentence that supports the statement, "The sun is much larger than anything else in the solar system."

FIGURE 1 ···

> INTERACTIVE ART **The Solar System**

The planets' sizes are shown to scale, but their distances from the sun are not.

✎ **Mark the position of each planet on the distance scale above.**

1. **Interpret Data** Where is the largest gap between planets?

_____

2. CHALLENGE Could you show the planets' relative sizes and distances from the sun in the same diagram on one page? Why or why not?

_____

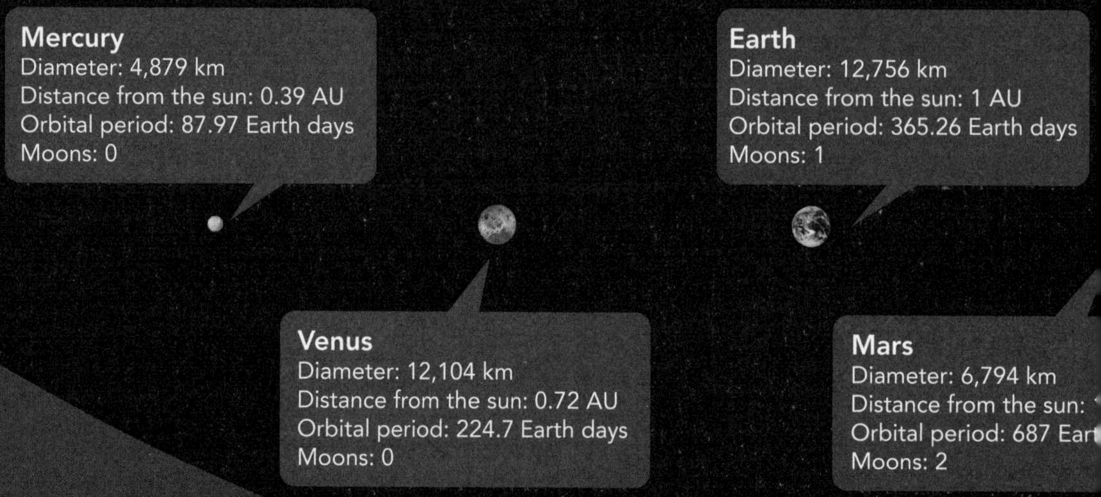

Mercury
Diameter: 4,879 km
Distance from the sun: 0.39 AU
Orbital period: 87.97 Earth days
Moons: 0

Earth
Diameter: 12,756 km
Distance from the sun: 1 AU
Orbital period: 365.26 Earth days
Moons: 1

Venus
Diameter: 12,104 km
Distance from the sun: 0.72 AU
Orbital period: 224.7 Earth days
Moons: 0

Mars
Diameter: 6,794 km
Distance from the sun:
Orbital period: 687 Ear
Moons: 2

Planets

There are many different objects in the solar system. How do you decide what is a planet and what isn't? In 2006, astronomers decided that a planet must be round, orbit the sun, and have cleared out the region of the solar system along its orbit. The first four planets are small and are mostly made of rock and metal. The last four planets are very large and are mostly made of gas and liquid. Like Earth, each planet has a "day" and a "year." Its day is the time it takes to rotate on its axis. Its year is the time it takes to orbit the sun. **Figure 1** shows some basic facts about the planets.

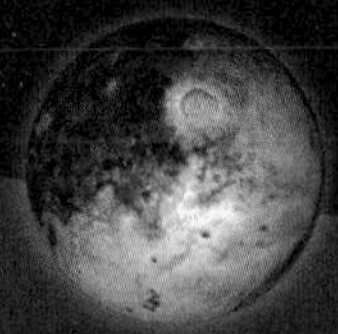

Dwarf Planets

For many years, Pluto was considered the planet in the solar system. But Pluto share area of its orbit with other objects. Pluto is considered a dwarf planet. A dwarf plane object that orbits the sun and has enough to be spherical, but has not cleared the are orbit. There are five known dwarf planets i solar system: Pluto, Eris, Ceres, Makemake (MAH keh MAH keh), and Haumea (how MAY scientists observe more distant objects, th

Satellites

Except for Mercury and Venus, every planet in the solar system has at least one natural satellite, or moon. Earth has the fewest moons, with just one. Jupiter and Saturn each have more than 60! Some dwarf planets also have satellites.

Smaller Objects

The solar system also includes many smaller objects that orbit the sun. Some, called asteroids, are small, mostly rocky bodies. Many asteroids are found in an area between the orbits of Mars and Jupiter. Comets are another large group of solar system objects. Comets are loose balls of ice and rock that usually have very long, narrow orbits.

Saturn
Diameter: 120,536 km
Distance from the sun: 9.54 AU
Orbital period: 29.47 Earth years
Moons: 60+

Neptune
Diameter: 49,258 km
Distance from the sun: 30.07 AU
Orbital period: 163.72 Earth years
Moons: 13+

Uranus
Diameter: 51,118 km
Distance from the sun: 19.19 AU
Orbital period: 83.75 Earth years
Moons: 20+

Jupiter
Diameter: 142,984 km
Distance from the sun: 5.20 AU
Orbital period: 11.86 Earth years
Moons: 60+

 Do the Lab Investigation
Speeding Around the Sun.

🔑 Assess Your Understanding

1a. Sequence List the planets in order of increasing distance from the sun.

_____

_____

_____

b. Make Generalizations What is the relationship between a planet's distance from the sun and the length of its year?

_____

_____

got it?

○ **I get it!** Now I know that the solar system includes _____

_____

_____

○ **I need extra help with** _____

_____

Go to **my science COACH** *online for help with this subject.*

How Did the Solar System Form?

Where did the objects in the solar system come from? ◯ **Scientists think the solar system formed about 4.6 billion years ago from a cloud of hydrogen, helium, rock, ice, and other materials pulled together by gravity.**

A Spinning Disk The process began as gravity pulled the cloud's material together. The cloud collapsed and started to rotate, forming a disk. Most of the material was pulled to the center. As this material became tightly packed, it got hotter and the pressure on it increased.

Eventually, the temperature and pressure became so high that hydrogen atoms were pressed together to form helium. This process, called nuclear fusion, releases large amounts of energy. Once nuclear fusion began, the sun gave off light and became a stable star. Sunlight is one form of the energy produced by fusion.

The Planets Form Away from the sun, planets began to form as gravity pulled rock, ice, and gas together. The rock and ice formed small bodies called **planetesimals** (pla nuh TE suh muhlz). Over time, planetesimals collided and stuck together, eventually combining to form all the other objects in the solar system.

Inner Planets Close to the sun, the solar system was very hot. Most water evaporated, preventing ice from forming. The bodies that formed in this region were comparatively low in mass. Their gravity was too weak to hold on to light gases such as hydrogen and helium. This is why the inner planets are small and rocky.

Outer Planets At greater distances from the sun, temperatures were cooler. Ice formed, adding mass to the planets that formed at these distances. As the planets grew, their gravity was strong enough to hold hydrogen and helium, forming the gas giant planets. Beyond the gas giants, temperatures were even lower. Ice and other materials produced comets and dwarf planets.

FIGURE 2 ·······························

▶ ART IN MOTION **Formation of the Solar System**

✎ **Sequence** Write the numbers 1 through 4 in the circles to put the images in order.

EXPLORE THE BIG ?

Solve THE SOLAR SYSTEM

Why are objects in the solar system different from each other?

FIGURE 3 ·····························
Use the clues to complete the puzzle.
Then answer the question.

ACROSS

3 The planet farthest from the sun
4 A loose, icy body with a long, narrow orbit
6 A gas giant planet that is smaller than Jupiter but larger than Neptune
7 The smallest planet in the solar system
8 An object that orbits a planet

DOWN

1 The largest planet in the solar system
2 A planet that formed closer to the sun than Earth but not closest to the sun
5 A small rocky body that orbits the sun

Why are the objects in clues 2 and 6 so different?

_____

_____

_____

Lab zone Do the Quick Lab *Clumping Planets.*

🔑 Assess Your Understanding

2a. Explain What force formed the solar system?

_____

b. ANSWER THE BIG ? Why are objects in the solar system different from each other?

_____

_____

_____

_____

got it?

○ **I get it!** Now I know that the solar system formed when _____

_____

_____

○ **I need extra help with** _____

Go to MY SCIENCE 🔎 COACH *online for help with this subject.*

The Sun

🔑 **What Is the Structure of the Sun?**

🔑 **What Features Can You See on the Sun?**

MY PLANET DIARY

DISASTER

Left in the Dark

On March 13, 1989, a flood of electric particles from the sun reached Earth, causing a magnetic storm. Bright streamers of color filled the sky as far south as Jamaica. But in Quebec, Canada, the storm brought problems. At 2:45 A.M., the entire electric power system collapsed. People woke up with no heat or light. Traffic snarled as traffic lights and subways stopped working.

How could particles from the sun take out a power system? The magnetic storm caused an electrical surge through the power lines. Electric stations couldn't handle the extra electricity, and they blew out, taking the power system with them.

✏️ **Communicate** Discuss the Quebec blackout with a partner. Then answer the questions below.

1. What caused the Quebec blackout of 1989?

_____

_____

2. How would your life be affected if a magnetic storm shut down electricity in your area?

_____

_____

_____

▶ **PLANET DIARY** Go to **Planet Diary** to learn more about the sun.

 Do the Inquiry Warm-Up *How Can You Safely Observe the Sun?*

Vocabulary

- core • nuclear fusion • radiation zone
- convection zone • photosphere • chromosphere
- corona • solar wind • sunspot • prominence
- solar flare

Skills

↺ **Reading:** Relate Cause and Effect

△ **Inquiry:** Interpret Data

What Is the Structure of the Sun?

Unlike Earth, the sun has no solid surface. About three fourths of the sun's mass is hydrogen, and about one fourth is helium. There are tiny amounts of other elements. ⌖ **The sun has an interior and an atmosphere. The interior includes the core, the radiation zone, and the convection zone. Figure 1** shows the sun's interior.

FIGURE 1 ···

Layers of the Sun

The diagram shows the layers of the sun's interior.

✎ **Apply Concepts** Draw arrows to show energy as it passes from the sun's core through the radiation and convection zones. Underline clues in the text that help you determine the path.

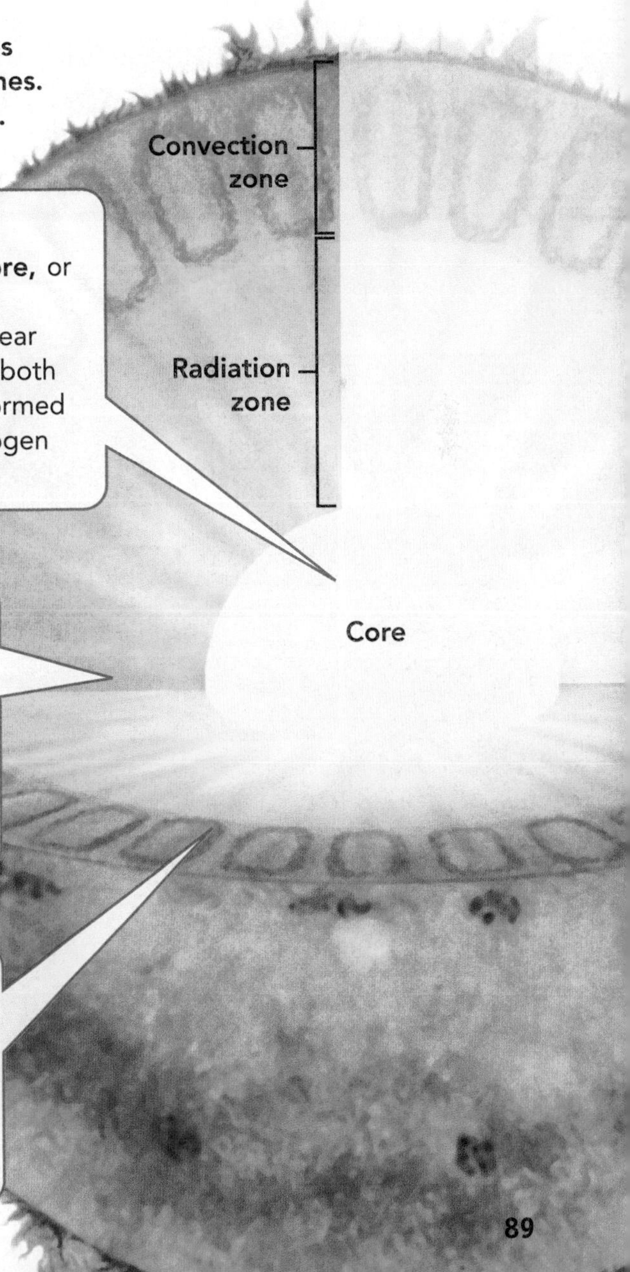

The Core

The sun produces an enormous amount of energy in its **core,** or central region, through nuclear fusion. In the process of **nuclear fusion,** hydrogen atoms join to form helium. Nuclear fusion requires extremely high temperature and pressure, both of which are found in the core. The total mass of helium formed by nuclear fusion is slightly less than the mass of the hydrogen that goes into it. The remaining mass becomes energy.

The Radiation Zone

The energy produced in the sun's core moves outward through the radiation zone. The **radiation zone** is a region of very tightly packed gas where energy moves mainly in the form of electromagnetic radiation. Because the radiation zone is so dense, energy can take more than 100,000 years to move through it.

The Convection Zone

The **convection zone** is the outermost layer of the sun's interior. Hot gases rise from the bottom of the convection zone and gradually cool as they approach the top. Cooler gases sink, forming loops of gas that move energy toward the sun's surface.

Convection — zone

Radiation — zone

Core

89

The sun has an atmosphere that stretches far into space, as you can see in **Figure 2**. The layers of the atmosphere become less dense the farther they are from the radiation zone. Like the sun's interior, the atmosphere is primarily composed of hydrogen and helium. 🔑 The sun's atmosphere includes the photosphere, the chromosphere, and the corona. Each layer has unique properties.

Vocabulary Greek Word Origins
The Greek word *photos* means "light." What does *photosphere* mean?

_____

_____

FIGURE 2

▶ INTERACTIVE ART **The Sun's Atmosphere**
This image is a combination of two photographs of the sun. One shows the sun's surface and was taken through a special filter that shows the sun's features. The other shows the corona and was taken during an eclipse.

✎ Relate Text and Visuals On the photograph, label the photosphere and corona. Shade in the area of the chromosphere.

CHALLENGE Why can the chromosphere and corona only be seen from Earth during an eclipse?

_____

_____

_____

The Photosphere
The inner layer of the sun's atmosphere is called the **photosphere** (FOH tuh sfeer). The sun does not have a solid surface, but the gases of the photosphere are thick enough to be visible. When you look at an image of the sun, you are looking at the photosphere. It is considered to be the sun's surface layer.

The Chromosphere
At the start and end of a total eclipse, a reddish glow is visible just around the photosphere. This glow comes from the middle layer of the sun's atmosphere, the **chromosphere** (KROH muh sfeer). The Greek word *chroma* means "color," so the chromosphere is the "color sphere."

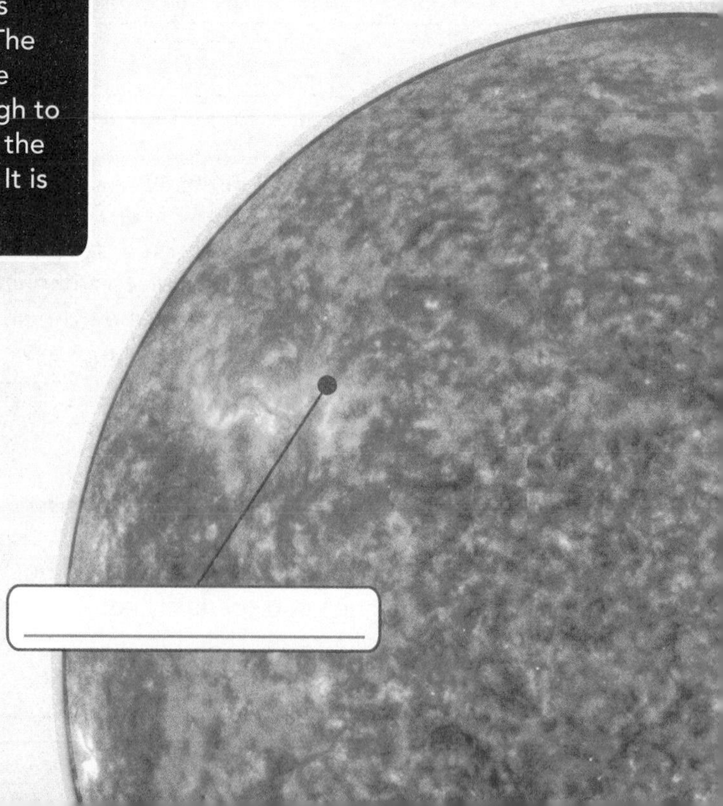

do the math! Analyzing Data

Solar Temperature

Use the table to answer the questions.

Layer	Temperature (°C)
Core	About 15,000,000
Radiation and Convection Zones	About 4,000,000
Photosphere	About 6,000
Inner Chromosphere	About 4,300
Outer Chromosphere	About 8,300
Corona	About 1,000,000

1 **Interpret Data** Which layer is hottest?

_____

2 **Compare and Contrast** How does the temperature change in the sun's atmosphere differ from the temperature change in the sun's interior?

_____

_____

The Corona

During a total solar eclipse, an even fainter layer of the sun becomes visible, as you can see in **Figure 2.** This outer layer, which looks like a white halo around the sun, is called the corona, which means "crown" in Latin. The corona extends into space for millions of kilometers. It gradually thins into streams of electrically charged particles called the solar wind.

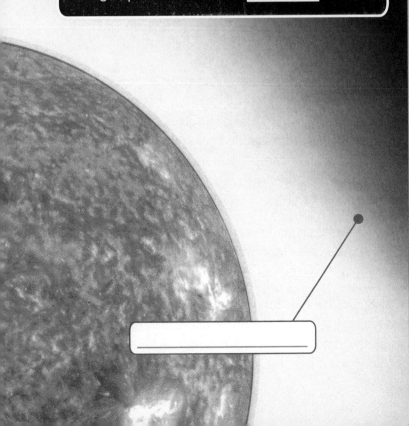

 Do the Quick Lab
Layers of the Sun.

🔑 Assess Your Understanding

1a. List List the layers of the sun's interior and atmosphere, starting from the center.

_____

_____

_____

b. Compare and Contrast What is one key difference between the radiation and convection zones?

_____

_____

_____

_____

got it? ....

○ **I get it!** Now I know that the sun's structure includes _____

_____

○ **I need extra help with** _____

_____

Go to MY SCIENCE ⑤ COACH *online for help with this subject.*

What Features Can You See on the Sun?

For hundreds of years, scientists have used special telescopes to study the sun. They have spotted a variety of features on the sun's surface. 🔑 **Features on or just above the sun's surface include sunspots, prominences, and solar flares.**

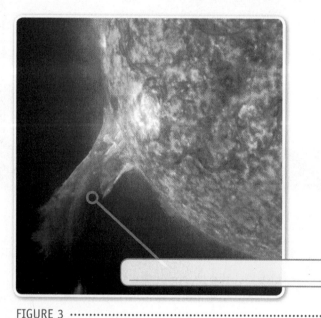

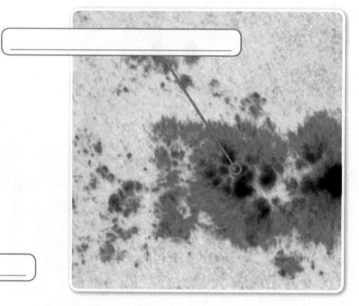

FIGURE 3 ··

Sunspots and Prominences

Sunspots look dark in regular photographs. Some photos of the sun are taken with special filters that show the sun's structure. Sunspots may appear white in these photos. Sunspots are visible in both of the photos above. ✏️ **Classify** Label a prominence and a sunspot in the photos.

Sunspots Photographs show dark areas on the sun's surface. These **sunspots** are areas of gas on the sun's surface that are cooler than the gases around them. Cooler gases don't give off as much light as hotter gases, which is why sunspots look dark. Sunspots look small, but in fact they can be larger than Earth. The number of sunspots varies in a regular cycle, with the most sunspots appearing about once every 11 years.

Prominences Sunspots usually occur in groups. Huge loops of gas called **prominences** often link different parts of sunspot regions. You can compare sunspots and prominences in **Figure 3.**

Solar Flares Sometimes the loops in sunspot regions suddenly connect, releasing large amounts of magnetic energy. The energy heats gas on the sun to millions of degrees Celsius, causing the gas to erupt into space. These eruptions are called **solar flares.**

··

🖊️ **Relate Cause and Effect**
When prominences join, they cause (sunspots/solar flares).

Solar Wind The solar wind is made up of electrical particles from the sun. Solar flares can greatly increase the solar wind, which means that more particles reach Earth's upper atmosphere. Earth's atmosphere and magnetic field normally block these particles. But near the North and South poles, the particles can enter Earth's atmosphere. There, they create powerful electric currents that cause gas molecules in the atmosphere to glow. These particles cause auroras near the poles. They can also cause magnetic storms like the one that caused the blackout in Quebec in 1989. **Figure 4** shows how the solar wind interacts with Earth's magnetic field.

FIGURE 4 ·······················

Solar Wind

Particles from the solar wind spread through the solar system. When they reach Earth, they interact with Earth's magnetic field. (Note: The diagram is not to scale.)

✎ **Make Generalizations** The corona is the least dense layer of the sun's atmosphere. How do you think the density of the solar wind compares to the density of the corona?

_____

_____

_____

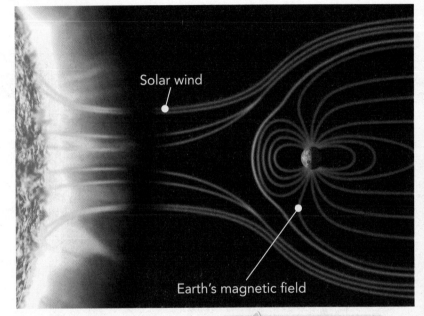

Solar wind

Earth's magnetic field

Do the Quick Lab
Viewing Sunspots.

🗝 Assess Your Understanding

2a. Define (Prominences/sunspots) are loops of gas that extend from the sun's surface.

b. Explain Why do sunspots look darker than the rest of the sun's photosphere?

_____

_____

_____

c. ⟳ Relate Cause and Effect How is the solar wind related to magnetic storms on Earth?

_____

_____

_____

_____

_____

got it? ··

○ **I get it!** Now I know that features on the sun include _____

○ **I need extra help with** _____

Go to my science ⓢ COACH online for help with this subject.

The Inner Planets

UNLOCK THE BIG ?

🔑 What Do the Inner Planets Have in Common?

🔑 What Are the Characteristics of the Inner Planets?

MY PLANET DIARY

What's in a Name?

Where in the solar system could you find Lewis and Clark's guide Sacagawea, artist Frida Kahlo, writer Helen Keller, and abolitionist Sojourner Truth all in the same place? On Venus! In fact, almost every feature on Venus is named for a real, fictional, or mythological woman.

In general, the person or people who discover an object or feature in the solar system get to choose its name. But scientists have agreed on some guidelines. Features on Mercury are named for authors, artists, and musicians. Many craters on Mars are named for towns on Earth. And most of the craters on Earth's moon are named for astronomers, physicists, and mathematicians.

FUN FACT

After you read the information to the left, answer the questions below.

1. Who decides what to name a newly discovered feature in the solar system?

_____

_____

2. If you discovered a new planet, how would you decide what to name its features?

_____

_____

_____

▷ PLANET DIARY Go to **Planet Diary** to learn more about the inner planets.

Lab zone® Do the Inquiry Warm-Up *Ring Around the Sun.*

Vocabulary
- terrestrial planet
- greenhouse effect

Skills
- Reading: Compare and Contrast
- Inquiry: Communicate

What Do the Inner Planets Have in Common?

Earth, Mercury, Venus, and Mars are more like each other than they are like the outer planets. **The inner planets are small and dense and have rocky surfaces.** The inner planets are often called the **terrestrial planets,** from the Latin word *terra,* which means "Earth." **Figure 1** summarizes data about the inner planets.

The terrestrial planets all have relatively high densities. They are rich in rocky and metallic materials, including iron and silicon. Each has a solid surface. All except Mercury have atmospheres.

FIGURE 1 ....

> INTERACTIVE ART

The Inner Planets

✎ **Interpret Data** Use the table to answer the questions below.

1. Which planet is largest?

   _____

2. Which planet has the most moons?

   _____

3. Which planet is most similar to Earth in size?

   _____

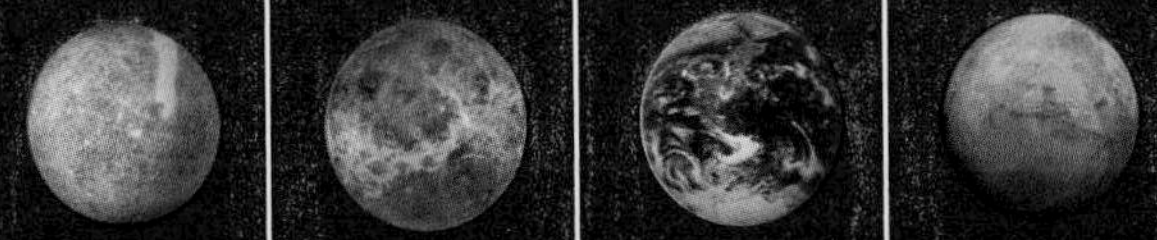

Planet	Mercury	Venus	Earth	Mars
Diameter (km)	4,879	12,104	12,756	6,794
Period of rotation (Earth days)	58.9	244	1.0	1.03
Average distance from sun (AU)	0.39	0.72	1.0	1.52
Period of revolution (Earth days)	88	224.7	365.2	687
Number of moons	0	0	1	2

Note: Planets are not shown to scale.

Do the Quick Lab *Characteristics of the Inner Planets.*

⌗ Assess Your Understanding

got it? ....

○ I get it! Now I know that the inner planets are _____

_____

○ I need extra help with _____

Go to **my science S coach** *online for help with this subject.*

What Are the Characteristics of the Inner Planets?

Though the four inner planets have many features in common, they differ in size and composition as well as distance from the sun.

Mercury Would you like to visit a place where the temperature can range from 430°C to below −170°C? ⚷ **Mercury is the smallest terrestrial planet and the planet closest to the sun.** Mercury is not much larger than Earth's moon. The interior of Mercury is probably made up mainly of the dense metal iron.

Mercury's Surface As you can see in **Figure 2,** Mercury has flat plains and craters on its surface. Most of these craters formed early in the history of the solar system. Since Mercury has no water and not much atmosphere, the craters have not worn away over time.

Mercury's Atmosphere Mercury has virtually no atmosphere. Because Mercury's mass is small, its gravity is weak. Gas particles can easily escape into space. However, astronomers have detected small amounts of sodium and other gases around Mercury.

During the day, the side of Mercury facing the sun can reach temperatures of 430°C. Because there is so little atmosphere, the planet's heat escapes at night. Then the temperature drops below −170°C.

Exploring Mercury Much of what astronomers know about Mercury has come from space probes. *Mariner 10* flew by Mercury three times in 1974 and 1975. *Mercury MESSENGER* has passed Mercury several times, and will begin orbiting Mercury in 2011.

Size of Mercury compared to Earth

I'm visiting the planets! As you read this lesson and the next one, keep track of how far I've traveled.

FIGURE 2 ···

Mercury

The photo shows Mercury's cratered surface.

✎ **Answer the questions below.**

1. **Solve Problems** List three things a visitor to Mercury would need to bring.

_____

_____

_____

2. CHALLENGE Refer to **Figure 1.** How many Mercury days are there in a Mercury year?

_____

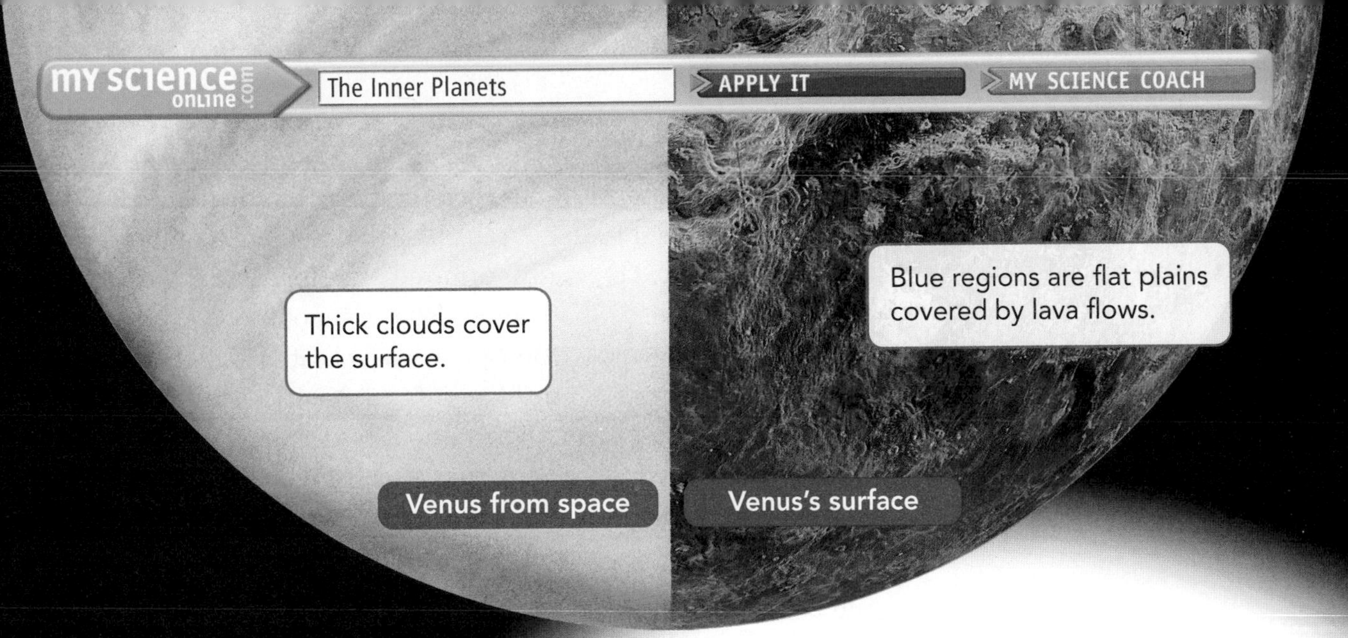

Thick clouds cover the surface.

Blue regions are flat plains covered by lava flows.

Venus from space

Venus's surface

FIGURE 3 ··

Venus

This figure combines images of Venus taken from space with a camera (left) and radar (right). Radar is able to penetrate Venus's thick clouds to reveal the surface. The colors in both images are altered to show more details.

✎ **Infer** Why do scientists need to use radar to study Venus's surface?

_____

_____

Size of Venus compared to Earth

Venus Venus is so similar in size and mass to Earth that it is sometimes called "Earth's twin." Venus's density and internal structure are similar to Earth's. But in other ways Venus and Earth are very different. 🔑 **Venus has a thick atmosphere, an unusual pattern of rotation, and the hottest surface of any planet.**

Venus's Atmosphere Venus's atmosphere is so thick that it is always cloudy. As you can see in **Figure 3,** astronomers can see only a smooth cloud cover over Venus. The thick clouds are made mostly of droplets of sulfuric acid.

At Venus's surface, you would quickly be crushed by the weight of its atmosphere. The pressure of Venus's atmosphere is 90 times greater than the pressure of Earth's atmosphere. You couldn't breathe on Venus because its atmosphere is mostly carbon dioxide.

Venus's Rotation Venus takes about 7.5 Earth months to revolve around the sun. It takes about 8 months for Venus to rotate once on its axis. Thus, Venus rotates so slowly that its day is longer than its year! Oddly, Venus rotates from east to west, the opposite direction from most other planets and moons. Astronomers hypothesize that this unusual rotation was caused by a very large object that struck Venus billions of years ago. Such a collision could have caused the planet to change its direction of rotation. Another hypothesis is that Venus's thick atmosphere could have somehow altered its rotation.

97

Compare and Contrast

List one feature Venus has in common with Earth and one feature that is different.

In common: _____

_____

Different: _____

_____

_____

A Hot Planet Because Venus is closer to the sun than Earth is, it receives more solar energy than Earth does. Much of this radiation is reflected by Venus's atmosphere. However, some radiation reaches the surface and is later given off as heat. The carbon dioxide in Venus's atmosphere traps heat so well that Venus has the hottest surface of any planet. At 460°C, its average surface temperature is hot enough to melt lead. This trapping of heat by the atmosphere is called the **greenhouse effect. Figure 4** shows how the greenhouse effect occurs.

Exploring Venus The first probe to land on Venus's surface and send back data, *Venera 7*, landed in 1970. It survived for only a few minutes because of the high temperature and pressure. Later probes were more durable and sent images and data back to Earth.

The *Magellan* probe reached Venus in 1990, carrying radar instruments. Radar works through clouds, so *Magellan* was able to map nearly the entire surface. The *Magellan* data confirmed that Venus is covered with rock. Venus's surface has more than 10,000 volcanoes. Lava flows from these volcanoes have formed plains.

More recent probes have included *Venus Express*, from the European Space Agency, as well as brief visits by space probes headed for other planets. Images from *Venus Express* have helped scientists understand how Venus's clouds form and change.

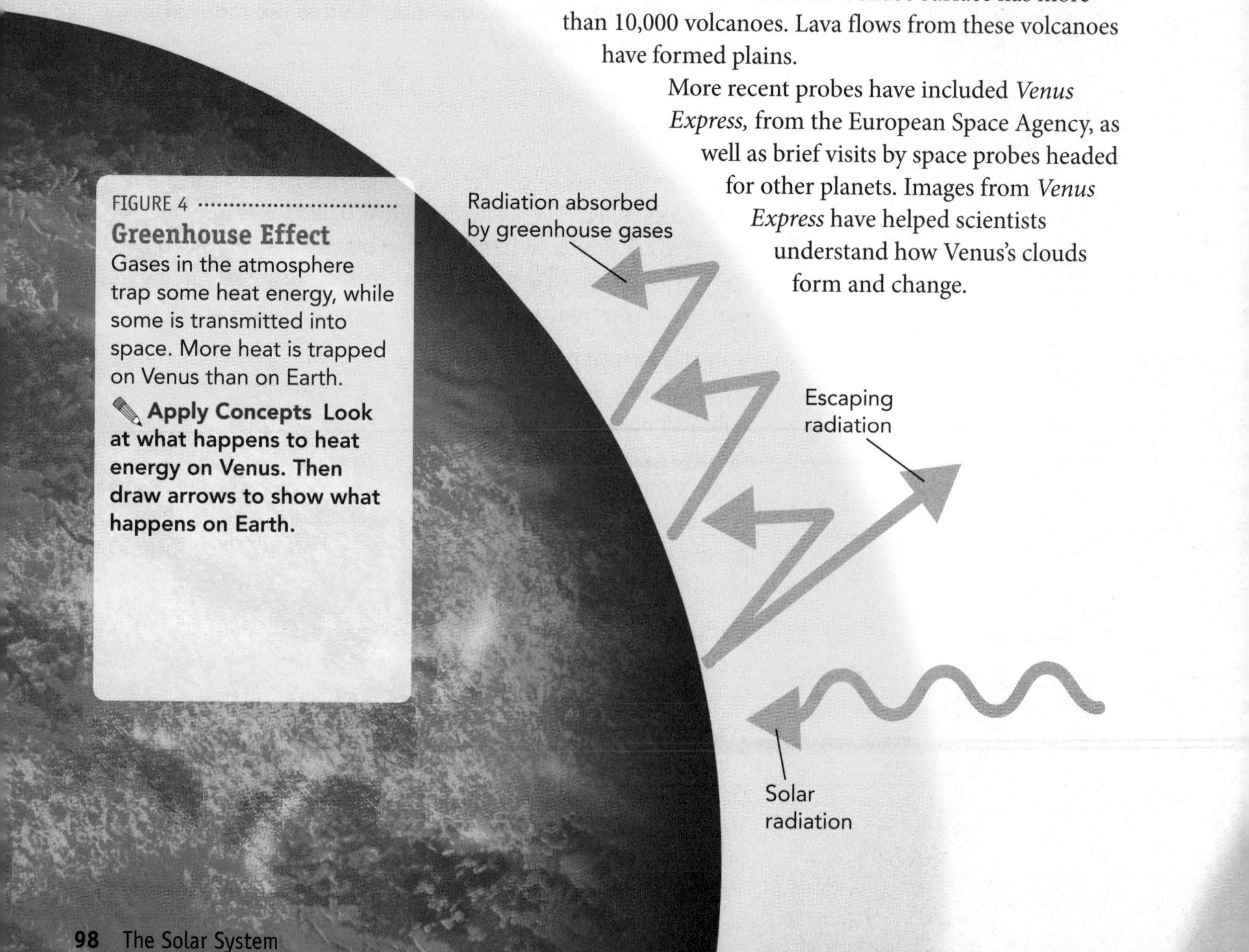

FIGURE 4 ··················

Greenhouse Effect

Gases in the atmosphere trap some heat energy, while some is transmitted into space. More heat is trapped on Venus than on Earth.

✎ **Apply Concepts Look at what happens to heat energy on Venus. Then draw arrows to show what happens on Earth.**

Radiation absorbed by greenhouse gases

Escaping radiation

Solar radiation

Earth

There's only one planet in the solar system where you could live easily: Earth. **Earth has liquid water and a suitable temperature range and atmosphere for living things to survive.**

The Water Planet Earth is unique in our solar system in having liquid water on its surface. In fact, most of Earth's surface, about 70 percent, is covered with water.

Earth's Temperature Scientists sometimes speak of Earth as having "Goldilocks" conditions—in other words, Earth is "just right" for life as we know it. Earth is not too hot and not too cold. If Earth were a little closer to the sun, it would be so hot that liquid water would evaporate. If it were a little farther away and colder, water would always be solid ice.

Earth's Atmosphere Earth has enough gravity to hold on to most gases. These gases make up Earth's atmosphere. Earth is the only planet with an atmosphere that is rich in oxygen. Oxygen makes up about 20 percent of Earth's atmosphere. Nearly all the rest is nitrogen, with small amounts of other gases such as argon, carbon dioxide, and water vapor.

Like Venus, Earth experiences a greenhouse effect. Earth's atmosphere traps heat, though less heat than Venus's atmosphere does. Without the atmosphere, Earth would be much colder.

FIGURE 5 ·····························
Earth's Structure
Earth has three main layers—a crust, a mantle, and a core. The crust includes the solid, rocky surface. Under the crust is the mantle, a layer of hot rock. Earth has a dense core made mainly of iron and nickel.

✎ **Relate Text and Visuals**
Label the layer of Earth with the highest density.

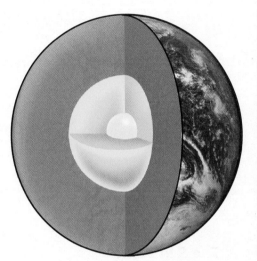

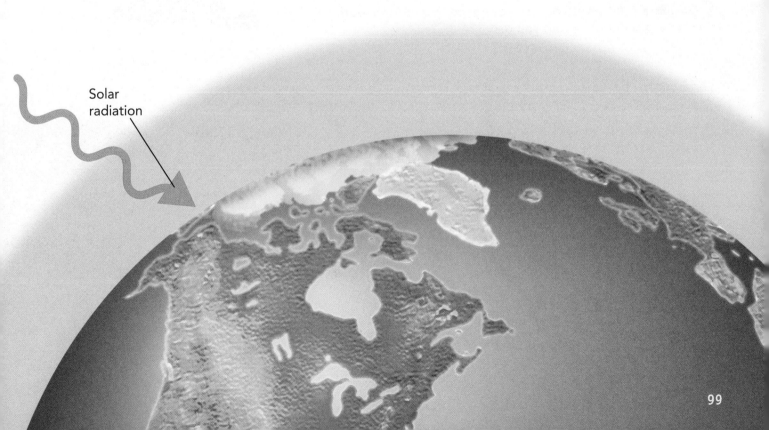

Solar radiation

Size of Mars
compared to Earth

Mars

Mars is called the "red planet." **Figure 6** shows why. This reddish color is due to the breakdown of iron-rich rocks, leaving a rusty dust behind. **Though Mars is mostly too cold for liquid water, it does have water ice now and shows evidence of intermittent seasonal flowing water today as well as liquid water in the past.**

Mars's Atmosphere

The atmosphere of Mars is more than 95 percent carbon dioxide. You could walk around on Mars, but you would have to wear an airtight suit and carry your own oxygen. Mars has few clouds, and they are very thin compared to clouds on Earth. Temperatures on the surface range from −140°C to 20°C.

Water and Ice

Images of Mars taken from space show a variety of features that look as if they were made by ancient streams, lakes, or floods. Scientists think that more liquid water flowed on Mars's surface in the distant past. Scientists infer that Mars must have been much warmer and had a thicker atmosphere at that time.

Today, Mars's atmosphere is so thin that most liquid water would quickly turn into a gas. Some water is located in the planet's two polar ice caps, which are almost entirely made of frozen water. Observations from the *Mars Reconnaissance Orbiter* in 2015 found evidence of flowing water in warmer areas today.

FIGURE 6 ···

The Red Planet

Remote-controlled landers such as *Phoenix*, *Spirit*, and *Opportunity* have sent back pictures of the surface of Mars.

✎ **Design a Solution** If you were designing a lander to work on Mars, where on Earth would you test it? Why?

apply it!

Communicate Choose one of the inner planets other than Earth. Describe an alien that could live there. Include at least three features of your alien that make it well suited for the planet you chose. Draw your alien to the right.

_____

_____

_____

_____

_____

FIGURE 7 ·······························

Olympus Mons

This computer-generated image is based on data from the *Mars Global Surveyor* mission.

Volcanoes Some regions of Mars have giant volcanoes. There are signs that lava flowed from the volcanoes in the past, but the volcanoes are rarely active today. Olympus Mons, shown in **Figure 7,** is the largest volcano in the solar system. It is as large as Missouri and is nearly three times as tall as Mount Everest!

Mars's Moons Mars has two very small moons. Phobos, the larger moon, is about 22 kilometers across. Deimos is even smaller, about 13 kilometers across. Like Earth's moon, Phobos and Deimos are covered with craters.

Exploring Mars Many space probes have visited Mars, looking for signs of water and possible life. Rovers called *Spirit* and *Opportunity* found traces of salts and minerals that form in the presence of water. The *Phoenix* mission found frozen water near the north polar cap, and the *Mars Reconnaissance Orbiter* found evidence of flowing water in warmer areas. *Mars Express* detected methane gas in Mars's atmosphere. This gas might be a clue that microscopic life forms exist on Mars, even today!

 Do the Quick Lab *Greenhouse Effect.*

Assess Your Understanding

1a. Name Which inner planet has the thickest atmosphere? _____

b. Relate Cause and Effect Why is Venus hotter than Mercury? _____

_____

_____

got it?

○ **I get it!** Now I know that the inner planets differ in _____

_____

○ **I need extra help with** _____

Go to MY SCIENCE COACH online for help with this subject.

LESSON
5 The Outer Planets

UNLOCK THE BIG ?

🔑 **What Do the Outer Planets Have in Common?**

🔑 **What Are the Characteristics of Each Outer Planet?**

my planet diary

Predicting a Planet

In the 1840s, astronomers were puzzled. Uranus didn't move as expected, based on the theory of gravity. Astronomers John Couch Adams and Urbain Leverrier independently hypothesized that Uranus was being affected by another planet's gravity. They calculated where this planet should be. Another astronomer, Johann Galle, aimed his telescope at the place Leverrier predicted. On September 23, 1846, he discovered the new planet—Neptune.

DISCOVERY

✏️ **Communicate Work with a partner to answer the question.**

What science skills did the astronomers use when they discovered Neptune?

_____

_____

_____

_____

▷ PLANET DIARY Go to **Planet Diary** to learn more about the outer planets.

Lab zone® Do the Inquiry Warm-Up How Big Are the Planets?

What Do the Outer Planets Have in Common?

If you could visit the outer planets, you wouldn't have a solid place to stand! 🔑 **The four outer planets are much larger and more massive than Earth, and they do not have solid surfaces.** Because these four planets are so large, they are often called **gas giants.** **Figure 1** summarizes some basic facts about the gas giants.

Composition Jupiter and Saturn are composed mainly of hydrogen and helium. Uranus and Neptune contain some of these gases, but also ices of ammonia and methane. Because they are so massive, the gas giants exert a very strong gravitational force. This gravity keeps gases from escaping, forming thick atmospheres.

Vocabulary
- gas giant
- ring

Skills
- Reading: Outline
- Inquiry: Pose Questions

Despite the name "gas giant," much of the material in these planets is actually liquid because the pressure inside the planets is so high. The outer layers are extremely cold because they are far from the sun. Temperatures increase greatly within the planets.

Moons and Rings All the gas giants have many moons, ranging from 13 around Neptune to more than 60 around Jupiter! These moons vary from tiny balls of rock and ice barely a kilometer across to moons larger than Mercury. Some of these moons even have their own atmospheres!

In addition, each of the gas giants is surrounded by a set of rings. A **ring** is a thin disk of small particles of ice and rock. Saturn's rings are the largest and most complex.

As you visit each planet, don't forget to keep track of how many AU you've collected!

TOTAL AU:

SOL TOURS

INTERPLANETARY FREQUENT TRAVELER REWARDS PROGRAM

Planet	Jupiter	Saturn	Uranus	Neptune
Diameter (km)	142,984	120,536	51,118	49,528
Period of rotation (Earth hours)	9.9	10.7	17.2	16.1
Average distance from sun (AU)	5.20	9.54	19.2	30.07
Period of revolution (Earth years)	11.9	29.5	83.8	163.8
Number of moons	at least 63	at least 61	at least 27	at least 13

Note: Planets are not shown to scale.

FIGURE 1 ·······························

> INTERACTIVE ART

The Outer Planets
The table summarizes data about the outer planets.

✏ **Estimate** Earth's diameter is about 12,750 km. About how many times larger is Jupiter's diameter than Earth's?

_____

Lab® zone Do the Quick Lab *Density Mystery.*

🔑 Assess Your Understanding

got it? ··

O I get it! Now I know that the gas giants all _____

_____

O I need extra help with _____

Go to MY SCIENCE ⓢ COACH online for help with this subject.

What Are the Characteristics of Each Outer Planet?

Since telescopes were first invented, scientists have studied the features of the outer planets and their moons. Today, space-based telescopes and space probes including the *Voyager, Galileo,* and *Cassini* missions have revealed many details of these planets that are not visible from Earth. Scientists are constantly discovering new information about these planets and their moons.

Jupiter  **Jupiter is the largest and most massive planet.** Jupiter's enormous mass dwarfs the other planets. In fact, its mass is about $2\frac{1}{2}$ times that of all the other planets combined!

Jupiter's Atmosphere Like all of the gas giants, Jupiter has a thick atmosphere made up mainly of hydrogen and helium. One notable feature of Jupiter's atmosphere is its Great Red Spot, a storm that is larger than Earth! The storm's swirling winds are similar to a hurricane, as you can see in **Figure 2.** Unlike hurricanes on Earth, however, the Great Red Spot shows no signs of going away.

Jupiter's Structure Astronomers think that Jupiter probably has a dense core of rock and iron at its center. A thick mantle of liquid hydrogen and helium surrounds this core. Because of the weight of Jupiter's atmosphere, the pressure at Jupiter's core is estimated to be about 30 million times greater than the pressure at Earth's surface.

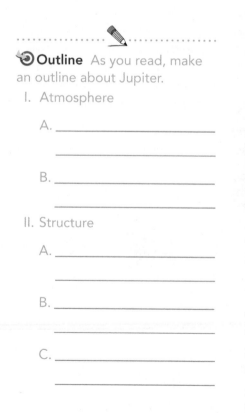

Size of Jupiter compared to Earth

🔄 **Outline** As you read, make an outline about Jupiter.

I. Atmosphere

   A. _____

      _____

   B. _____

      _____

II. Structure

   A. _____

      _____

   B. _____

      _____

   C. _____

      _____

FIGURE 2 ···

The Great Red Spot
This storm is about 20,000 km long and 12,000 km wide. The largest tropical storm on Earth was 2,200 km across.

✏️ **Calculate** Think of the storm on Earth as a square and the Great Red Spot as a rectangle. About how many Earth storms would fit inside the Great Red Spot?

_____

Jupiter's Moons The Italian astronomer Galileo Galilei discovered Jupiter's largest moons in 1610. These moons, shown in **Figure 3,** are named Io, Europa, Ganymede, and Callisto. Since Galileo's time, astronomers have discovered dozens of additional moons orbiting Jupiter. Many of these are small moons that have been found in the last few years thanks to improved technology.

FIGURE 3 ....

The Moons of Jupiter

Jupiter's four largest moons are larger than Earth's moon. Each has characteristics that set it apart from the others.

✎ **Relate Text and Visuals** Based on the photograph, match each description below to its moon.

1 **Ganymede** is Jupiter's largest moon. It is larger than Mercury! Its surface is divided into dark and bright areas.

2 **Callisto** is second to Ganymede in size, but has less ice. It has the most craters of any of Jupiter's moons.

3 **Io** is not icy, unlike most of Jupiter's moons. It may have as many as 300 active volcanoes. The eruptions from those volcanoes constantly change the moon's surface.

4 **Europa** is covered with ice. There may be liquid water below the ice—and if there's water, there might be life!

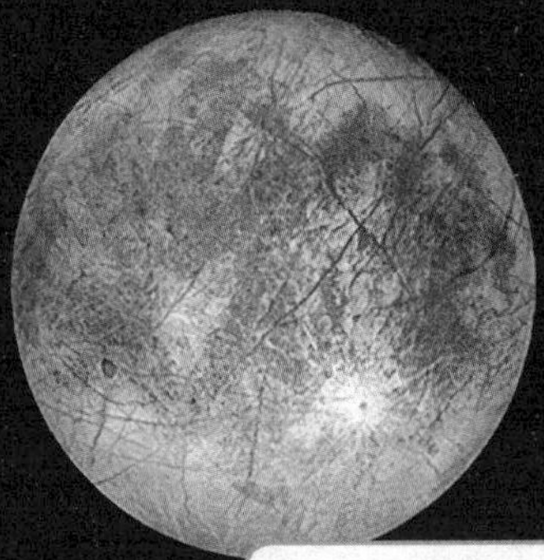

TOTAL AU:

SOL TOURS

INTERPLANETARY
FREQUENT TRAVELER
REWARDS PROGRAM

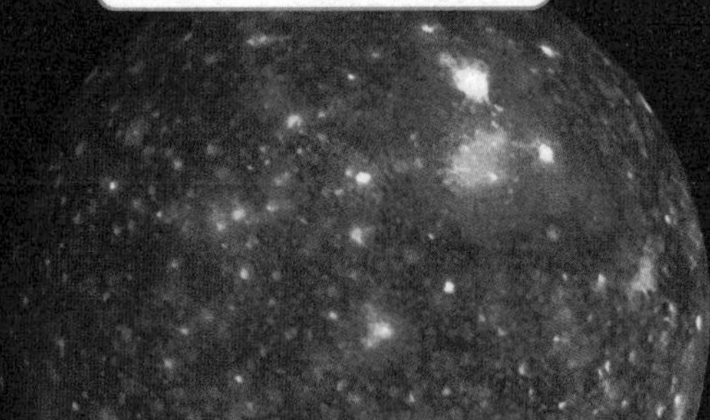

Iapetus This moon has light and dark areas.

✎ **Develop Hypotheses** What might the light areas be?

_____

Saturn The second-largest planet in the solar system is Saturn. Saturn, like Jupiter, has a thick atmosphere made up mainly of hydrogen and helium. Saturn's atmosphere also contains clouds and storms, but they are less dramatic than those on Jupiter. The *Cassini* space probe found unusual six-sided cloud patterns around Saturn's north pole. Scientists aren't sure what causes these patterns.

Saturn's Rings 🔑 **Saturn has the most spectacular rings of any planet.** These rings are made of chunks of ice and rock, each traveling in its own orbit around Saturn. From Earth, it looks as though Saturn has only a few rings and that they are divided from each other by narrow, dark regions. Space probes have shown that each of these obvious rings is divided into many thinner rings. Saturn's rings are broad and thin, like a compact disc. Some rings are kept in place by gravity from tiny moons that orbit on either side of the ring.

Saturn's Moons Saturn's largest moon, Titan, is larger than the planet Mercury. It is also the only moon in the solar system that has a thick atmosphere. The atmosphere is composed mostly of nitrogen and methane. Some of these gases break down high in the atmosphere, forming a haze that is somewhat like smog on Earth. In 2005, the *Huygens* probe landed on Titan's surface. Photos from *Huygens* show features that may have been formed by flowing liquid. A few scientists think that Titan might support life.

Scientists have learned a great deal about Saturn's moons from the *Cassini* space probe. Giant craters and trenches cut across Mimas (MY mus) and Tethys (TEE this). Ice and water erupt in geysers from the surface of Enceladus (en SEL uh dus), which was found in 2015 to have a warm ocean. In 2009, scientists discovered a ring of material that may come from the outermost moon, Phoebe (FEE bee). **Figure 4** shows some of the members of the Saturn system.

Size of Saturn compared to Earth

did you know?

Saturn has the lowest density of any planet. If you could build a bathtub big enough, Saturn would float!

Tethys In this photo, you can just see a group of canyons that circle this moon.

Enceladus This photo shows faint bluish plumes erupting from the surface of Enceladus.

✏️ **Make Generalizations** Eruptions from Enceladus form one of Saturn's rings. What is that ring most likely made of?

_____

Size of Uranus
compared to Earth

Uranus Although the gas giant Uranus (YOOR uh nus) is about four times the diameter of Earth, it is still much smaller than Jupiter and Saturn. Uranus is twice as far from the sun as Saturn, so it is much colder. Uranus looks blue-green because of traces of methane in its atmosphere. Like the other gas giants, Uranus is surrounded by a group of thin, flat rings, although they are much darker than Saturn's rings.

Uranus's Moons Photographs from *Voyager 2* show that Uranus's five largest moons have icy, cratered surfaces. The craters show that rocks from space have hit the moons. Uranus's moons also have lava flows on their surfaces, suggesting that material has erupted from inside each moon. *Voyager 2* images revealed 10 moons that had never been seen before. Recently, astronomers discovered several more moons, for a total of at least 27.

A Tilted Planet 🔑 **Uranus's axis of rotation is tilted at an angle of about 90 degrees from the vertical.** Viewed from Earth, Uranus rotates from top to bottom instead of from side to side, as other planets do. You can see the tilt in **Figure 5.** Uranus's rings and moons rotate around this tilted axis. Astronomers think that billions of years ago, an object hit Uranus and knocked it on its side. Images from the *Voyager 2* space probe allowed scientists to determine that Uranus rotates in about 17 hours.

FIGURE 5 ···
A Sideways Planet
✎ **Compare and Contrast** How do day and night at Uranus's equator change as Uranus revolves around the sun?

_____

_____

_____

_____

_____

_____

_____

_____

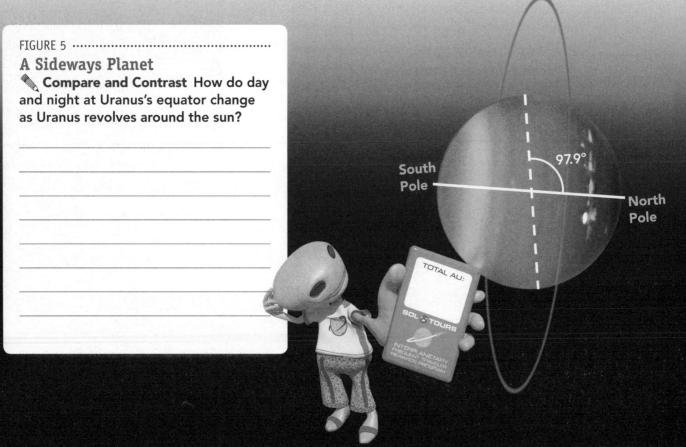

South Pole

97.9°

North Pole

TOTAL AU:

SOL TOURS

INTERPLANETARY
FREQUENT TRAVELER
REWARDS PROGRAM

Neptune Neptune is similar in size and color to Uranus. 🔑 **Neptune is a cold, blue planet. Its atmosphere contains visible clouds.** The color comes from methane in the atmosphere. Neptune's interior is hot due to energy left over from its formation. As this energy rises, it produces clouds and storms in the atmosphere.

Neptune's Atmosphere In 1989, *Voyager 2* flew by Neptune and photographed a Great Dark Spot about the size of Earth. Like the Great Red Spot on Jupiter, the Great Dark Spot was probably a giant storm. But it didn't last long. Images taken five years later showed that the spot was gone.

Neptune's Moons Astronomers have discovered at least 13 moons orbiting Neptune. The largest moon is Triton, which has a thin atmosphere. *Voyager 2* images show that the area of Triton's south pole is covered by nitrogen ice.

Size of Neptune compared to Earth

FIGURE 6 ·····

Changing Neptune
The photograph above was taken in 1989. The photograph below was taken in 2002.

✏️ **Interpret Photos** How did Neptune change?

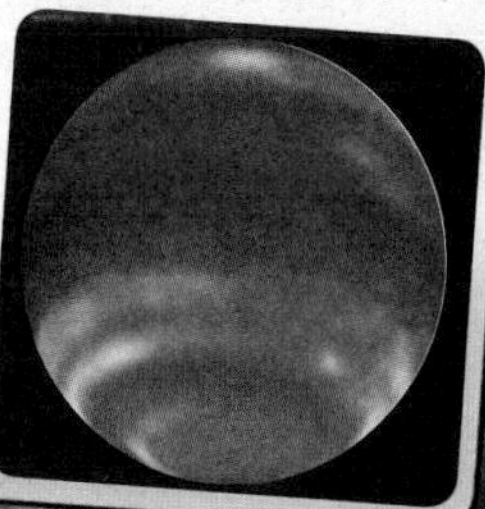

_____

_____

_____

_____

apply it!

Congratulations! You've earned enough AU in your travels to qualify for a free mission to one planet or moon of your choice!

1 Make Judgments Which planet or moon do you choose? List three reasons for your choice.

_____

_____

2 Pose Questions What is one question you would want your mission to answer?

_____

Lab zone ® Do the Quick Lab *Make a Model of Saturn.*

🔑 **Assess Your Understanding**

1. Describe Describe one feature of each outer planet that distinguishes it from the others.

_____

_____

_____

got it?

○ **I get it!** Now I know that the outer planets differ in _____

_____

○ **I need extra help with** _____

Go to **MY SCIENCE COACH** online for help with this subject.

Small Solar System Objects

How Do Scientists Classify Small Objects in the Solar System?

my planet Diary

BLOG

Posted by: Haley

Location: Constantia, New York

During the summer my dad and I go outside when it gets dark. We like to go stargazing. I have even seen shooting stars! Shooting stars are very hard to spot. You have to stare at the sky and sometimes you will see one shoot by. They only stick around for one split second, but it is really amazing to see one. This is my favorite thing to do when it gets dark during the summer!

Communicate Discuss your answers to these questions with a partner.

1. What do you think shooting stars are?

_____

_____

_____

_____

2. What do you like to observe in the night sky?

_____

_____

_____

> PLANET DIARY Go to **Planet Diary** to learn more about small solar system objects.

Lab zone Do the Inquiry Warm-Up Collecting Micrometeorites.

Vocabulary

- asteroid belt • Kuiper belt • Oort cloud
- comet • coma • nucleus • asteroid
- meteoroid • meteor • meteorite

Skills

- Reading: Summarize
- Inquiry: Classify

How Do Scientists Classify Small Objects in the Solar System?

The solar system contains many small objects that, like the planets, orbit the sun. 🔑 **Scientists classify these objects based on their sizes, shapes, compositions, and orbits. The major categories include dwarf planets, comets, asteroids, and meteoroids.**

Areas of the Solar System Most of the small objects in the solar system are found in three areas: the asteroid belt, the Kuiper belt, and the Oort cloud. The **asteroid belt** is a region of the solar system between Mars and Jupiter. Beyond Neptune's orbit is a region called the **Kuiper belt** (KY per) which extends to about 100 times Earth's distance from the sun. Beyond the Kuiper belt, the **Oort cloud** (ort) stretches out more than 1,000 times the distance between the sun and Neptune. **Figure 1** shows these areas.

FIGURE 1 ···

Areas of the Solar System
The diagram below shows the relative positions of the asteroid belt, the Kuiper belt, and the Oort cloud.

✎ **Relate Text and Visuals** As you read this lesson, write a C to show where a comet would most likely come from. Write a P to show where you would expect to find a plutoid. Write an A to show where you would expect to find an asteroid.

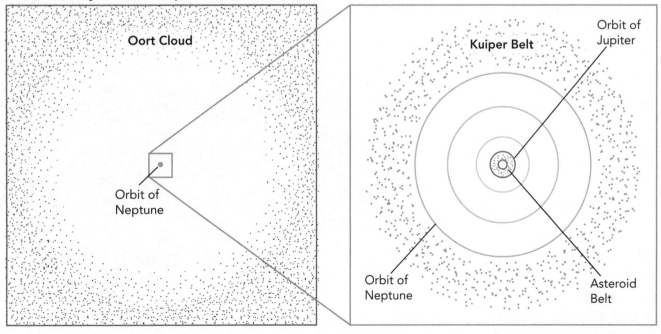

Oort Cloud

Orbit of Neptune

Kuiper Belt

Orbit of Jupiter

Orbit of Neptune

Asteroid Belt

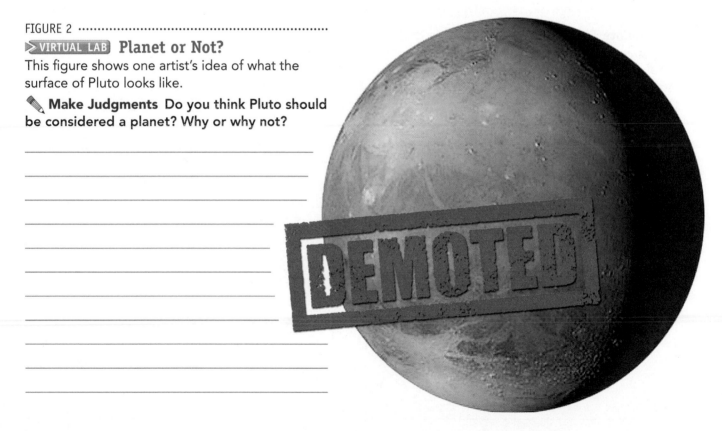

Vocabulary Greek Word Origins The word *comet* comes from the Greek word *kometes*, meaning "long hair." Why do you think this word is used?

_____

_____

_____

Dwarf Planets "What happened to Pluto?" You may have found yourself asking this question as you have learned about the solar system. For many years, Pluto was considered a planet. But then scientists discovered other objects that were at least Pluto's size. Some were even farther away than Pluto. Scientists began debating how to define a planet.

Defining Dwarf Planets In 2006, astronomers developed a new category of objects, called dwarf planets. These objects orbit the sun and have enough gravity to pull themselves into spheres, but they have other objects in the area of their orbits. As of 2009, scientists had identified five dwarf planets: Pluto, Eris, Makemake, Haumea, and Ceres. Eris is believed to be the largest dwarf planet so far. There are at least a dozen more objects that may turn out to be dwarf planets, once scientists are able to study them.

Like planets, dwarf planets can have moons. Pluto has three moons: Charon, Nix, and Hydra. Haumea has two and Eris has one.

Kuiper Belt Objects All the known dwarf planets except Ceres orbit beyond Neptune. (Ceres orbits in the asteroid belt.) A dwarf planet that orbits beyond Neptune is also called a plutoid. Most plutoids orbit the sun in the Kuiper belt, though Eris may be beyond it. The Kuiper belt also includes many other objects that are too small to be considered dwarf planets.

FIGURE 2 ⋯⋯⋯⋯⋯⋯⋯⋯⋯⋯⋯⋯⋯⋯⋯⋯⋯⋯⋯

▷ **VIRTUAL LAB** **Planet or Not?**
This figure shows one artist's idea of what the surface of Pluto looks like.

✎ **Make Judgments** Do you think Pluto should be considered a planet? Why or why not?

_____

_____

_____

_____

_____

_____

_____

_____

Comets A comet is one of the most dramatic objects you can see in the night sky. On a dark night, you can see its fuzzy white head and long, streaming tails. **Comets** are loose collections of ice, dust, and small rocky particles whose orbits can be very long, narrow ellipses. Some comets have smaller orbits that bring them near Earth regularly. Most comets originate in the Oort cloud.

A Comet's Head When a comet gets close to the sun, the energy in sunlight turns the ice into gas, releasing gas and dust. Clouds of gas and dust form a fuzzy outer layer called a **coma. Figure 3** shows the coma and the **nucleus,** the solid inner core of a comet. The nucleus is usually only a few kilometers across.

A Comet's Tail As a comet approaches the sun, it heats up and starts to glow. Some of its gas and dust stream outward, forming a tail. Most comets have two tails—a gas tail and a dust tail. The gas tail points away from the sun and the dust tail points along the path the comet has taken. A comet's tail can be more than 100 million kilometers long and from Earth, appears to stretch across most of the sky. The material is stretched out very thinly, however.

⟳ Summarize Write a few sentences to summarize the structure of a comet.

_____
_____
_____
_____
_____
_____

FIGURE 3 ··································
A Comet's Orbit
Comets, as shown here, have long, narrow orbits. Their tails tend to grow longer as they approach the sun.
✎ **Apply Concepts** Complete the diagram above by adding the comet's tails.

Gas tail

Dust tail

Nucleus

Coma

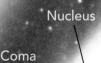

Asteroids Hundreds of small, irregular, rocky objects orbit the sun. These **asteroids** are rocky objects, most of which are too small and too numerous to be considered planets or dwarf planets. Astronomers have discovered more than 100,000 asteroids, and they are constantly finding more.

Small Bodies Most asteroids are small—less than a kilometer in diameter. Only Ceres, Pallas, Vesta, and Hygiea are more than 300 kilometers across. (Ceres is both a dwarf planet and the largest asteroid.) Most asteroids are not spherical. Scientists hypothesize that asteroids are leftover pieces of the early solar system that never came together to form a planet.

Asteroid Orbits Most asteroids orbit the sun in the asteroid belt. Some, however, have very elliptical orbits that bring them closer to the sun than Earth's orbit. Someday, an asteroid will hit Earth. One or more large asteroids did hit Earth about 65 million years ago, filling the atmosphere with dust and smoke and blocking out sunlight around the world. Scientists hypothesize that many species of organisms, including the dinosaurs, became extinct as a result.

apply it!

Classify For each description below, classify the object as a dwarf planet, comet, asteroid, or meteoroid.

❶ This object is slightly smaller than Pluto. It orbits the sun beyond Neptune and is spherical. _____

❷ This object is irregularly shaped. It orbits the sun just outside the orbit of Mars. _____

❸ This object is a chunk of rock and metal. It was once part of another object that orbited the sun. _____

❹ This object is composed of ice and rock. It orbits the sun in an elongated orbit, taking many years to complete one orbit.

_____

❺ [CHALLENGE] Which two types of objects are hardest to tell apart? Why? _____

_____

_____

Meteoroids Chunks of rock or dust smaller than asteroids are called **meteoroids.** Meteoroids are generally less than 10 meters across. Some meteoroids form when asteroids collide. Others form when comets break up, creating dust clouds.

Meteors and Meteorites When a meteoroid enters Earth's atmosphere, friction with the air creates heat and produces a streak of light. This streak is a **meteor.** (People often call meteors shooting stars, but they are not stars.) Most meteors come from tiny bits of rock or dust that burn up completely. But some larger meteoroids do not burn up. Meteoroids that pass through the atmosphere and are found on Earth's surface are called **meteorites.** Meteorite impacts can leave craters, such as the one shown in **Figure 4.**

Meteor Showers Meteor showers occur when Earth passes through an area with many meteoroids. Some of these groups of meteoroids are bits of comets that broke up. These meteor showers occur every year as Earth passes through the same areas. Meteor showers are often named for the constellation from which they appear to come. The Perseids, Geminids, and Orionids are examples of meteor showers.

FIGURE 4 ···

Meteor Crater

Meteor Crater in Arizona formed about 50,000 years ago from the impact of a meteorite 50–100 meters wide. ✎ **Predict** How would a large meteorite impact affect Earth today?

_____

_____

_____

Approximate size of meteorite relative to crater

 Lab zone ® Do the Quick Lab *Changing Orbits.*

🗝 Assess Your Understanding

1a. Review (Comets/Asteroids) are rocky, while (comets/asteroids) are made of ice and dust.

b. Compare and Contrast What is the difference between a dwarf planet and an asteroid?

_____

_____

c. Relate Cause and Effect How and why does a comet change as it approaches the sun?

_____

_____

_____

_____

got it? ···

○ **I get it!** Now I know that small solar system objects include _____

_____

○ **I need extra help with** _____

Go to **MY SCIENCE** Ⓢ **COACH** online for help with this subject.

Objects in the solar system are different because they formed _____

_____

LESSON 1 Models of the Solar System

🗝 In a geocentric model, Earth is at the center.

🗝 Copernicus worked out the arrangement of the known planets and how they orbit the sun.

🗝 Kepler found that planets' orbits are ellipses.

🗝 Evidence from Galileo Galilei convinced others that the heliocentric model was correct.

Vocabulary
• geocentric • heliocentric • ellipse

LESSON 2 Introducing the Solar System

🗝 Our solar system consists of the sun, the planets, their moons, and smaller objects.

🗝 The solar system formed about 4.6 billion years ago from a cloud of hydrogen, helium, rock, ice, and other materials pulled together by gravity.

Vocabulary
• solar system • astronomical unit • planet
• dwarf planet • planetesimal

LESSON 3 The Sun

🗝 The sun's interior consists of the core, the radiation zone, and the convection zone. The sun's atmosphere includes the photosphere, the chromosphere, and the corona.

🗝 Features on or just above the sun's surface include sunspots, prominences, and solar flares.

Vocabulary
• core • nuclear fusion • radiation zone
• convection zone • photosphere
• chromosphere • corona • solar wind
• sunspot • prominence • solar flare

LESSON 4 The Inner Planets

🗝 The inner planets are small and dense and have rocky surfaces.

🗝 Mercury is the smallest terrestrial planet and the planet closest to the sun. Venus has a thick atmosphere and the hottest surface of any planet. Earth has a suitable temperature range and atmosphere for living things to survive. Mars has ice and evidence of flowing liquid water.

Vocabulary
• terrestrial planet • greenhouse effect

LESSON 5 The Outer Planets

🗝 The outer planets are much larger than Earth and do not have solid surfaces.

🗝 Jupiter is the largest and most massive planet. Saturn has the most spectacular rings of any planet. Uranus's axis of rotation is tilted at an angle of about 90 degrees from the vertical. Neptune is a cold, blue planet with visible clouds.

Vocabulary
• gas giant • ring

LESSON 6 Small Solar System Objects

🗝 Scientists classify small objects based on their sizes, shapes, compositions, and orbits. The major categories include dwarf planets, comets, asteroids, and meteoroids.

Vocabulary
• asteroid belt • Kuiper belt • Oort cloud
• comet • coma • nucleus • asteroid
• meteoroid • meteor • meteorite

Review and Assessment

LESSON 1 Models of the Solar System

1. What object is at the center of a geocentric system?

  a. Earth   **b.** the moon

  c. a star   **d.** the sun

2. Kepler discovered that planets move in

_____

3. Relate Cause and Effect How did Tycho Brahe's work contribute to the development of the heliocentric model?

_____

_____

_____

4. Write About It Suppose you lived at the time of Copernicus. Write a letter to a scientific journal supporting the heliocentric model.

LESSON 2 Introducing the Solar System

5. Pluto is an example of a(n)

  a. dwarf planet.   **b.** inner planet.

  c. outer planet.   **d.** planetesimal.

6. An astronomical unit is equal to _____

_____

7. Compare and Contrast Compare the conditions that led to the formation of the inner planets with those that led to the formation of the outer planets.

_____

_____

_____

_____

LESSON 3 The Sun

8. In which part of the sun does nuclear fusion take place?

  a. chromosphere   **b.** convection layer

  c. core   **d.** corona

9. Relatively cool areas on the sun's surface are called _____

10. Explain How can the solar wind affect life on Earth? _____

_____

_____

11. math! The density of the sun's core is about 160 g/cm^3. The density of Earth's core is about 13.0 g/cm^3. About how many times denser is the sun's core than Earth's?

_____

LESSON 4 The Inner Planets

12. What feature is shared by all the inner planets?

  a. thick atmosphere   **b.** rocky surface

  c. ring system   **d.** liquid water

13. The inner planets are also called _____

_____

14. Apply Concepts Explain why Venus has the hottest surface of any planet.

_____

_____

_____

_____

15. Write About It Choose one inner planet. Write a news article describing a visit to that planet's surface. Include descriptive details.

LESSON 5 The Outer Planets

16. Which planet's orbit is farthest from Earth's?

   a. Jupiter   **b.** Neptune

   c. Saturn   **d.** Uranus

17. All the gas giants are surrounded by _____

_____

Use the illustration to answer Question 18.

18. Interpret Diagrams What planet is shown above? What is unusual about it? What do scientists think caused that unusual feature?

_____

_____

_____

_____

_____

19. Predict Do you think astronomers have found all the moons of the outer planets? Explain.

_____

_____

_____

_____

_____

_____

LESSON 6 Small Solar System Objects

20. Where are most dwarf planets found?

   a. asteroid belt   **b.** Kuiper belt

   c. Oort cloud   **d.** plutoid belt

21. A _____ is a meteoroid that reaches Earth's surface.

22. Compare and Contrast Compare and contrast asteroids, comets, and meteoroids.

_____

_____

_____

_____

_____

23. **Write About It** Suppose you could witness a large meteorite or asteroid striking Earth. Write a news report explaining the event.

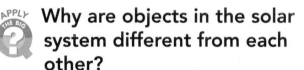

APPLY THE BIG Q

Why are objects in the solar system different from each other?

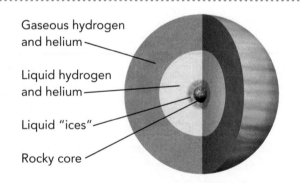

Gaseous hydrogen and helium

Liquid hydrogen and helium

Liquid "ices"

Rocky core

24. What type of planet is shown? Under what conditions would it most likely have formed?

_____

_____

_____

_____

_____

Standardized Test Prep

Multiple Choice

Circle the letter of the best answer.

1. The table below shows data for five planets.

Planet	Period of Rotation (Earth days)	Period of Revolution (Earth years)	Average Distance from the Sun (million km)
Mars	1.03	1.9	228
Jupiter	0.41	12	779
Saturn	0.45	29	1,434
Uranus	0.72	84	2,873
Neptune	0.67	164	4,495

According to the table, which planet has a "day" that is most similar in length to a day on Earth?

A Mars   B Jupiter
C Neptune   D Uranus

2. What characteristic do all of the outer planets share?

A They have rocky surfaces.
B They are larger than the sun.
C They have many moons.
D They have thin atmospheres.

3. Which layer of the sun has the highest density?

A core
B corona
C photosphere
D radiation zone

4. Mercury has a daytime temperature of about 430°C and a nighttime temperature below –170°C. What is the *best* explanation for this?

A Mercury has a greenhouse effect.
B Mercury is the closest planet to the sun.
C Mercury has little to no atmosphere.
D Mercury has no liquid water.

5. From what region do *most* comets come?

A asteroid belt
B inner solar system
C Kuiper belt
D Oort cloud

Constructed Response

Use the diagram below to answer Question 6.

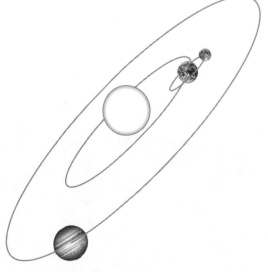

6. What model of the solar system is shown above? Give at least two pieces of evidence that support the model.

Mars Rovers

High school students came up with the names—*Spirit* and *Opportunity*—and scientists at the National Aeronautics and Space Administration (NASA) came up with the plan. Mars is too far away for humans to explore directly. So robot rovers would be dropped onto the surface of Mars and do the exploring for us. The rovers landed on Mars in January 2004. Their assignment was to collect images that would help answer the question: Was there ever water on Mars and could there have been life?

Chemical and physical data from the rovers suggested that there once was water on Mars. The rovers found evidence of erosion as well as of chemicals that would exist in an acidic lake or hot springs. Then, in 2015, NASA's *Mars Reconnaissance Orbiter* found evidence of flowing liquid water on Mars even today. It is still impossible to know for sure whether life ever existed on Mars.

Organize It Find three articles about the rover mission. Organize the information in the articles into a two-column chart. In one column, list any data about Mars described in the articles. In the second column, list any conclusions that scientists made about Mars based on that evidence. Circle any conclusions that were confirmed by later Mars missions.

Maria Mitchell

In the mid-1800s, the idea of a woman astronomer seemed far-fetched. But then Maria Mitchell changed everything. In 1847, Mitchell was the first American woman astronomer to use a telescope to find a comet. Later, she taught astronomy at Vassar College, and inspired other young women to follow in her footsteps. She was a true astronomical pioneer.

Write About It Research more about Maria Mitchell's career. Write a biographical essay about her life and work.

Maria Mitchell (left) and Mary Whitney in the observatory at Vassar. Mary Whitney studied with Maria Mitchell, and later taught with her. ▶

GOODBYE, PLUTO!

What is a planet? That question was hotly debated by astronomers in 2006. Everyone agreed that a planet must be round and orbit the sun. But some said that a planet must also be dominant in its area of space. And then, the astronomers voted. The result: Pluto was demoted to a dwarf planet.

Research It Find out more about the Pluto decision. Participate in a debate and vote on the definition of *planet*. Write a newspaper article about the result of your debate. Be sure to include information from both sides of the argument.

HOW CAN YOU GAZE DEEP INTO SPACE?

How do astronomers learn about distant objects in the universe?

Two galaxies are colliding! It all started 40 million years ago and will take millions more for these two spiral galaxies to actually combine. Astronomers know that the galaxy on the left, NGC 2207, and the galaxy on the right, IC 2163, are 140 million light-years from Earth. A light-year is the distance light travels in one year, or 9.46 trillion kilometers. That makes these galaxies about 1,320,000,000,000,000,000,000 kilometers away. **Infer** How can astronomers see so far into space?

_____

_____

_____

_____

▷ UNTAMED SCIENCE Watch the **Untamed Science** video to learn more about the universe.

Stars, Galaxies, and the Universe

4 Getting Started

Check Your Understanding

1. **Background** Read the paragraph below and then answer the question.

The children all held onto the edge of the giant parachute and shook it. The fabric moved up and down as a **wave** moved across it. "There's **energy** traveling across the fabric," their teacher said. "If we shake the edge quickly, the **distance** between the tops of the waves will get smaller."

A **wave** is a disturbance that transfers energy from place to place.

Energy is the ability to do work or cause change.

Distance is the length of a path between two points.

• What will happen if the students shake the parachute more slowly?

_____

_____

> **MY READING WEB** If you had trouble completing the question above, visit **My Reading Web** and type in *Stars, Galaxies, and the Universe*.

Vocabulary Skill

Suffixes A suffix is a letter or group of letters added to the end of a word to form a new word with a slightly different meaning. Adding a suffix to a word often changes its part of speech.

Suffix	Meaning	Part of Speech	Example
-tion/-ion	Process of, action of	Noun	scientific nota*tion*
-ory	Place or thing connected with or used for	Noun	observat*ory*

2. **Quick Check** Use the information in the chart to suggest a meaning for each vocabulary term below.

• observatory: _____

_____

• scientific notation: _____

radio telescope

supernova

spiral galaxy

big bang

Chapter Preview

LESSON 1
- electromagnetic radiation
- visible light • wavelength
- spectrum • telescope
- optical telescope
- refracting telescope • convex lens
- reflecting telescope • observatory
- radio telescope

 ↻ **Ask Questions**
 △ **Infer**

LESSON 2
- parallax • universe
- light-year • scientific notation

 ↻ **Summarize**
 △ **Calculate**

LESSON 3
- spectrograph
- apparent brightness
- absolute brightness
- Hertzsprung-Russell diagram
- main sequence

 ↻ **Identify the Main Idea**
 △ **Interpret Data**

LESSON 4
- nebula • protostar • white dwarf
- supernova • neutron star
- pulsar • black hole

 ↻ **Compare and Contrast**
 △ **Predict**

LESSON 5
- binary star • eclipsing binary
- open cluster • globular cluster
- galaxy • spiral galaxy
- elliptical galaxy • irregular galaxy
- quasar

 ↻ **Relate Cause and Effect**
 △ **Draw Conclusions**

LESSON 6
- big bang • Hubble's law
- cosmic background radiation
- dark matter • dark energy

 ↻ **Identify Supporting Evidence**
 △ **Make Models**

125

Telescopes

UNLOCK THE BIG **?**

🔑 **What Are the Regions of the Electromagnetic Spectrum?**

🔑 **What Are Telescopes and How Do They Work?**

my planet diary

TECHNOLOGY

Infrared Goggles

Suppose you're a spy on a dark street, hoping to spot another spy. How would you see the other spy in the dark? Wear a pair of infrared goggles.

All objects give off radiation that you can't see. The glowing coils of an electric heater give off infrared radiation, which you feel as heat. Human beings also glow infrared, and with the infrared goggles you can see a green outline of a person in the dark. Some objects in space also give off invisible radiation that we can detect with special telescopes.

Communicate Answer the following question. Then discuss your answer with a partner.

In what other situations might you want to use infrared goggles?

_____

_____

_____

_____

> PLANET DIARY Go to **Planet Diary** to learn more about telescopes.

Lab zone® Do the Inquiry Warm-Up *How Does Distance Affect an Image?*

What Are the Regions of the Electromagnetic Spectrum?

To understand how telescopes work, it's useful to understand **electromagnetic radiation** (ih LEK troh mag NET ik), or energy that can travel through space in the form of waves.

Scientists call the light you can see **visible light.** Visible light is just one of many types of electromagnetic radiation. Many objects give off radiation that you can't see. Objects in space give off all types of electromagnetic radiation.

Vocabulary
- electromagnetic radiation • visible light • wavelength • spectrum
- telescope • optical telescope • refracting telescope • convex lens
- reflecting telescope • observatory • radio telescope

Skills
- ⊙ Reading: Ask Questions
- △ Inquiry: Infer

The distance between the crest of one wave and the crest of the next wave is called the **wavelength.** Visible light has very short wavelengths, less than one millionth of a meter. There are some electromagnetic waves that have even shorter wavelengths. Other waves have much longer wavelengths, even several meters long.

If you shine white light through a prism, the light spreads out to make a range of different colors with different wavelengths, called a **spectrum.** The spectrum of visible light is made of the colors red, orange, yellow, green, blue, and violet. 🗝 **The electromagnetic spectrum includes the entire range of radio waves, infrared radiation, visible light, ultraviolet radiation, X-rays, and gamma rays.** Look at **Figure 1** to see the spectrum.

Flower seen in visible light

FIGURE 1 ·············
The Electromagnetic Spectrum
Humans see visible light, but bees can see ultraviolet light, so flowers look different to a bee.

✏️ CHALLENGE **What advantage does having ultraviolet vision give bees?**

_____
_____
_____
_____

Flower seen in ultraviolet light

Lab zone® Do the Quick Lab *Observing a Continuous Spectrum.*

🗝 Assess Your Understanding

got it? ·············

O **I get it!** Now I know that the electromagnetic spectrum includes _____

O **I need extra help with** _____
Go to my science ⓢ coach online for help with this subject.

What Are Telescopes and How Do They Work?

On a clear night, your eyes can see at most a few thousand stars. But with a telescope, you can see many millions. Why? The light from stars spreads out as it moves through space and your eyes are too small to gather much light.

🔑 **Telescopes are instruments that collect and focus light and other forms of electromagnetic radiation.** Telescopes make distant objects appear larger and brighter. A telescope that uses lenses or mirrors to collect and focus visible light is called an **optical telescope.** There are also nonoptical telescopes. These telescopes collect and focus different types of electromagnetic radiation, just as optical telescopes collect visible light.

Optical Telescopes The two major types of optical telescopes are refracting telescopes and reflecting telescopes.

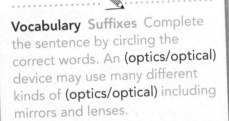
Refracting Telescopes

A **refracting telescope** is a telescope that uses convex lenses to gather and focus light. A **convex lens** is a piece of glass that is curved, so the middle is thicker than the edges.

A simple refracting telescope has two convex lenses, one at each end of a long tube. Light enters the telescope through the large objective lens at the top. The objective lens focuses the light at a certain distance from the lens. This distance is the focal length of the lens. A larger objective lens means that the telescope can collect more light. This makes it easier for astronomers to see faint objects, or objects that are far away.

The smaller lens at the lower end of a refracting telescope is the eyepiece lens. The eyepiece lens magnifies the image produced by the objective lens. A magnified image can be easier to study.

Reflecting Telescopes

In 1668, Isaac Newton built the first reflecting telescope. A **reflecting telescope** uses a curved mirror to collect and focus light. Like the objective lens in a refracting telescope, the curved mirror in a reflecting telescope focuses a large amount of light onto a small area. A larger mirror means that the telescope can collect more light. The largest optical telescopes today are all reflecting telescopes.

Why are the largest optical telescopes reflecting telescopes? Because the mirror can be supported from below. But the lens of a refracting telescope must be supported from the edges, so light can pass through it.

Objective lens — Light rays — Eyepiece lens

Light rays — Eyepiece lens — Objective (curved mirror)

FIGURE 2

> INTERACTIVE ART **Refracting and Reflecting Telescopes**
A refracting telescope uses convex lenses to focus light.
A reflecting telescope uses a curved mirror to focus light.

✎ Compare and Contrast **After reading about refracting and reflecting telescopes, circle the correct answers in the table showing the similarities and differences between the two.**

TELESCOPE	Objective	Eyepiece	Typical size	Light collection
Refracting	Lens / Mirror	Lens / Mirror	Smaller / Larger	Less / More
Reflecting	Lens / Mirror	Lens / Mirror	Smaller / Larger	Less / More

The Hubble telescope

FIGURE 3

The Hubble Space Telescope
The Hubble telescope is a reflecting telescope with a mirror 2.4 meters in diameter. The Hubble telescope orbits Earth above the atmosphere. As a result, it produces very detailed images in visible light. It also collects ultraviolet and infrared radiation. Images such as the ones shown here have changed the way astronomers view the universe.

The glowing shell of a supernova remnant

The Cone Nebula

A supernova remnant in the Large Magellanic Cloud

The Sombrero Galaxy

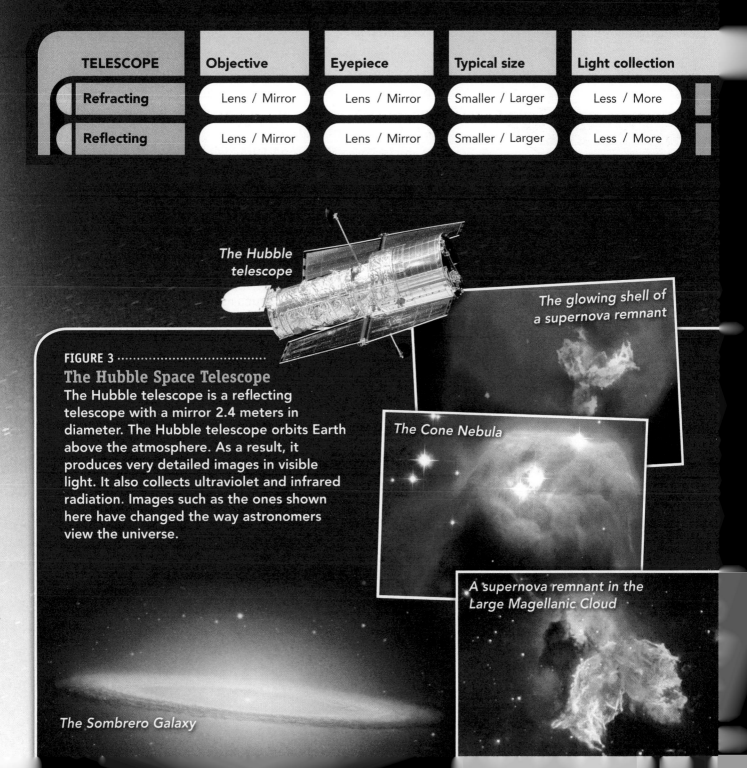

know?

Astronomers are concerned about "light pollution," artificial lighting that makes it hard to see the skies at night. Some cities have replaced their street lamps with ones that point down. With these lamps, light isn't beamed into the night sky and people can once again see the stars.

✏️ **Ask Questions** Write a question you would like answered about telescopes.

_____

_____

_____

_____

_____

Other Telescopes

Telescopes are usually located in observatories. An **observatory** is a building that contains one or more telescopes. Many large observatories are located on the tops of mountains or in space. Why? Earth's atmosphere makes objects in space look blurry. The sky on some mountaintops is clearer than at sea level and is not brightened by city lights.

- **Radio telescopes** detect radio waves from objects in space. Most radio telescopes have curved, reflecting surfaces. These surfaces focus faint radio waves the way the mirror in a reflecting telescope focuses light waves. Radio telescopes need to be large to collect and focus more radio waves, because radio waves have long wavelengths. Some radio telescopes, like the one in **Figure 4**, are placed in valleys.
- The Spitzer Space Telescope, launched in 2003, produces images in the infrared portion of the spectrum.
- Very hot objects in space give off X-rays. The Chandra X-ray Observatory produces images in the X-ray portion of the spectrum. X-rays are blocked by Earth's atmosphere, so this telescope is located in outer space.

Some new telescopes are equipped with computer systems that correct images for problems such as telescope movement and changes in air temperature or mirror shape.

FIGURE 4 ⋯⋯⋯⋯⋯⋯⋯⋯⋯⋯⋯⋯⋯⋯⋯⋯⋯⋯⋯

Arecibo Radio Telescope

The Arecibo telescope in Puerto Rico is 305 meters in diameter.

✏️ **Evaluate the Design** Why are radio telescopes so large?

_____

_____

apply it!

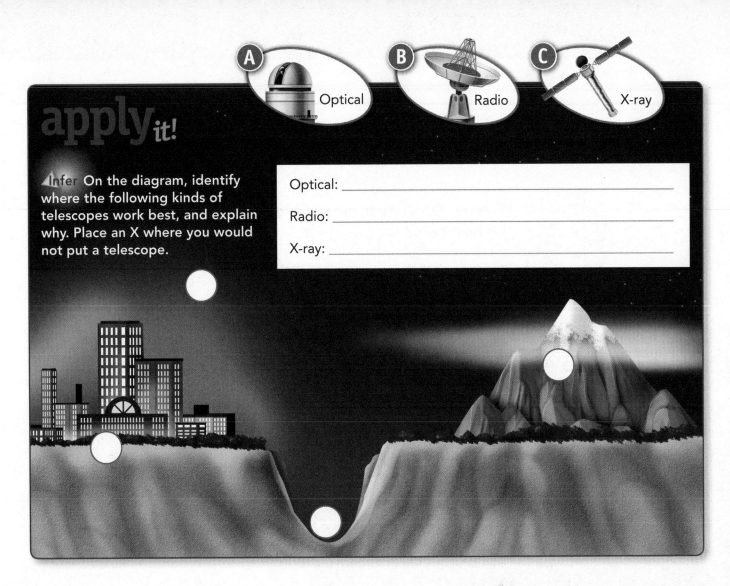

A **Optical**
B **Radio**
C **X-ray**

Infer On the diagram, identify where the following kinds of telescopes work best, and explain why. Place an X where you would not put a telescope.

Optical: _____

Radio: _____

X-ray: _____

 Lab zone ® Do the Lab Investigation *Design and Build a Telescope.*

🔑 Assess Your Understanding

1a. Sequence List the electromagnetic waves, from longest to shortest wavelength.

_____
_____
_____
_____
_____

b. Identify Faulty Reasoning A student of astronomy suggests locating a radio telescope near a radio station. Is this a good idea? Why or why not?

_____
_____
_____
_____
_____

got it? ....

○ **I get it!** Now I know that telescopes are _____
_____

○ **I need extra help with** _____

Go to **MY SCIENCE** 🌐 **COACH** *online for help with this subject.*

131

The Scale of the Universe

🔑 How Do Astronomers Measure Distances to the Stars?

🔑 How Do Astronomers Describe the Scale of the Universe?

MY PLANET DiARY

FUN FACT

Voyager Golden Record

Sixteen billion kilometers away flies a gold-plated copper disk with a voice saying "Hello from the children of planet Earth." The disk is carried aboard *Voyager 1*, a spacecraft launched in 1977 that once sent back information about the planets of the outer solar system. The disk is filled with images and sounds of Earth. One day, aliens might find *Voyager 1* and learn all about us!

Communicate Discuss the Voyager Record with a partner. Then answer the question below.

What images and sounds would you put on a recording for aliens?

_____

_____

_____

_____

▷ **PLANET DIARY** Go to **Planet Diary** to learn more about the scale of the universe.

Lab ® Do the Inquiry Warm-Up
zone *Stringing Along.*

How Do Astronomers Measure Distances to the Stars?

Standing on Earth looking up at the sky, it may seem as if there is no way to tell how far away the stars are. However, astronomers have found ways to measure those distances. 🔑 **Astronomers often use parallax to measure distances to nearby stars.**

Parallax is the apparent change in position of an object when you look at it from different places. Astronomers can measure the parallax of nearby stars to determine their distances.

Vocabulary
- parallax
- light-year
- universe
- scientific notation

Skills
- Reading: Summarize
- Inquiry: Calculate

FIGURE 1 ·······································

Parallax of Stars

The apparent movement of a star when seen from a different position is called parallax. Note that the diagram is not to scale.

✏️ CHALLENGE Hold a finger about half an arm's length away from your face, as shown in the picture below. Switch back and forth between closing your left and right eye and watch how your finger appears to move against the background. Why does your finger seem to move? How is this related to the parallax of stars?

_____
_____
_____
_____
_____
_____
_____
_____
_____
_____

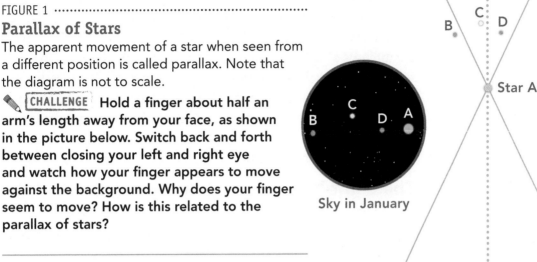

Sky in January   Star A   Sky in July

January   July

As shown in **Figure 1,** astronomers look at a nearby star when Earth is on one side of the sun. Then they look at the same star again six months later, when Earth is on the opposite side of the sun. Astronomers measure how much the nearby star appears to move against a background of stars that are much farther away. They can then use this measurement to calculate the distance to the nearby star. The less the nearby star appears to move, the farther away it is.

Astronomers can use parallax to measure distances up to a few hundred light-years from Earth. The parallax of any star that is farther away is too small to measure accurately.

Lab zone ® Do the Quick Lab
How Far Is That Star?

🔑 Assess Your Understanding

got it? ·····························

O **I get it!** Now I know that astronomers often measure the distances to nearby stars using _____, which is _____

_____
_____

O **I need extra help with** _____

_____

Go to my science ⑤ coach *online for help with this subject.*

How Do Astronomers Describe the Scale of the Universe?

Astronomers define the **universe** as all of space and everything in it. The universe is enormous, almost beyond imagination. Astronomers study objects as close as the moon and as far away as quasars. They study incredibly large objects, such as clusters of galaxies that are millions of light-years across. They also study the behavior of tiny particles, such as the atoms within the stars. 🔑 **Since the numbers astronomers use are often very large or very small, they frequently use scientific notation to describe sizes and distances in the universe. They use a unit called the light-year to measure distances between the stars.**

The Light-Year
Distances to the stars are so large that meters are not very practical units. In space, light travels at a speed of about 300,000,000 meters per second. A **light-year** is the distance that light travels in one year, about 9.46 trillion kilometers.

The light-year is a unit of distance, not time. To understand this better, consider an example. If you bicycle at 10 kilometers per hour, it would take you 1 hour to go to a mall 10 kilometers away. You could say that the mall is "1 bicycle-hour" away.

Scientific Notation
Scientific notation uses powers of ten to write very large or very small numbers in shorter form. Each number is written as the product of a number between 1 and 10 and a power of 10. For example: 1,200 is written as 1.2×10^3.

One light-year is about 9,460,000,000,000,000 meters. To express this number in scientific notation, first insert a decimal point in the original number so that you have a number between one and ten. In this case, the rounded number is 9.5. To determine the power of ten, count the number of places that the decimal point moved. Since there are 15 digits after the first digit, in scientific notation this number can now be written as 9.5×10^{15} meters.

The Immensity of Space
The objects in the universe vary greatly in their distance from Earth. To understand the scale of these distances, imagine that you are going on a journey through the universe. Refer to **Figure 2** as you take your imaginary trip. Start on Earth. Now shift to the right and change the scale by 100,000,000,000, or 10^{11}. You're now close to the sun, which is located 1.5×10^{11} meters away. As you move from left to right across **Figure 2,** the distance increases. The nearest star to our sun, Alpha Centauri, is 4.2×10^{16} meters or 4.3 light-years away. The nearest galaxy to the Milky Way, the Andromeda galaxy, is about 2.4×10^{22} meters away.

✏️ **Summarize** Explain why astronomers use scientific notation to describe sizes.

_____

_____

_____

do the
math!
Scientific Notation

To express a number in scientific notation, first insert a decimal point in the original number so you have a number between one and ten. Then count the number of places that the decimal point moved. That gives you the power of ten.

1 ⚠️ **Calculate** The sun takes about 220,000,000 years to revolve once around the center of the galaxy. Express this length of time in scientific notation.

_____

_____

2 ⚠️ **Calculate** The distant star Deneb is thought by some astronomers to be 3,230 light-years away. Write this distance in scientific notation.

_____

_____

FIGURE 2 ·················

> INTERACTIVE ART **Scale of the Universe**

Scientists often use scientific notation to help describe the vast distances in space. The sun is 1.5×10^{11} m away from Earth, but the next star, Alpha Centauri, is 4.2×10^{16} m away, almost 300,000 times as far.

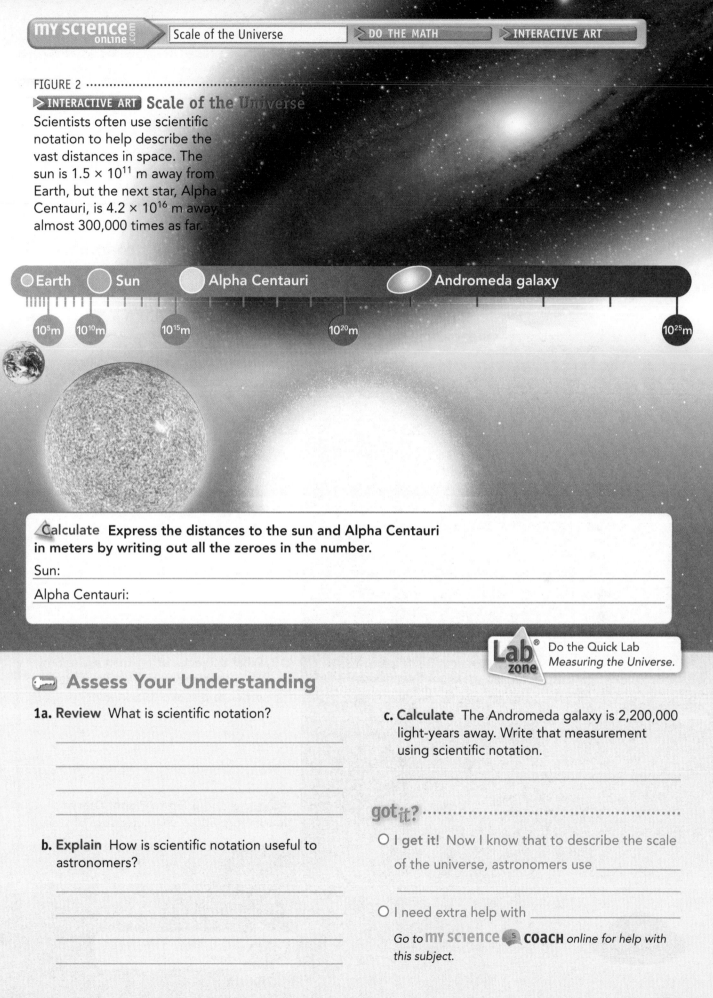

Earth   Sun   Alpha Centauri   Andromeda galaxy

10^5m 10^{10}m 10^{15}m 10^{20}m 10^{25}m

Calculate Express the distances to the sun and Alpha Centauri in meters by writing out all the zeroes in the number.

Sun: _____

Alpha Centauri: _____

Lab zone Do the Quick Lab *Measuring the Universe.*

🔑 Assess Your Understanding

1a. Review What is scientific notation?

_____

_____

_____

_____

b. Explain How is scientific notation useful to astronomers?

_____

_____

_____

c. Calculate The Andromeda galaxy is 2,200,000 light-years away. Write that measurement using scientific notation.

_____

got it? ···

○ **I get it!** Now I know that to describe the scale

of the universe, astronomers use _____

_____

○ **I need extra help with** _____

Go to my science ⓢ coach *online for help with this subject.*

Characteristics of Stars

UNLOCK THE BIG ?

🔑 **How Are Stars Classified?**

🔑 **What Is an H-R Diagram and How Do Astronomers Use It?**

my planet Diary

Black Holes

If you were an astronomer, you might study some of the strangest objects in the universe. For almost 100 years, scientists believed that some stars became black holes when they died. But a black hole is an object with gravity so strong that not even light can escape. So scientists couldn't prove that black holes existed because they couldn't see them. Eventually, astronomers discovered a way to prove black holes exist. They realized that they could detect the matter being pulled into the black hole. That matter reaches such high temperatures that it releases X-rays. In the 1960s, astronomers launched a rocket to record X-rays from outer space. On this first mission, they found evidence for black holes!

Communicate Answer the questions below. Then discuss your answers with a partner.

1. Why was it so hard to prove that black holes exist?

_____

_____

_____

_____

2. What subjects, other than astronomy, would astronomers have to study in order to discover black holes?

_____

_____

_____

> **PLANET DIARY** Go to **Planet Diary** to learn more about characteristics of stars.

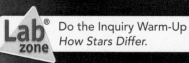
Do the Inquiry Warm-Up
How Stars Differ.

Vocabulary
- spectrograph
- absolute brightness
- main sequence
- apparent brightness
- Hertzsprung-Russell diagram

Skills
- Reading: Identify the Main Idea
- Inquiry: Interpret Data

How Are Stars Classified?

All stars are huge spheres of glowing gas. Made up mostly of hydrogen, stars produce energy through the process of nuclear fusion. Astronomers classify stars according to their physical characteristics. **Characteristics used to classify stars include color, temperature, size, composition, and brightness.**

Color and Temperature If you look at the night sky, you can see slight differences in the colors of the stars. Some stars look reddish. Others are yellow or blue-white, as shown in **Figure 1.**

A star's color reveals its surface temperature. The coolest stars—with a surface temperature of about 3,200°C—appear red. Our yellow sun has a surface temperature of about 5,500°C. The hottest stars, with surface temperatures of over 20,000°C, appear bluish.

Size When you look at stars in the sky, they all appear to be points of light of the same size. Many stars are actually about the size of the sun. However, some stars are much larger than the sun. Very large stars are called giant stars or supergiant stars.

Most stars are smaller than the sun. White dwarf stars are about the size of Earth. Neutron stars are even smaller, about 20 kilometers in diameter.

Identify the Main Idea
Write a sentence that says what the color of a star indicates.

_____

_____

_____

_____

FIGURE 1
Star Color and Temperature
Stars vary in size, color, and temperature.
Draw Conclusions Which of the four stars shown has the highest temperature? Why?

_____

_____

_____

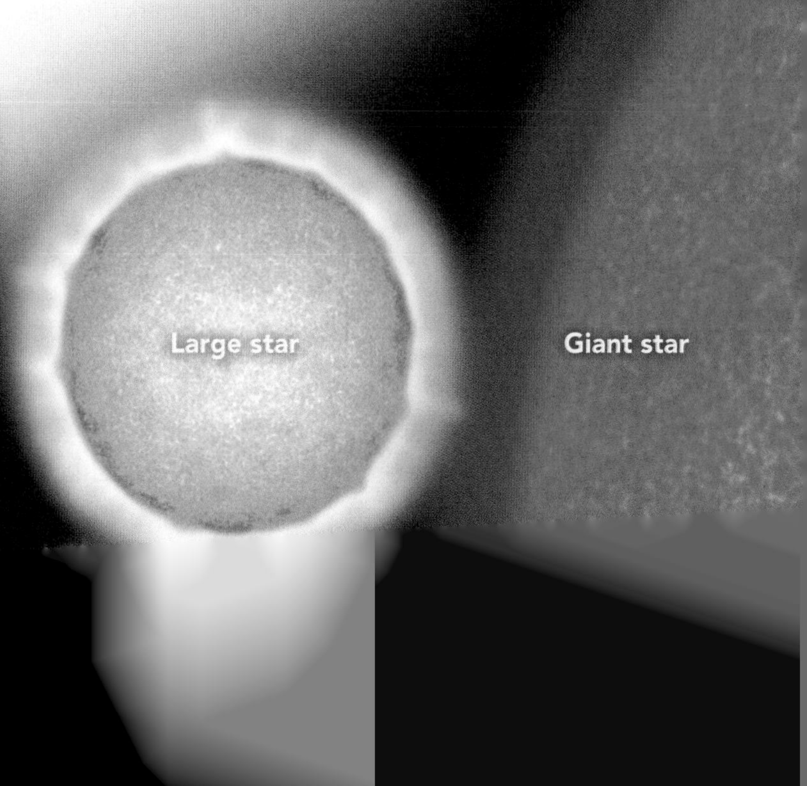

Large star

Giant star

Chemical Composition Stars vary in their chemical composition. The chemical composition of most stars is about 73 percent hydrogen, 25 percent helium, and 2 percent other elements by mass. This is close to the composition of the sun.

Astronomers use spectrographs to determine the elements found in stars. A **spectrograph** (SPEK truh graf) is a device that breaks light into colors and produces an image of the resulting spectrum. Today, most large telescopes have spectrographs to analyze light.

The gases in a star's atmosphere absorb some wavelengths of light produced within the star. When the star's light is seen through a spectrograph, each absorbed wavelength is shown as a dark line on a spectrum. Each chemical element absorbs light at particular wavelengths. Just as each person has a unique set of fingerprints, each element has a unique set of spectral lines for a given temperature.

Alnitak
approximately
800
light-years away

Alnilam
approximately
1,300
light-years away

apply it!

The lines on the spectrums below are from four different elements. By comparing a star's spectrum with the spectrums of known elements, astronomers can infer each element found in the star. Each star's spectrum is an overlap of the spectrums from the individual elements.

⚠ **Interpret Data** Identify the elements with the strongest lines in Stars A, B, and C.

Hydrogen

Helium

Sodium

Calcium

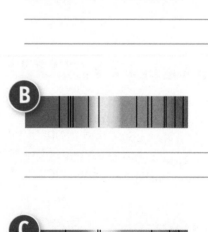

A

_____

_____

B

_____

_____

C

_____

_____

Brightness of Stars

Stars also differ in brightness, the amount of light they give off. **The brightness of a star depends upon both its size and temperature.** A larger star tends to be brighter than a smaller star. A hotter star tends to be brighter than a cooler star.

How bright a star appears depends on both its distance from Earth and how bright the star truly is. Because of these two factors, the brightness of a star is described in two ways: apparent brightness and absolute brightness.

Apparent Brightness A star's **apparent brightness** is its brightness as seen from Earth. Astronomers can measure apparent brightness fairly easily using electronic devices. However, astronomers can't tell how much light a star gives off just from the star's apparent brightness. Just as a flashlight looks brighter the closer it is to you, a star looks brighter the closer it is to Earth. For example, the sun looks very bright. This does not mean that the sun gives off more light than all other stars. The sun looks so bright simply because it is so close.

Absolute Brightness A star's **absolute brightness** is the brightness the star would have if it were at a standard distance from Earth. Finding absolute brightness is more complex than finding its apparent brightness. An astronomer must first find out both the star's apparent brightness and its distance from Earth. The astronomer can then calculate the star's absolute brightness.

Astronomers have found that the absolute brightness of stars can vary tremendously. The brightest stars are more than a billion times brighter than the dimmest stars!

FIGURE 2 ·······························

Apparent and Absolute Brightness

The three stars Alnitak, Alnilam, and Mintaka in the constellation Orion all seem to have the same apparent brightness from Earth. But Alnilam is actually farther away than the other two stars.

✎ [CHALLENGE] **Which star has the greatest absolute brightness? How do you know?**

_____

_____

_____

_____

Mintaka
approximately
900
light-years away

Do the Quick Lab
Star Bright.

⚷ Assess Your Understanding

got it? ·······························

○ **I get it!** Now I know that stars are classified by _____

_____

_____

○ **I need extra help with** _____

_____

Go to MY SCIENCE ⓢ COACH *online for help with this subject.*

What Is an H-R Diagram and How Do Astronomers Use It?

About 100 years ago, two scientists working independently made the same discovery. Both Ejnar Hertzsprung (EYE nahr HURT sprung) in Denmark and Henry Norris Russell in the United States made graphs to find out if the temperature and the absolute brightness of stars are related. They plotted the surface temperatures of stars on the *x*-axis and their absolute brightness on the *y*-axis. The points formed a pattern. The graph they made is still used by astronomers today. It is called the **Hertzsprung-Russell diagram,** or H-R diagram.

FIGURE 3 ···

Hertzsprung-Russell Diagram

The H-R diagram shows the relationship between surface temperature and absolute brightness of stars.

✎ **Interpret Diagrams** Place the stars listed in the table on the diagram, and note on the table the classification of each star.

H-R DIAGRAM

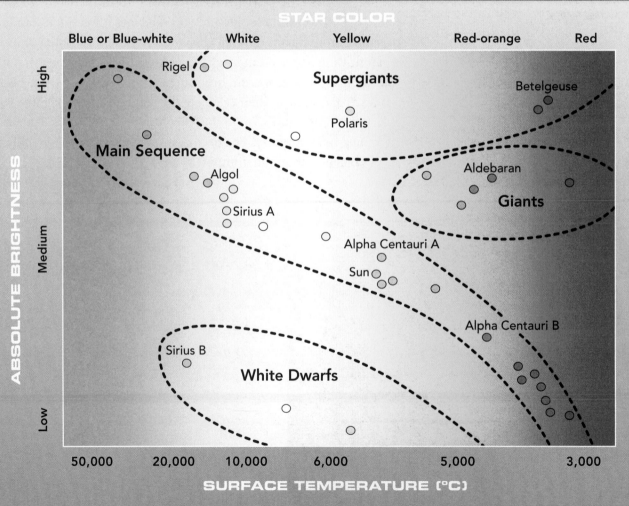

Astronomers use H-R diagrams to classify stars and to understand how stars change over time. As shown in **Figure 3,** most of the stars in the H-R diagram form a diagonal area called the **main sequence.** More than 90 percent of all stars, including the sun, are main-sequence stars. Within the main sequence, the surface temperature increases as absolute brightness increases. Thus, hot bluish stars are located at the left of an H-R diagram and cooler reddish stars are located at the right of the diagram.

The brightest stars are located near the top of an H-R diagram, while the dimmest stars are located at the bottom. Giant and supergiant stars are very bright. They can be found near the top center and right of the diagram. White dwarfs are hot, but not very bright, so they appear at either the bottom left or bottom center of the diagram.

STAR A

Color	Red-orange
Temperature	5,000°C
Brightness	High
Type	

STAR B

Color	Yellow
Temperature	6,000°C
Brightness	Medium
Type	

STAR C

Color	White
Temperature	10,000°C
Brightness	Low
Type	

Lab zone Do the Quick Lab *Interpreting the H-R Diagram.*

Assess Your Understanding

1a. Review What two characteristics of stars are shown in an H-R diagram?

_____

_____

_____

_____

b. Explain What is the relationship between brightness and temperature shown within the main sequence?

_____

_____

_____

_____

_____

c. Interpret Diagrams The star Procyon B has a surface temperature of 7,500°C and a low absolute brightness. What type of star is it?

_____

_____

got it? ....

○ **I get it!** Now I know that astronomers use H-R diagrams to _____

_____

_____

_____

○ **I need extra help with** _____

_____

Go to MY SCIENCE COACH *online for help with this subject.*

Lives of Stars

🔑 **How Does a Star Form and What Determines Its Life Span?**

🔑 **What Happens to a Star When It Runs Out of Fuel?**

my planet Diary

DISCOVERY

The Supernova of 1054

In the summer of 1054, some Chinese astronomers noticed a "guest star" in the night sky. The star was so bright people could see it during the day! The star remained visible for almost two years. How did these ancient astronomers interpret it? Was it a sign that the emperor would be visited by an important guest? People from around the world recorded and interpreted the event differently. Almost 1,000 years later, scientists realized the "guest star" was the explosion of a giant star 4,000 light-years away. So powerful was the explosion that all life within about 50 light-years would have been wiped out. Now called Supernova 1054, its remains are known as the Crab Nebula.

Communicate Discuss the supernova with a partner and answer the questions below.

1. Why was Supernova 1054 so notable?

_____

_____

_____

_____

2. How do you think ancient astronomers might have interpreted the event differently than astronomers today?

_____

_____

_____

 Lab® **zone** Do the Inquiry Warm-Up *What Determines How Long Stars Live?*

▷ **PLANET DIARY** Go to **Planet Diary** to learn more about stars.

Vocabulary

- nebula • protostar • white dwarf • supernova
- neutron star • pulsar • black hole

Skills

↻ Reading: Compare and Contrast
△ Inquiry: Predict

How Does a Star Form and What Determines Its Life Span?

Stars do not last forever. Each star is born, goes through its life cycle, and eventually dies. (Of course, stars are not really alive. The words *born, live,* and *die* are just helpful comparisons.) 🔑 **A star is born when the contracting gas and dust from a nebula become so dense and hot that nuclear fusion starts. How long a star lives depends on its mass.**

A Star Is Born All stars begin their lives as parts of nebulas, such as the one in **Figure 1**. A **nebula** is a large cloud of gas and dust spread out in an immense volume. A star, on the other hand, is made up of a large amount of gas in a relatively small volume.

In the densest part of a nebula, gravity pulls gas and dust together. A contracting cloud of gas and dust with enough mass to form a star is called a **protostar.** *Proto-* means "earliest" in Greek, so a protostar is the earliest stage of a star's life.

Recall that nuclear fusion is the process by which atoms combine to form heavier atoms. In the sun, for example, hydrogen atoms combine to form helium. During nuclear fusion, enormous amounts of energy are released. Nuclear fusion begins in a protostar.

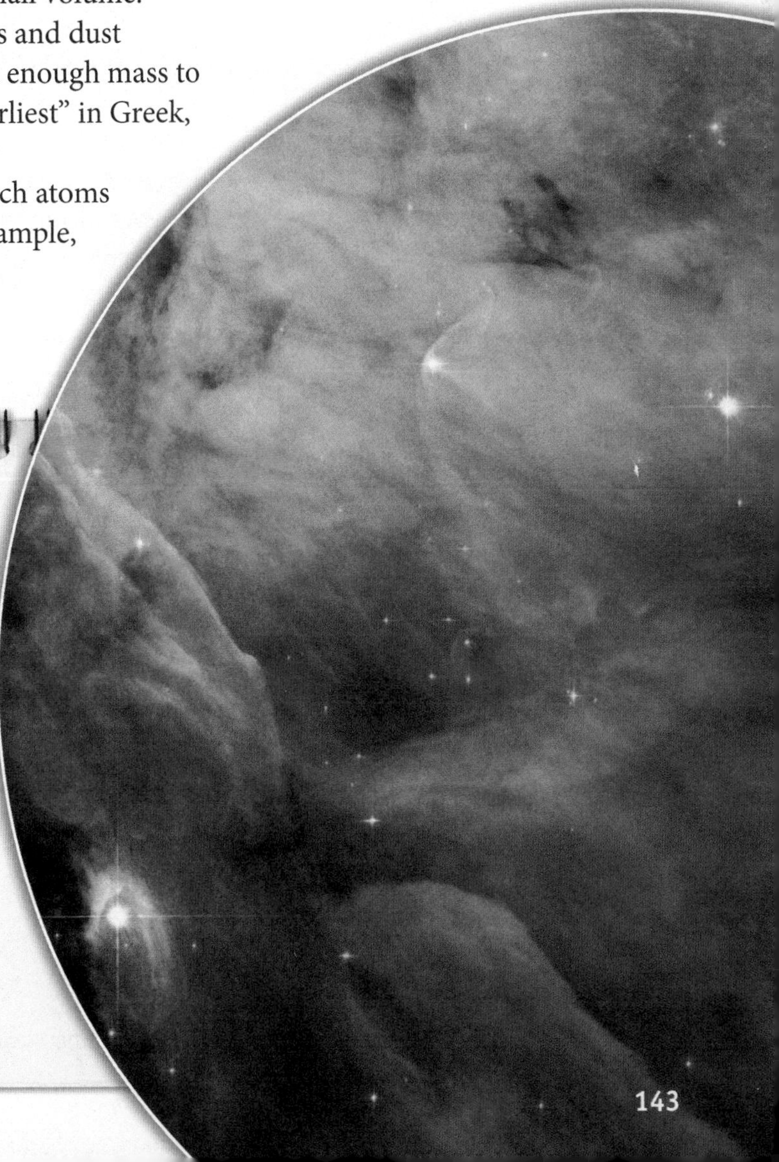

FIGURE 1 ·······························
A Stellar Nursery
New stars are forming in the nebula.

✏ **Summarize Describe the process of star formation.**

_____

_____

_____

_____

_____

_____

_____

143

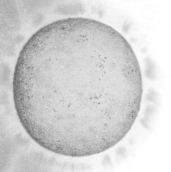

Lifetimes of Stars How long a star lives depends on the star's mass. You might think that stars with more mass would last longer than stars with less mass. But the reverse is true. You can think of stars as being like cars. A small car has a small gas tank, but it also has a small engine that burns gas slowly. A large car has a larger gas tank, but it also has a larger engine that burns gas rapidly. So the small car can travel farther on a tank of gas than the larger car. Small-mass stars use up their fuel more slowly than large-mass stars, so they have much longer lives.

Generally, stars that have less mass than the sun use their fuel slowly, and can live for up to 200 billion years. A medium-mass star like the sun will live for about 10 billion years. The sun is about 4.6 billion years old, so it is about halfway through its lifetime. In **Figure 2**, the yellow star is similar to the sun.

Stars that have more mass than the sun have shorter lifetimes. A star that is more massive than the sun, such as the blue star shown in **Figure 2,** may live only about 10 million years. That may seem like a very long time, but it is only one tenth of one percent of the lifetime of the sun.

FIGURE 2 ··········
Life of a Star
A star's lifetime depends on its mass.

✎ **Explain** The yellow star has much less mass than the blue star and so will live longer. Explain why.

_____
_____
_____
_____
_____
_____

Lab zone ® Do the Quick Lab
Life Cycle of Stars.

🔑 Assess Your Understanding

1a. Review How does a star form from a nebula?

_____
_____
_____
_____

b. Summarize What factor determines how long a star lives?

_____
_____

c. Predict A star is twice as massive as the sun. How will its lifespan compare?

_____
_____

got it? ···

O **I get it!** Now I know that stars are born when _____

_____

and how long a star lives depends on _____

O I need extra help with _____

Go to MY SCIENCE ⓢ COACH *online for help with this subject.*

What Happens to a Star When It Runs Out of Fuel?

When a star begins to run out of fuel, its core shrinks and its outer portion expands. Depending on its mass, the star becomes either a red giant or a supergiant. Red giants and supergiants evolve in very different ways. **After a star runs out of fuel, it becomes a white dwarf, a neutron star, or a black hole.**

White Dwarfs Low-mass stars and medium-mass stars like the sun take billions of years to use up their nuclear fuel. As they start to run out of fuel, their outer layers expand, and they become red giants. Eventually, the outer parts grow larger still and drift out into space, forming a glowing cloud of gas called a planetary nebula. The blue-white core of the star that is left behind cools and becomes a **white dwarf.**

White dwarfs are about the size of Earth, but they have about as much mass as the sun. A white dwarf is about one million times as dense as the sun. White dwarfs have no fuel, but they glow faintly from leftover energy. After billions of years, a white dwarf stops glowing. Then it is called a black dwarf.

Supernovas The life cycle of a high-mass star is quite different. These stars quickly evolve into brilliant supergiants. When a supergiant runs out of fuel, it can explode suddenly. Within hours, the star blazes millions of times brighter. The explosion is called a **supernova.** After a supernova, some of the material from the star expands into space. This material may become part of a nebula. This nebula can then contract to form a new, partly recycled star. Recall that nuclear fusion creates heavy elements. A supernova provides enough energy to create the heaviest elements. Astronomers think that the matter in the sun and the planets around it came from a gigantic supernova. If so, this means that the matter all around you was created in a star, and all matter on Earth is a form of stardust.

Compare and Contrast
How does the mass and size of a white dwarf compare with the mass and size of the sun?

○ Same mass; greater size
○ Less mass; greater size
○ Same mass; smaller size
○ Less mass; smaller size

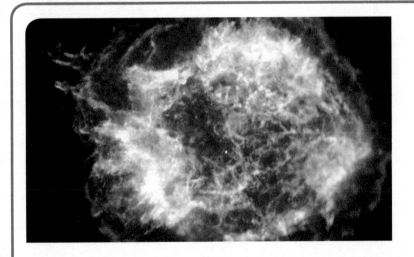

FIGURE 3 ·······················
Supernova Remnant Cassiopeia A
Cassiopeia A is the remnant of a once-massive star that died in a supernova explosion seen 325 years ago.

✎ [CHALLENGE] **Explain the connection between your body and a supernova.**

_____
_____
_____
_____

145

FIGURE 4 ·····································

> INTERACTIVE ART **Lives of Stars**

✏ **Relate Text and Visuals** Fill in the missing stages on the diagram. Now, think about where the sun fits on the diagram. On the lines below, describe what will happen to the sun when it runs out of fuel.

_____

_____

_____

_____

_____

_____

_____

_____

_____

_____

_____

_____

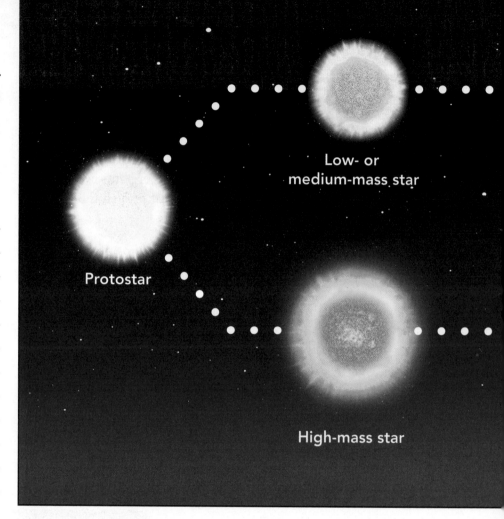

Protostar

Low- or
medium-mass star

High-mass star

apply it!

Predict An alien civilization is in orbit around a high-mass supergiant star. Should they stay or should they go elsewhere? Why?

_____

_____

_____

_____

Neutron Stars After a supergiant explodes, some of the material from the star is left behind. This material may form a neutron star. **Neutron stars** are the remains of high-mass stars. They are even smaller and denser than white dwarfs. A neutron star may contain as much as three times the mass of the sun but be only about 25 kilometers in diameter, the size of a city.

In 1967, Jocelyn Bell, a British astronomy student working with Antony Hewish, detected an object in space that appeared to give off regular pulses of radio waves. Some astronomers thought the pulses might be signals from an extraterrestrial civilization. At first, astronomers even named the source LGM, for the "Little Green Men" in early science-fiction stories. Soon, however, astronomers concluded that the source of the radio waves was really a rapidly spinning neutron star. Spinning neutron stars are called **pulsars,** short for pulsating radio sources. Some pulsars spin hundreds of times per second!

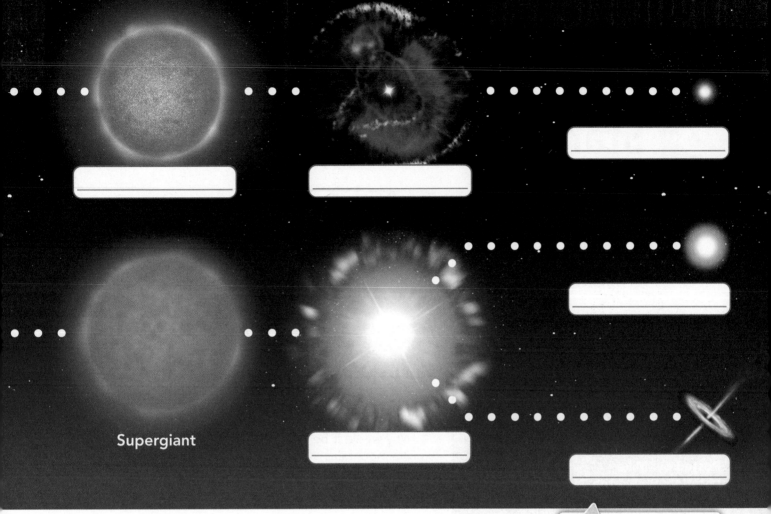

Supergiant

Black Holes

The most massive stars—those that have more than 10 times the mass of the sun—may become black holes when they die. A **black hole** is an object with gravity so strong that nothing, not even light, can escape. After a very massive star dies in a supernova explosion, more than five times the mass of the sun may be left. The gravity of this mass is so strong that the gas is pulled inward, packing the gas into a smaller and smaller space. The star's gas becomes squeezed so hard that the star converts into a black hole, and its intense gravity will not allow even light to escape.

No light, radio waves, or any other form of radiation can ever get out of a black hole, so it is not possible to detect directly. But astronomers can detect black holes indirectly. For example, gas near a black hole is pulled so strongly that it revolves faster and faster around the black hole. Friction heats the gas up. Astronomers can detect X-rays coming from the hot gas and infer that a black hole is present.

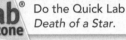 Do the Quick Lab
Death of a Star.

🔑 Assess Your Understanding

2a. Review What determines if a star becomes a white dwarf, neutron star, or black hole?

_____

b. Predict Which will the sun become: a white dwarf, neutron star, or a black hole? Why?

_____

_____

got it? ....

○ **I get it!** Now I know that after a star runs

out of fuel, it becomes _____

_____

○ **I need extra help with** _____

Go to MY SCIENCE Ⓢ COACH *online for help with this subject.*

147

Star Systems and Galaxies

UNLOCK THE BIG Q

🔑 **What Is a Star System?**

🔑 **What Are the Major Types of Galaxies?**

my planeT DiaRY

Posted by: Mike
Location: Brewerton, New York

When I was ten, I went to visit a friend in the Adirondack Mountains. We were outside on a clear, dark night until 2:00 A.M., and we saw the Milky Way. It was a big, white stream in the sky. The Milky Way was filled with stars.

Communicate Answer these questions. Discuss your answers with a partner.

1. Why would it be easier to see the Milky Way from the mountains?

_____

_____

2. Why does the Milky Way appear more like a white stream than separate stars?

_____

_____

_____

_____

▶ PLANET DIARY Go to **Planet Diary** to learn more about galaxies.

Lab zone Do the Inquiry Warm-Up *Why Does the Milky Way Look Hazy?*

What Is a Star System?

Our solar system has only one star: the sun. But this is not a common situation for stars. 🔑 **Most stars are members of groups of two or more stars, called star systems.** If you were on a planet in one of these star systems, at times you might see two or more suns in the sky! At other times, one or more of these suns might be below the horizon.

Vocabulary

- binary star • eclipsing binary • open cluster
- globular cluster • galaxy • spiral galaxy
- elliptical galaxy • irregular galaxy • quasar

Skills

⟳ Reading: Relate Cause and Effect
△ Inquiry: Draw Conclusions

FIGURE 1 ....
Invisible Partner
A dim companion star might not
be visible from Earth, but its
existence can be inferred, like
the invisible dancer.

✎ **Identify** Name another
situation when you can't see
something but you know it's there.

_____

_____

_____

Multiple Star Systems

Star systems that have two
stars are called double stars or **binary stars.** (The prefix *bi-*
means "two.") Those with three stars are called triple stars.

Often one star in a binary star is much brighter and more
massive than the other. Astronomers can sometimes detect a
binary star even if only one of the stars can be seen from Earth.
Astronomers can often tell that there is a dim star in a binary
system by observing the effects of its gravity. As the dim
companion star revolves around a bright star, the dim star's
gravity causes the bright star to wobble. Imagine watching a
pair of dancers who are twirling each other around, as shown
in **Figure 1**. Even if one dancer were invisible, you could tell the
invisible dancer was there from the motion of the visible dancer.

Eclipsing Binaries

A wobble is not the only clue that a star
has a dim companion. A dim star in a binary star may pass in front
of a brighter star and eclipse it. From Earth, the bright star would
suddenly look much dimmer. A system in which one star blocks the
light from another periodically is called an **eclipsing binary.**

✎ **⟳ Relate Cause and Effect**
What causes a binary star to
wobble back and forth?
○ Gravity of another star
○ Eclipsing by another star

149

Planets Around Other Stars

In 1995, astronomers first discovered a planet revolving around another ordinary star. They used a method similar to the one used in studying binary stars. The astronomers observed that the star was moving slightly toward and then away from us. They knew that the invisible object causing the movement didn't have enough mass to be a star. They inferred that it must be a planet.

Since then, astronomers have discovered more than 300 planets around other stars, and new ones are being discovered all of the time. Most of these new planets are very large, with at least half of the mass of Jupiter. A small planet would be hard to detect because it would have little gravitational effect on the star it orbited.

Could there be life on planets in other solar systems? Some scientists think it is possible. A few astronomers are using radio telescopes to search for signals that could not have come from natural sources. Such signals might be evidence that an alien civilization was sending out radio waves.

Star Clusters

Many stars belong to larger groupings called star clusters. All of the stars in a particular cluster formed from the same nebula at about the same time and are about the same distance from Earth.

There are two major types of star clusters: open clusters and globular clusters. **Open clusters** have a loose, disorganized appearance as shown in **Figure 3** and contain up to a few thousand stars. They often contain many bright supergiants and much gas and dust. In contrast, **globular clusters** are large groupings of older stars. Globular clusters are round and packed with stars. Some may contain more than a million stars.

FIGURE 3 ••
Star Cluster Pleiades
✏️ [CHALLENGE] Why did some ancient astronomers call the Pleiades the "seven sisters"?

_____

_____

EXPLORE THE BIG ?

Searching for Alien Life

How do astronomers learn about distant objects in the universe?

FIGURE 2 ••
▶ REAL-WORLD INQUIRY Imagine you are an astronomer looking for intelligent alien life around a faraway star. All you can get from the star is visible light and other parts of the electromagnetic spectrum.

① Suppose you detect a slight wobble of the star. What might that tell you?

_____

_____

_____

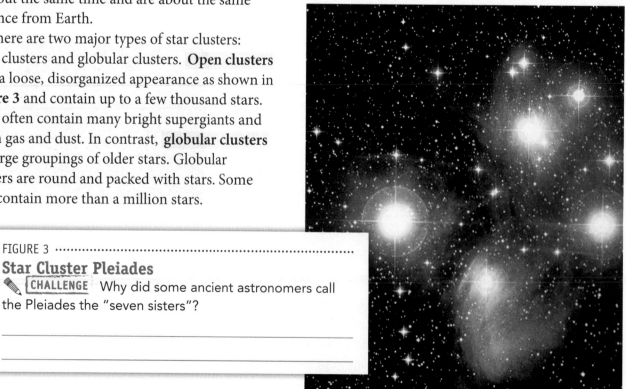

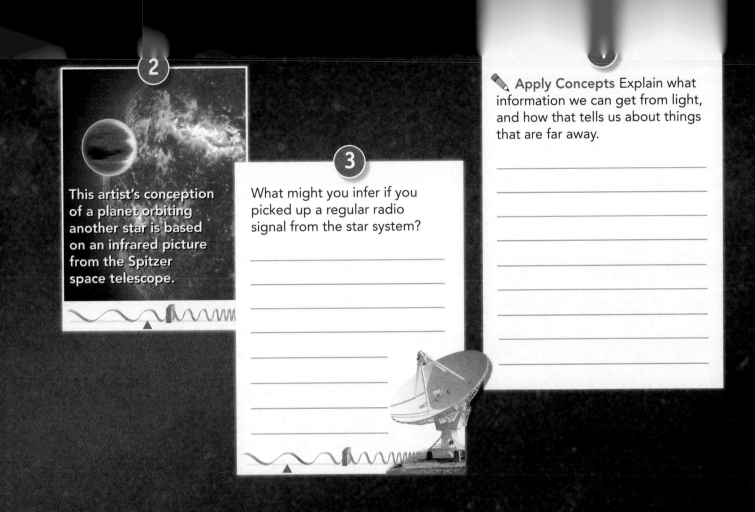

2

This artist's conception of a planet orbiting another star is based on an infrared picture from the Spitzer space telescope.

3

What might you infer if you picked up a regular radio signal from the star system?

_____

_____

_____

_____

_____

_____

_____

_____

✎ **Apply Concepts** Explain what information we can get from light, and how that tells us about things that are far away.

_____

_____

_____

_____

_____

_____

_____

_____

_____

_____

Lab ® Do the Quick Lab *Planets*
zone *Around Other Stars.*

🔑 Assess Your Understanding

1a. Define What is a binary star?

_____

_____

b. Apply Concepts In what two ways can we tell if a star is a binary star?

_____

_____

_____

_____

c. 🅰️❓ How do astronomers learn about distant objects in the universe?

_____

_____

_____

_____

_____

_____

got it? ....

○ **I get it!** Now I know that star systems are _____

○ **I need extra help with** _____

Go to **MY SCIENCE ⑤ COACH** *online for help with this subject.*

What Are the Major Types of Galaxies?

A **galaxy** is a huge group of single stars, star systems, star clusters, dust, and gas bound together by gravity. There are billions of galaxies in the universe. The largest galaxies have more than a trillion stars. 🔑 **Astronomers classify most galaxies into the following types: spiral, elliptical, and irregular.**

① ② ③ ④

Spiral Galaxies

Some galaxies appear to have a bulge in the middle and arms that spiral outward, like pin-wheels. These galaxies are spiral galaxies. The arms contain gas, dust, and many bright, young stars. Most new stars in spiral galaxies form in these arms. Barred-spiral galaxies have a bar-shaped area of stars and gas that passes through the center.

Elliptical Galaxies

Not all galaxies have spiral arms. Elliptical galaxies look like round or flattened balls. These galaxies contain billions of stars but have little gas and dust between the stars. Because there is little gas or dust, stars are no longer forming. Most elliptical galaxies contain only old stars.

Irregular Galaxies

Some galaxies do not have regular shapes. These are known as irregular galaxies. Irregular galaxies are typically smaller than other types of galaxies. They generally have many bright, young stars and lots of gas and dust to form new stars.

Quasars

Astronomers in the 1960s discovered distant, extremely bright objects that looked like stars. Since *quasi* means "something like" in Latin, these objects were called quasi-stellar objects, or quasars. Quasars are active young galaxies with huge black holes at their centers. Gas spins around the black hole, heats up, and glows.

FIGURE 4 ·········

Types of Galaxies

✏️ **Relate Text and Visuals** Identify the four galaxies shown on these pages and explain.

Ⓐ _____

_____

Ⓑ _____

_____

Ⓒ _____

_____

Ⓓ _____

_____

Ⓐ

○ Spiral   ○ Elliptical

○ Irregular   ○ Quasar

apply it!

Our solar system is located in a galaxy called the Milky Way. From the side, the Milky Way would look like a narrow disk with a large bulge in the middle. But from the top or bottom, the Milky Way would have a pinwheel shape. You can't see the shape of the Milky Way from Earth because our solar system is inside one of the arms.

When you see the Milky Way at night during the summer, you are looking toward the center of our galaxy. The center of the galaxy is about 25,000 light-years away, but it is hidden from view by large clouds of dust and gas. But astronomers can study the center using X-rays, infrared radiation, and radio waves.

Draw Conclusions What kind of galaxy is the Milky Way? Explain why and draw a sketch of what the Milky Way might look like from outside.

_____

_____

_____

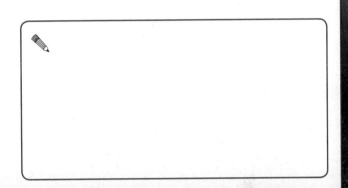

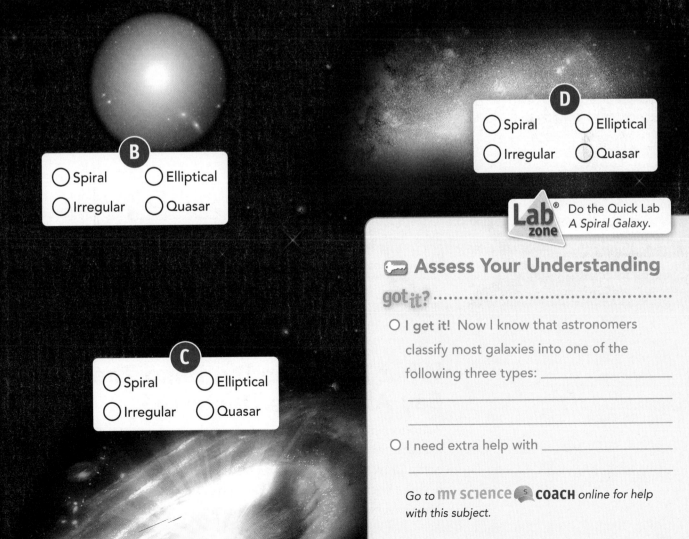

B
○ Spiral   ○ Elliptical
○ Irregular ○ Quasar

C
○ Spiral   ○ Elliptical
○ Irregular ○ Quasar

D
○ Spiral   ○ Elliptical
○ Irregular ○ Quasar

Lab zone Do the Quick Lab
A Spiral Galaxy.

🔑 Assess Your Understanding

got it? ....

○ **I get it!** Now I know that astronomers classify most galaxies into one of the following three types: _____

_____

_____

○ **I need extra help with** _____

_____

Go to MY SCIENCE Ⓢ COACH *online for help with this subject.*

LESSON
6 The Expanding Universe

UNLOCK THE BIG ?

🔑 **What Does the Big Bang Theory Say About the Universe?**

MY PLANET DIARY

BLOG

Posted by: David
Location: Bowie, Maryland

On Sunday, March 15, 2009, I flew to Orlando, Florida, to see the launch of *Discovery* in Cape Canaveral, the first launch I ever saw. At 5 seconds, the engines ignited and at 0 seconds, *Discovery* went into the sky. I could feel the vibrations. *Discovery* looked like a ball of fire the color of autumn leaves, and it left a trail of smoke.

Communicate Write your answer to the question below. Then discuss your answer with a partner.

What would you want scientists to learn about the universe from a space shuttle mission?

_____

_____

_____

_____

_____

▶ PLANET DIARY Go to **Planet Diary** to learn more about the universe.

Lab® **zone** Do the Inquiry Warm-Up *How Does the Universe Expand?*

What Does the Big Bang Theory Say About the Universe?

Astronomers have learned a lot about the universe. They theorize that the universe began 13.7 billion years ago. At that time, the part of the universe we can see was no larger than the period at the end of this sentence. This tiny universe was incredibly hot and dense. The universe then exploded in what astronomers call the **big bang.**

Vocabulary

- big bang • Hubble's law
- cosmic background radiation
- dark matter • dark energy

Skills

- Reading: Identify Supporting Evidence
- Inquiry: Make Models

According to the big bang theory, the universe formed in an instant, billions of years ago, in an enormous explosion. New observations lead many astronomers to conclude that the universe will likely expand forever. Since the big bang, the size of the universe has been increasing. The universe is immensely larger now than it once was.

As the universe expanded, it gradually cooled. After a few hundred thousand years, atoms formed. Within about the first 500 million years after the big bang, the first stars and galaxies formed.

Moving Galaxies

In the 1920s, an American astronomer, Edwin Hubble, discovered important evidence that led to the big bang theory. Hubble studied the spectrums of many galaxies at various distances from Earth. By examining a galaxy's spectrum, Hubble could tell how fast the galaxy was moving and whether it was moving toward our galaxy or away from it.

Hubble discovered that almost all galaxies are moving away from us and from each other. Hubble found the relationship between the distance to a galaxy and its speed. **Hubble's law** states that the farther away a galaxy is, the faster it is moving away from us. Hubble's law strongly supports the big bang theory.

Cosmic Background Radiation

Another piece of evidence for the big bang was discovered by accident. In 1965, two American physicists, Arno Penzias and Robert Wilson, detected faint radiation on their radio telescope coming from all directions. Scientists later concluded that this **cosmic background radiation** is the leftover thermal energy from the big bang. This energy was distributed in every direction as the universe expanded.

Identify Supporting Evidence Underline the main evidence Hubble found that the universe is expanding.

apply it!

The galaxies in the universe are like raisins in rising bread dough.

Make Models Draw the raisins in their new positions on the bottom picture. Explain why the raisins are like galaxies.

_____
_____
_____
_____
_____

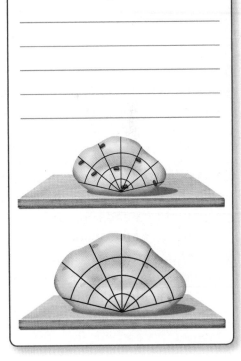

FIGURE 1 ··············

Age of the Universe

By measuring how fast the universe is expanding, astronomers can infer how long it has been expanding. The COBE satellite shown measured the cosmic background radiation, which also gave clues to the age of the universe.

155

The Big Bang and the Future of the Universe

What will happen to the universe in the future? One possibility is that the universe will continue to expand. All of the stars will eventually run out of fuel and burn out, and the universe will be cold and dark. Another possibility is that the force of gravity will begin to pull the galaxies back together, as shown in **Figure 2**. The result would be a reverse big bang, or "big crunch." The universe would be crushed in an enormous black hole.

FIGURE 2 ·································
The Big Crunch
The small diagram represents the expansion of the universe until now. The big bang is at the bottom.

✏️ [CHALLENGE] **On the top part of the diagram, draw a sketch of the universe collapsing to a big crunch. Explain your drawing.**

_____

_____

_____

_____

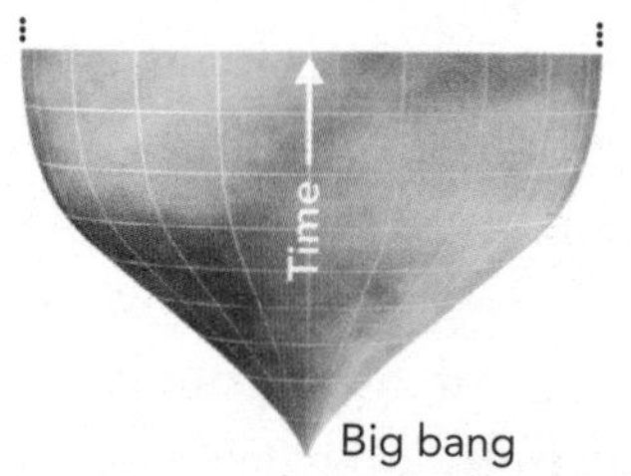

Big bang

Which of these possibilities is more likely? Recent discoveries have produced a surprising new view of the universe that is still not well understood. But many astronomers conclude that the universe will likely expand forever.

Dark Matter Until recently, astronomers assumed that the universe consisted solely of the matter they could observe directly. But this idea was disproved by American astronomer Vera Rubin. Rubin studied the rotation of spiral galaxies. She discovered that the matter that astronomers can see makes up as little as ten percent of the mass in galaxies. The rest exists in the form of dark matter.

Dark matter is matter that does not give off electromagnetic radiation. It cannot be seen directly. However, its presence can be inferred by observing the effect of its gravity on visible objects.

An Accelerating Expansion In the late 1990s, astronomers observed that the expansion of the universe appeared to be accelerating. That is, galaxies seemed to be moving apart at a faster rate than in the past. This observation was puzzling, as no known force could account for it. Astronomers infer that a mysterious new force, which they call **dark energy,** is causing the expansion of the universe to accelerate, as shown in **Figure 3**.

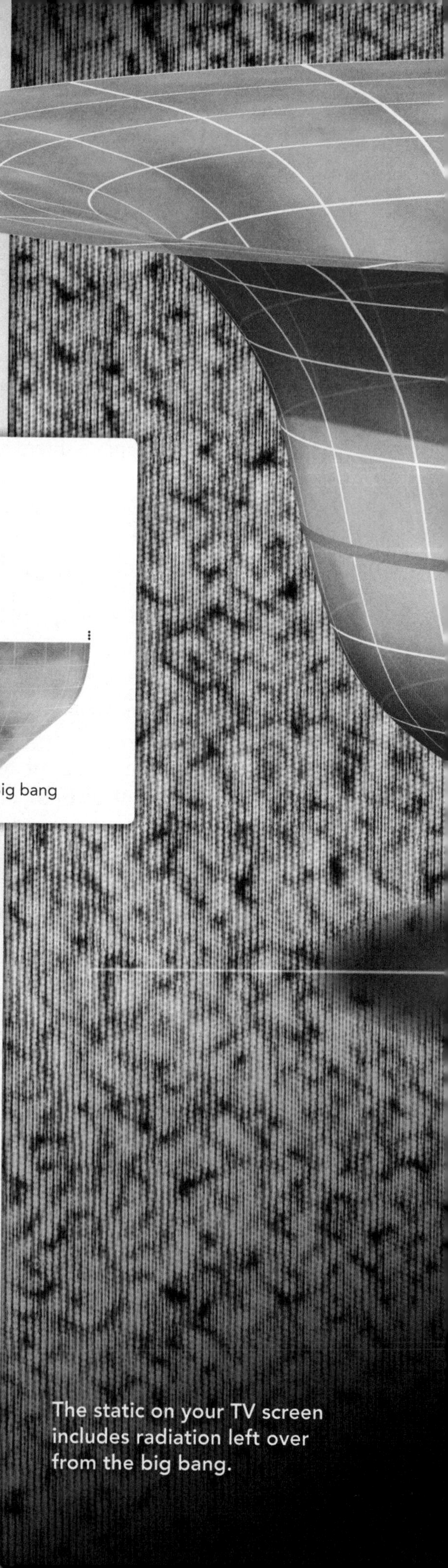

The static on your TV screen includes radiation left over from the big bang.

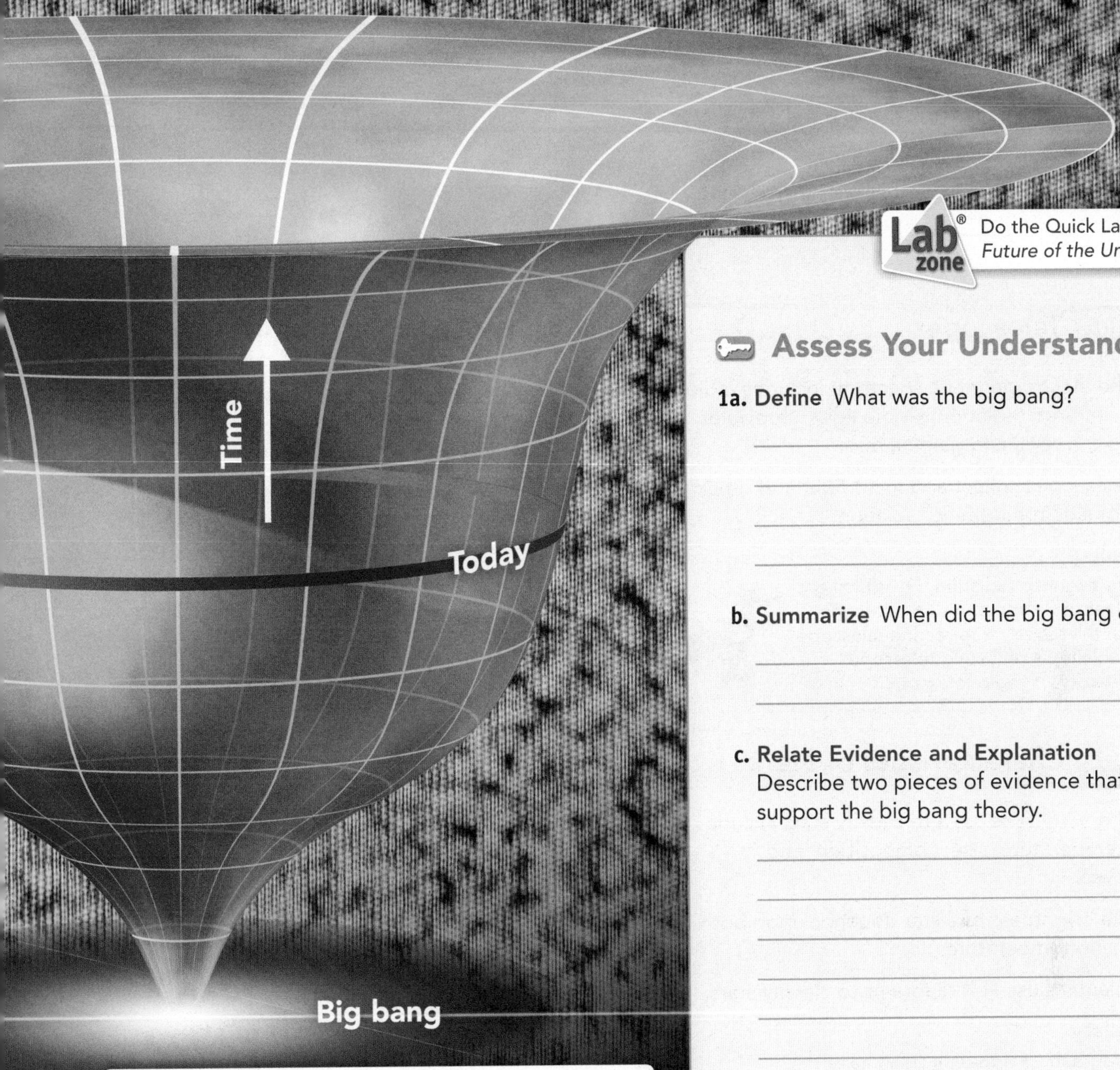

Time

Today

Big bang

FIGURE 3 ··

▶ **ART IN MOTION** **Expansion of the Universe**

✎ **Interpret Diagrams** The diagram represents a universe that is expanding forever. Explain why scientists think this might happen.

_____

_____

_____

_____

_____

_____

_____

🔑 **Assess Your Understanding**

1a. Define What was the big bang?

_____

_____

_____

_____

b. Summarize When did the big bang occur?

_____

_____

c. Relate Evidence and Explanation Describe two pieces of evidence that support the big bang theory.

_____

_____

_____

_____

_____

_____

_____

_____

got it? ··

○ **I get it!** Now I know that the big bang theory says that _____

_____

_____

_____

○ **I need extra help with** _____

_____

Go to **my science 🔵 COACH** online for help with this subject.

4 Study Guide

Astronomers learn about distant objects in the universe by studying _____

_____

LESSON 1 Telescopes

🔑 The electromagnetic spectrum includes radio waves, infrared radiation, visible light, ultraviolet radiation, X-rays, and gamma rays.

🔑 Telescopes collect and focus light and other forms of electromagnetic radiation.

Vocabulary
- electromagnetic radiation • visible light
- wavelength • spectrum • telescope
- optical telescope • refracting telescope
- convex lens • reflecting telescope
- observatory • radio telescope

LESSON 2 The Scale of the Universe

🔑 Astronomers often use parallax to measure distances to nearby stars.

🔑 Since the numbers astronomers use are often very large or very small, they frequently use scientific notation to describe sizes and distances in the universe. They use a unit called the light-year to measure distances between the stars.

Vocabulary
- parallax • universe
- light-year • scientific notation

LESSON 3 Characteristics of Stars

🔑 Characteristics used to classify stars include color, temperature, size, composition, and brightness.

🔑 The brightness of a star depends upon both its size and temperature.

🔑 Scientists use H-R diagrams to classify stars.

Vocabulary
- spectrograph • apparent brightness
- absolute brightness • Hertzsprung-Russell diagram
- main sequence

LESSON 4 Lives of Stars

🔑 A star is born when the contracting gas and dust from a nebula becomes so dense and hot that nuclear fusion starts. How long a star lives depends on its mass.

🔑 After a star runs out of fuel, it becomes a white dwarf, a neutron star, or a black hole.

Vocabulary
- nebula • protostar • white dwarf
- supernova • neutron star • pulsar
- black hole

LESSON 5 Star Systems and Galaxies

🔑 Most stars are members of groups of two or more stars, called star systems.

🔑 Astronomers classify most galaxies into the following types: spiral, elliptical, and irregular.

Vocabulary
- binary star • eclipsing binary
- open cluster • globular cluster
- galaxy • spiral galaxy • elliptical galaxy
- irregular galaxy • quasar

LESSON 6 The Expanding Universe

🔑 According to the big bang theory, the universe formed in an instant, billions of years ago, in an enormous explosion. New observations lead many astronomers to conclude that the universe will expand forever.

Vocabulary
- big bang • Hubble's law
- cosmic background radiation
- dark matter • dark energy

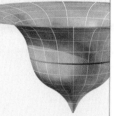

Review and Assessment

LESSON 1 Telescopes

1. What is visible light?

   a. gamma rays and X-rays

   b. the spectrum of rays

   c. a particular wavelength

   d. a form of electromagnetic radiation

2. Explain An optical telescope works by

_____

_____

_____

3. Draw Conclusions What advantage might there be in placing a telescope on the moon?

_____

_____

_____

_____

LESSON 2 The Scale of the Universe

4. Which type of numbers does scientific notation best describe?

   a. very small or very large

   b. very large only

   c. very small only

   d. large and small combined

5. Develop Hypotheses Why can't astronomers measure the parallax of a star that is a million light-years away?

_____

_____

_____

_____

6. math! The star Antares is about 604 light-years from Earth. Write this distance in scientific notation.

_____

LESSON 3 Characteristics of Stars

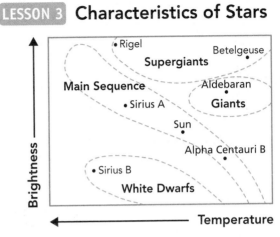

Use the diagram to answer the questions below.

7. Interpret Diagrams On the diagram, circle the star that has a greater absolute brightness: Aldebaran or Sirius B.

8. Apply Concepts On the diagram, underline the star that is most likely to be red: Rigel, Sirius B, or Betelgeuse.

LESSON 4 Lives of Stars

9. Relate Cause and Effect How does a star's mass affect its lifetime?

_____

_____

_____

_____

10. Sequence Explain how a black hole forms.

_____

_____

_____

_____

_____

_____

_____

159

CHAPTER 4 Review and Assessment

LESSON 5 **Star Systems and Galaxies**

11. In what kind of star system does one star block the light from another?

a. open cluster
b. binary star system
c. quasar system
d. eclipsing binary

12. Compare and Contrast How is the number of stars different in an open cluster than in a globular cluster?

_____

_____

_____

_____

_____

13. **Write About It** Describe the "life story" of a star in a spiral galaxy. Explain where it was born and what it was like there.

LESSON 6 **The Expanding Universe**

14. What is the name of the explosion that began the universe?

a. solar nebula
b. big bang
c. dark matter
d. supernova

15. Classify Radio telescopes are able to detect cosmic background radiation, which is

_____

_____

16. Compare and Contrast Explain the difference between a big crunch and an ever-expanding universe.

_____

_____

_____

_____

_____

APPLY THE BIG **How do astronomers learn about distant objects in the universe?**

17. Write the introduction of a manual for young astronomers. Briefly describe different tools astronomers have for learning about distant objects in the universe. Tell what kind of information each tool can provide.

_____

_____

_____

_____

_____

_____

_____

_____

_____

_____

_____

_____

_____

_____

_____

_____

_____

_____

_____

_____

_____

_____

_____

Standardized Test Prep

Multiple Choice

Circle the letter of the best answer.

1. The table below gives an estimate of star distribution in the Milky Way galaxy. According to the table, what is the most common type of star in the Milky Way?

Type of Star	Percentage of Total
Main sequence	90.75 %
Red giant	0.50 %
Supergiant	< 0.0001 %
White dwarf	8.75 %

A main-sequence star
B red giant
C supergiant
D white dwarf

2. What is the main factor that affects the evolution of a star?

A color   B brightness
C mass   D parallax

3. What does a light-year measure?

A time   B volume
C brightness   D distance

4. Which of the following best describes a reflecting telescope?

A Isaac Newton invention
B has an objective lens
C is the smallest telescope
D has a mirror lens

5. Which statement explains the big bang theory?

A The universe formed from a series of explosions over billions of years.
B The universe will explode in 10 million years and destroy our solar system.
C The universe formed very quickly from an enormous explosion.
D The universe gradually heated up until it exploded.

Constructed Response

Use the diagram below and your knowledge of science to help you answer Question 6. Write your answer on a separate sheet of paper.

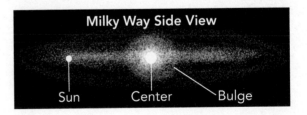

Milky Way Side View
Sun   Center   Bulge

6. Describe the appearance of the Milky Way as you would see it both from Earth and from a point directly above the galaxy. Why does the galaxy look different from different places?

BLACK HOLES

Scientists can't see them, but they keep studying them. For years, astronomers have known that black holes exist. The extreme gravity of a black hole allows nothing to escape, not even light. So astronomers need to use some pretty high-powered tools to study them.

Astronomers use data from space telescopes to measure the visible light, X-rays, and radio waves emitted from objects near a black hole. Astronomers have used this data to learn a lot about black holes. They know that black holes come in two main sizes— stellar-sized, formed when massive stars collapse inward, and supermassive.

Supermassive black holes are found in the center of galaxies. The gravity from the black hole helps bind the stars, star systems, star clusters, dust, and gas into a galaxy.

Evaluate It Black holes are often described in movies and science fiction novels. Find one example of a black hole in a novel, graphic novel, TV show, or movie. Write an essay that explains how the black hole is described in your sources. Evaluate the source's scientific accuracy, and correct any inaccurate information.

◀ This image of two galaxies colliding was taken by the Hubble Space Telescope in 2008. Astronomers believe that supermassive black holes are at the center of galaxies.

APPRENTICE ASTRONOMERS

Kids in the Boston area have their heads in the stars. At least the lucky ones do. They're part of the Youth Astronomy Apprenticeship (YAA) program run by four astronomical and educational institutions in the area.

The goal of YAA is to give urban kids more exposure to astronomers and astronomy. In after-school programs, apprentices learn many things, including how to understand and interpret images from a network of telescopes students control online, and how to prepare the images to illustrate their own research. In Stage 2 of the program, apprentices can go on to a summer apprentice program. In the summer program, participants are paid to help make museum exhibits and perform science and astronomy plays. Participants also help teach other people about the universe. Some students go on to become youth assistants, teaching the next group of young stargazers.

Are the apprentices "star-struck"? The YAA program hopes they are.

Design It Choose a topic in astronomy that interests you. Working with a partner, prepare an exhibit about that topic. Present your exhibit to members of your school community.

APPENDIX A

Star Charts

Use these star charts to locate bright stars and major constellations in the night sky at different times of year. Choose the appropriate star chart for the current season.

Autumn Sky This chart works best at the following dates and times: September 1 at 10:00 P.M., October 1 at 8:00 P.M., or November 1 at 6:00 P.M. Look for the constellations Ursa Minor (the Little Dipper) and Cassiopeia in the northern sky, and for the star Deneb, which is nearly overhead in autumn.

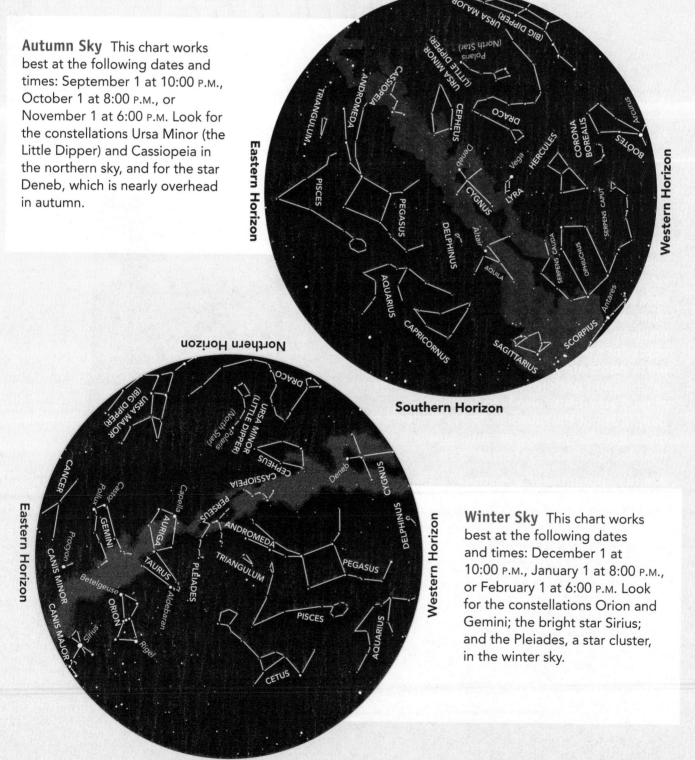

Winter Sky This chart works best at the following dates and times: December 1 at 10:00 P.M., January 1 at 8:00 P.M., or February 1 at 6:00 P.M. Look for the constellations Orion and Gemini; the bright star Sirius; and the Pleiades, a star cluster, in the winter sky.

How to Use the Star Charts

Using a flashlight and a compass, hold the appropriate chart and turn it so that the direction you are facing is at the bottom of the chart. These star charts work best at 34° north latitude, but can be used at other central latitudes.

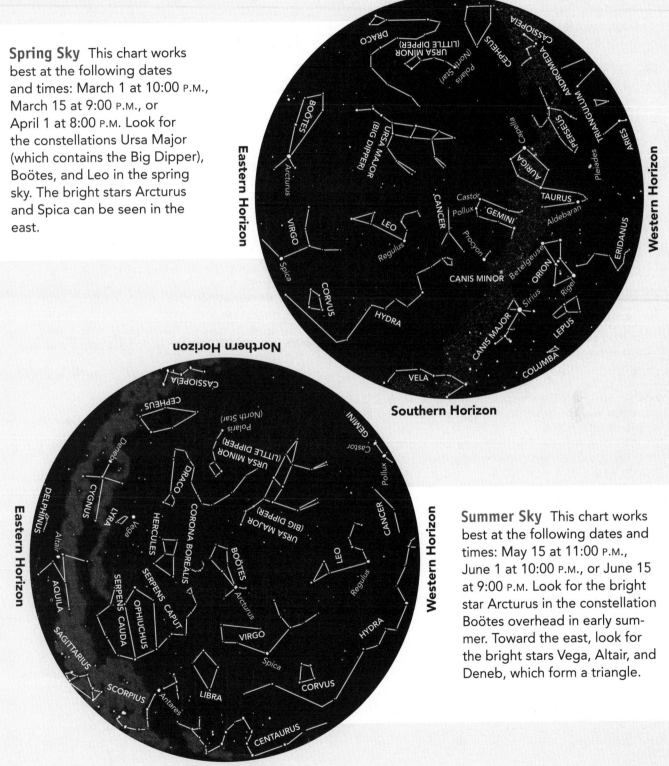

Spring Sky This chart works best at the following dates and times: March 1 at 10:00 P.M., March 15 at 9:00 P.M., or April 1 at 8:00 P.M. Look for the constellations Ursa Major (which contains the Big Dipper), Boötes, and Leo in the spring sky. The bright stars Arcturus and Spica can be seen in the east.

Summer Sky This chart works best at the following dates and times: May 15 at 11:00 P.M., June 1 at 10:00 P.M., or June 15 at 9:00 P.M. Look for the bright star Arcturus in the constellation Boötes overhead in early summer. Toward the east, look for the bright stars Vega, Altair, and Deneb, which form a triangle.

GLOSSARY

A

absolute brightness The brightness a star would have if it were at a standard distance from Earth. (139)
magnitud absoluta Brillo que tendría una estrella si estuviera a una distancia estándar de la Tierra.

apparent brightness The brightness of a star as seen from Earth. (139)
magnitud aparente Brillo de una estrella vista desde la Tierra.

asteroid belt The region of the solar system between the orbits of Mars and Jupiter, where many asteroids are found. (111)
cinturón de asteroides Región del sistema solar entre las órbitas de Marte y Júpiter, donde se encuentran muchos asteroides.

asteroid One of the rocky objects revolving around the sun that are too small and numerous to be considered planets. (114)
asteroide Uno de los cuerpos rocosos que se mueven alrededor del Sol y que son demasiado pequeños y numerosos como para ser considerados planetas.

astronomical unit A unit of distance equal to the average distance between Earth and the sun, about 150 million kilometers. (83)
unidad astronómica Unidad de medida equivalente a la distancia media entre la Tierra y el Sol, aproximadamente 150 millones de kilómetros.

axis An imaginary line that passes through a planet's center and its north and south poles, about which the planet rotates. (11)
eje Línea imaginaria alrededor de la cual gira un planeta, y que atraviesa su centro y sus dos polos, norte y sur.

B

big bang The initial explosion that resulted in the formation and expansion of the universe. (154)
Big bang Explosión inicial que resultó en la formación y expansión del universo.

binary star A star system with two stars. (149)
estrella binaria Sistema estelar de dos estrellas.

black hole An object whose gravity is so strong that nothing, not even light, can escape. (147)
agujero negro Cuerpo cuya gravedad es tan fuerte que nada, ni siquiera la luz, puede escapar.

C

calendar A system of organizing time that defines the beginning, length, and divisions of a year. (12)
calendario Sistema de organización del tiempo que define el principio, la duración y las divisiones de un año.

chromosphere The middle layer of the sun's atmosphere. (90)
cromósfera Capa central de la atmósfera solar.

coma The fuzzy outer layer of a comet. (113)
coma Capa exterior y difusa de un cometa.

comet A loose collection of ice and dust that orbits the sun, typically in a long, narrow orbit. (5, 113)
cometa Cuerpo poco denso de hielo y polvo cuya órbita alrededor del Sol es típicamente excéntrica.

constellation A pattern or grouping of stars that people imagine to represent a figure or object. (6)
constelación Patrón de estrellas que se dice se asemeja a una figura u objeto.

convection zone The outermost layer of the sun's interior. (89)
zona de convección Capa más superficial del interior del Sol.

convex lens A lens that is thicker in the center than at the edges. (128)
lente convexa Lente que es más gruesa en el centro que en los extremos.

core The central region of the sun, where nuclear fusion takes place. (89)
núcleo Región central del Sol, donde ocurre la fusión nuclear.

corona The outer layer of the sun's atmosphere. (91)
corona Capa externa de la atmósfera solar.

cosmic background radiation The electromagnetic radiation left over from the big bang. (155)
radiación cósmica de fondo Radiación electromagnética que quedó del *Big bang*.

crater **1.** A large round pit caused by the impact of a meteoroid. (33) **2.** A bowl-shaped area that forms around a volcano's central opening.
cráter **1.** Hoyo grande causado por el impacto de un meteoroide. **2.** Depresión de forma más o menos circular que se forma alrededor de la parte central de un volcán.

D

dark energy A mysterious force that appears to be causing the expansion of the universe to accelerate. (156)
energía negra Misteriosa fuerza que parece acelerar la expansión del universo.

dark matter Matter that does not give off electromagnetic radiation but is quite abundant in the universe. (156)
materia negra Materia que es muy abundante en el universo y no despide radiación electromagnética.

dwarf planet An object that orbits the sun and is spherical, but has not cleared the area of its orbit. (84)
planeta enano Un cuerpo esférico que orbita alrededor del Sol, pero que no ha despejado las proximidades de su órbita.

E

eclipse The partial or total blocking of one object in space by another. (25)
eclipse Bloqueo parcial o total de un cuerpo en el espacio por otro.

eclipsing binary A binary star system in which one star periodically blocks the light from the other. (149)
eclipse binario Sistema estelar binario en el que una estrella bloquea periódicamente la luz de la otra.

electromagnetic radiation The energy transferred through space by electromagnetic waves. (126)
radiación electromagnética Energía transferida a través del espacio por ondas electromagnéticas.

ellipse An oval shape, which may be elongated or nearly circular; the shape of the planets' orbits. (81)
elipse Forma ovalada que puede ser alargada o casi circular; la forma de la órbita de los planetas.

elliptical galaxy A galaxy shaped like a round or flattened ball, generally containing only old stars. (152)
galaxia elíptica Galaxia de forma redonda o semejante a una pelota desinflada, que generalmente sólo contiene estrellas viejas.

equinox Either of the two days of the year on which neither hemisphere is tilted toward or away from the sun. (16)
equinoccio Cualquiera de los de dos días del año en el que ningún hemisferio se retrae o inclina hacia el Sol.

escape velocity The velocity an object must reach to fly beyond a planet's or moon's gravitational pull. (49)
velocidad de escape Velocidad que debe alcanzar un cohete para salir del empuje gravitacional de un planeta o luna.

F

force A push or pull exerted on an object. (18)
fuerza Empuje o atracción que se ejerce sobre un cuerpo.

G

galaxy A huge group of single stars, star systems, star clusters, dust, and gas bound together by gravity. (152)
galaxia Enorme grupo de estrellas individuales, sistemas estelares, cúmulos de estrellas, polvo y gases unidos por la gravedad.

gas giant The name often given to the outer planets: Jupiter, Saturn, Uranus, and Neptune. (102)
gigantes gaseosos Nombre que normalmente se da a los cuatro planetas exteriores: Júpiter, Saturno, Urano y Neptuno.

geocentric Term describing a model of the universe in which Earth is at the center of the revolving planets and stars. (79)
geocéntrico Término que describe un modelo del universo en el cual la Tierra se encuentra al centro de los planetas y estrellas que circulan a su alrededor.

geostationary orbit An orbit in which a satellite orbits Earth at the same rate as Earth rotates and thus stays over the same place all the time. (66)
órbita geoestacionaria Órbita en la que un satélite orbita alrededor de la Tierra a la misma velocidad que rota la Tierra y que, por lo tanto, permanece en el mismo lugar todo el tiempo.

globular cluster A large, round, densely-packed grouping of older stars. (150)
cúmulo globular Conjunto grande y redondo de estrellas viejas densamente agrupadas.

greenhouse effect The trapping of heat near a planet's surface by certain gases in the planet's atmosphere. (98)
efecto invernadero Retención del calor irradiado por un planeta en su atmósfera ocasionada por ciertos gases atmosféricos.

gravity The attractive force between objects; the force that moves objects downhill. (19)
gravedad Propiedad de atracción entre los cuerpos; la fuerza que mueve un cuerpo hacia abajo.

H

heliocentric Term describing a model of the solar system in which Earth and the other planets revolve around the sun. (80)
heliocéntrico Término que describe un modelo del universo en el cual la Tierra y los otros planetas giran alrededor del Sol.

Hertzsprung-Russell diagram A graph relating the surface temperatures and absolute brightnesses of stars. (140)
diagrama Hertzsprung-Russell Gráfica que muestra la relación entre la temperatura de la superficie de una estrella y su magnitud absoluta.

Hubble's law The observation that the farther away a galaxy is, the faster it is moving away. (155)
ley de Hubble Observación que enuncia que mientras más lejos se encuentre una galaxia, se aleja con mayor rapidez.

I

inertia The tendency of an object to resist a change in motion. (20)
inercia Tendencia de un cuerpo de resistirse a cambios de movimiento.

irregular galaxy A galaxy that does not have a regular shape. (152)
galaxia irregular Galaxia que no tiene una forma regular.

K

Kuiper belt A region where many small objects orbit the sun and that stretches from beyond the orbit of Neptune to about 100 times Earth's distance from the sun. (111)
cinturón de Kuiper Región en la cual muchos cuerpos pequeños giran alrededor del Sol y que se extiende desde más allá de la órbita de Neptuno hasta aproximadamente cien veces la distancia entre la Tierra y el Sol.

L

law of universal gravitation The scientific law that states that every object in the universe attracts every other object. (19)
ley de gravitación universal Ley científica que establece que todos los cuerpos del universo se atraen entre sí.

light-year The distance that light travels in one year, about 9.5 million million kilometers. (134)
año luz Distancia a la que viaja la luz en un año; aproximadamente 9.5 millones de millones de kilómetros.

lunar eclipse The blocking of sunlight to the moon that occurs when Earth is directly between the sun and the moon. (26)
eclipse lunar Bloqueo de la luz solar que ilumina la Luna que ocurre cuando la Tierra se interpone entre el Sol y la Luna.

M

main sequence A diagonal area on an Hertzsprung-Russell diagram that includes more than 90 percent of all stars. (141)
secuencia principal Área diagonal en un diagrama de Hertzsprung-Russell que incluye más del 90 por ciento de todas las estrellas.

maria Dark, flat areas on the moon's surface formed from huge ancient lava flows. (33)
maria Áreas oscuras y llanas de la superficie lunar formadas por enormes flujos de lava antiguos.

mass The amount of matter in an object. (19)
masa Cantidad de materia que hay en un cuerpo.

meteor A streak of light in the sky produced by the burning of a meteoroid in Earth's atmosphere. (5,115)
meteoro Rayo de luz en el cielo producido por el incendio de un meteoroide en la atmósfera terrestre.

meteorite A meteoroid that passes through the atmosphere and hits Earth's surface. (115)
meteorito Meteoroide que pasa por la atmósfera y toca la superficie terrestre.

meteoroid A chunk of rock or dust in space, generally smaller than an asteroid. (33, 115)
meteoroide Un trozo de roca o polvo, generalmente más pequeño que un asteroide, que existe en el espacio.

microgravity The condition of experiencing weightlessness in orbit. (63)
microgravedad Manifestación de la falta de pesadez al estar en órbita.

N

neap tide The tide with the least difference between consecutive low and high tides. (30)
marea muerta Marea con la mínima diferencia entre las mareas altas y bajas consecutivas.

nebula A large cloud of gas and dust in space. (143)
nebulosa Gran nube de gas y polvo en el espacio.

neutron star The small, dense remains of a high-mass star after a supernova. (146)
estrella de neutrones Restos pequeños y densos de una estrella de gran masa tras ocurrir una supernova.

Newton's first law of motion The scientific law that states that an object at rest will stay at rest and an object in motion will stay in motion with a constant speed and direction unless acted on by a force. (20)
Primera ley de movimiento de Newton Ley científica que establece que un cuerpo en reposo se mantendrá en reposo y un cuerpo en movimiento se mantendrá en movimiento con una velocidad y dirección constantes a menos que se ejerza una fuerza sobre él.

nuclear fusion The process in which two atomic nuclei combine to form a larger nucleus, forming a heavier element and releasing huge amounts of energy; the process by which energy is produced in stars. (89)
fusión nuclear Unión de dos núcleos atómicos que produce un elemento con una mayor masa atómica y que libera una gran cantidad de energía; el proceso mediante el cual las estrellas producen energía.

nucleus 1. In cells, a large oval organelle that contains the cell's genetic material in the form of DNA and controls many of the cell's activities. 2. The central core of an atom which contains protons and neutrons. 3. The solid inner core of a comet. (113)
núcleo 1. Orgánulo ovalado de una célula que contiene el material genético en forma de ADN y controla las distintas funciones celulares. 2. Parte central de un átomo que contiene los protones y los neutrones. 3. Centro denso e interior de un cometa.

O

observatory A building that contains one or more telescopes. (130)
observatorio Edificio que contiene uno o más telescopios.

Oort cloud A spherical region of comets that surrounds the solar system. (111)
nube de Oort Región esférica de cometas que rodea al sistema solar.

open cluster A star cluster that has a loose, disorganized appearance and contains no more than a few thousand stars. (150)
cúmulo abierto Cúmulo de estrellas que tiene una apariencia no compacta y desorganizada, y que no contiene más de unas pocos miles de estrellas.

optical telescope A telescope that uses lenses or mirrors to collect and focus visible light. (128)
telescopio óptico Telescopio que usa lentes o espejos para captar y enfocar la luz visible.

orbit The path of an object as it revolves around another object in space. (12)
órbita Trayectoria de un cuerpo a medida que gira alrededor de otro en el espacio.

orbital velocity The velocity a rocket must achieve to establish an orbit around a body in space. (49)
velocidad orbital Velocidad que un cohete debe alcanzar para establecer una órbita alrededor de un cuerpo en el espacio.

P

parallax The apparent change in position of an object when seen from different places. (132)
paralaje Cambio aparente en la posición de un cuerpo cuando es visto desde distintos lugares.

penumbra The part of a shadow surrounding the darkest part. (25)
penumbra Parte de la sombra que rodea su parte más oscura.

phase One of the different apparent shapes of the moon as seen from Earth. (22)
fase Una de las distintas formas aparentes de la Luna vistas desde la Tierra.

photosphere The inner layer of the sun's atmosphere that gives off its visible light; the sun's surface. (90)
fotósfera Capa más interna de la atmósfera solar que provoca la luz que vemos; superficie del Sol.

planet An object that orbits a star, is large enough to have become rounded by its own gravity, and has cleared the area of its orbit. (5, 84)
planeta Cuerpo que orbita alrededor de una estrella, que tiene suficiente masa como para permitir que su propia gravedad le dé una forma casi redonda, y que además ha despejado las proximidades de su órbita.

planetesimal One of the small asteroid-like bodies that formed the building blocks of the planets. (86)
planetesimal Uno de los cuerpos pequeños parecidos a asteroides que dieron origen a los planetas.

prominence A huge, reddish loop of gas that protrudes from the sun's surface, linking parts of sunspot regions. (92)
prominencia Enorme burbuja de gas rojiza que sobresale de la superfice solar, y conecta partes de las manchas solares.

protostar A contracting cloud of gas and dust with enough mass to form a star. (143)
protoestrella Nube de gas y polvo que se contrae, con suficiente masa como para formar una estrella.

pulsar A rapidly spinning neutron star that produces radio waves. (146)
pulsar Estrella de neutrones que gira rápidamente y produce ondas de radio.

Q

quasar An enormously bright, distant galaxy with a giant black hole at its center. (152)
quásar Galaxia extraordinariamente luminosa y distante con un agujero negro gigante en el centro.

R

radiation zone A region of very tightly packed gas in the sun's interior where energy is transferred mainly in the form of electromagnetic radiation. (89)
zona radioactiva Región al interior del Sol de gases densamente acumulados y donde se transmite energía principalmente en la forma de radiación electromagnética.

radio telescope A device used to detect radio waves from objects in space. (130)
radiotelescopio Aparato usado para detectar ondas de radio de los cuerpos en el espacio.

reflecting telescope A telescope that uses a curved mirror to collect and focus light. (128)
telescopio de reflexión Telescopio que usa un espejo curvado para captar y enfocar la luz.

refracting telescope A telescope that uses convex lenses to gather and focus light. (128)
telescopio de refracción Telescopio que usa lentes convexas para captar y enfocar la luz.

remote sensing The collection of information about Earth and other objects in space using satellites or probes. (66)
percepción remota Recolección de información sobre la Tierra y otros cuerpos del espacio usando satélites o sondas.

revolution The movement of an object around another object. (12)
revolución Movimiento de un cuerpo alrededor de otro.

ring A thin disk of small ice and rock particles surrounding a planet. (103)
anillo Disco fino de pequeñas partículas de hielo y roca que rodea un planeta.

rocket A device that expels gas in one direction to move in the opposite direction. (46)
cohete Aparato que expulsa gases en una dirección para moverse en la dirección opuesta.

rotation The spinning motion of a planet on its axis. (11)
rotación Movimiento giratorio de un planeta sobre su eje.

rover A small robotic space probe that can move about the surface of a planet or moon. (59)
rover Pequeña sonda espacial robótica que puede desplazarse sobre la superficie de un planeta o sobre la Luna.

S

satellite An object that orbits a planet. (5, 53)
satélite Cuerpo que orbita alrededor de un planeta.

scientific notation A mathematical method of writing numbers using powers of ten. (134)
notación científica Método matemático de escritura de números que usa la potencia de diez.

solar eclipse The blocking of sunlight to Earth that occurs when the moon is directly between the sun and Earth. (25)
eclipse solar Bloqueo de la luz solar que ilumina la Tierra que ocurre cuando la Luna se interpone entre el Sol y la Tierra.

solar flare An eruption of gas from the sun's surface that occurs when the loops in sunspot regions suddenly connect. (92)
destello solar Erupción de los gases de la superficie solar que ocurre cuando las burbujas de las manchas solares se conectan repentinamente.

solar system The system consisting of the sun and the planets and other objects that revolve around it. (83)
sistema solar Sistema formado por el Sol, los planetas y otros cuerpos que giran alrededor de él.

solar wind A stream of electrically charged particles that emanate from the sun's corona. (91)
viento solar Flujo de partículas cargadas que emanan de la corona del Sol.

solstice Either of the two days of the year on which the sun reaches its greatest distance north or south of the equator. (16)
solsticio Uno de los dos días del año en el que el Sol alcanza la mayor distancia al norte o al sur del ecuador.

space probe A spacecraft that has various scientific instruments that can collect data, including visual images, but has no human crew. (59)
sonda espacial Nave espacial que tiene varios instrumentos científicos que pueden reunir datos e imágenes, pero que no tiene una tripulación.

space shuttle A spacecraft that can carry a crew into space, return to Earth, and then be reused for the same purpose. (57)
transbordador espacial Nave espacial que puede llevar a una tripulación al espacio, volver a la Tierra, y luego volver a ser usada para el mismo propósito.

space spinoff An item that has uses on Earth but was originally developed for use in space. (64)
derivación espacial Objeto que se puede usar en la Tierra, pero que originalmente se construyó para ser usado en el espacio.

space station A large artificial satellite on which people can live and work for long periods. (58)
estación espacial Enorme satélite artificial en el que la gente puede vivir y trabajar durante largos períodos.

spectrograph An instrument that separates light into colors and makes an image of the resulting spectrum. (138)
espectrógrafo Instrumento que separa la luz en colores y crea una imagen del espectro resultante.

spectrum The range of wavelengths of electromagnetic waves. (127)
espectro Gama de las longitudes de ondas electromagnéticas.

spiral galaxy A galaxy with a bulge in the middle and arms that spiral outward in a pinwheel pattern. (152)
galaxia espiral Galaxia con una protuberancia en el centro y brazos que giran en espiral hacia el exterior, como un remolino.

spring tide The tide with the greatest difference between consecutive low and high tides. (30)
marea viva Marea con la mayor diferencia entre las mareas altas y bajas consecutivas.

star A ball of hot gas, primarily hydrogen and helium, that undergoes nuclear fusion. (5)
estrella Bola de gases calientes, principalmente hidrógeno y helio, en cuyo interior se produce una fusión nuclear.

sunspot A dark area of gas on the sun's surface that is cooler than surrounding gases. (92)
mancha solar Área gaseosa oscura de la superficie solar, que es más fría que los gases que la rodean.

supernova The brilliant explosion of a dying supergiant star. (145)
supernova Explosión brillante de una estrella supergigante en extinción.

T

telescope An optical instrument that forms enlarged images of distant objects. (128)
telescopio Instrumento óptico que provee ampliaciones de los cuerpos lejanos.

terrestrial planets The name often given to the four inner planets: Mercury, Venus, Earth, and Mars. (95)
planetas telúricos Nombre dado normalmente a los cuatro planetas interiores: Mercurio, Venus, Tierra y Marte.

thrust The reaction force that propels a rocket forward. (48)
empuje Fuerza de reacción que propulsa un cohete hacia delante.

tide The periodic rise and fall of the level of water in the ocean. (29)
marea La subida y bajada periódica del nivel de agua del océano.

GLOSSARY

---------- **U** ----------

umbra The darkest part of a shadow. (25)
  umbra La parte más oscura de una sombra.

universe All of space and everything in it. (134)
  universo Todo el espacio y todo lo que hay en él.

---------- **V** ----------

vacuum A place that is empty of all matter. (63)
  vacío Lugar en donde no existe materia.

velocity Speed in a given direction. (48)
  velocidad Rapidez en una dirección dada.

visible light Electromagnetic radiation that can be seen with the unaided eye. (126)
  luz visible Radiación electromagnética que se puede ver a simple vista.

---------- **W** ----------

wavelength The distance between the crest of one wave and the crest of the next wave. (127)
  longitud de onda Distancia entre la cresta de una onda y la cresta de la siguiente onda.

weight A measure of the force of gravity on an object. (19)
  peso Medida de la fuerza de gravedad sobre un cuerpo.

white dwarf The blue-white hot core of a star that is left behind after its outer layers have expanded and drifted out into space. (145)
  enana blanca Núcleo caliente y azul blanquecino de una estrella que queda después de que sus capas externas se han expandido y esparcido por el espacio.

INDEX

Page numbers for key terms are printed in **boldface** type.

outer, 86, 102–108
  Jupiter, 85, 102–105
  Neptune, 85, 102–103, 109
  Saturn, 85, 102–103,
  106–107
  Uranus, 85, 102–103, 108
in star systems, 150
Pluto, 61, 84, 112, 121
Plutoids, 112
Process Skills. *See* Science Inquiry
  Skills; Science Literacy Skills
Prominences, solar, 92
Protostar, 143
Ptolemy, 79, 81
Pulsars, 146

—————— **Q** ——————

Quasars, 152

—————— **R** ——————

Radiation
  cosmic background, 155
  electromagnetic, 126, 127
Radiation zone, solar, 89
Radio telescope, 130
Reading Skills
  reading/thinking support
  strategies
    apply concepts, 12, 16, 69,
    83, 89, 98, 113, 117, 139,
    151, 159
    define, 17, 65, 93, 151, 157
    describe, 51, 56, 58, 109, 157
    estimate, 103
    explain, 9, 13, 27, 37, 38, 49,
    87, 93, 117, 135, 141, 144,
    145
    identify, 13, 21, 56, 147
    interpret data, 31, 49, 84, 91,
    95, 138
    interpret diagrams, 6, 11, 24,
    29, 38, 49, 57, 118, 140, 141,
    156, 157, 159
    interpret photos, 109, 150
    list, 35, 67, 91, 153
    make generalizations, 9, 15,
    21, 38, 54, 69, 70, 85, 93,
    107
    make judgments, 61, 106,
    109, 112
    mark text, 8, 14, 29, 66, 83,
    89, 137, 155
    name, 101, 149

read graphs, 21, 70
review, 31, 81, 115, 135, 141,
  144, 153
solve problems, 35, 96
target reading skills
  ask questions, 20, 59, 128,
  130
  compare and contrast, 19,
  34, 35, 37, 58, 65, 69, 91, 98,
  108, 115, 117, 118, 129, 145,
  160
  identify supporting evidence,
  83, 155
  identify the main idea, 8, 66,
  137
  outline, 104
  relate cause and effect, 17,
  29, 31, 37, 38, 69, 92, 93,
  101, 115, 117, 149, 159
  relate text and visuals, 25,
  26, 33, 50, 53, 90, 99, 105,
  111, 146, 152
  sequence, 11, 12, 80, 85, 86,
  131, 159
  summarize, 55, 61, 65, 113,
  134, 143, 144, 157
Reflecting telescope, 128
Refracting telescope, 128
Remote sensing by satellites, 66
Revolution of earth, 12
Rings, 103
  of Saturn, 74–75, 107
Rocket, 46
Rocket science, 46–51
  components of, 48–49
  history of, 46–47
  multistage rockets, 50–51
Rotation of earth, 11
Rovers (space probe), 59, 120

—————— **S** ——————

Satellites
  artificial, **53**
  natural, **5**
Saturn, 74–75, 85, 102–103,
  106–107
Science Inquiry Skills
  basic process skills
    calculate, 17, 83, 104, 134,
    135, 153
    classify, 69, 70, 92, 114, 153
    communicate, 4, 32, 52, 62,
    88, 101, 102, 110, 126, 132,
    136, 142, 148, 154
    design solutions, 100
    infer, 13, 14, 17, 23, 26, 30,
    37, 67, 97, 127

make models, 24, 60, 80, 155
observe, 5, 31, 133
predict, 8, 9, 17, 20, 37, 115,
  118, 131, 144, 146, 147
Science Literacy Skills
  integrated process skills
    demonstrate consumer
    literacy, 67
    develop hypotheses, 35, 42,
    74, 106, 122, xxii
    draw conclusions, 21, 56, 63,
    64, 137, 159
    evaluate the design, 130
    identify faulty reasoning, 131
    pose questions, 109
    relate evidence and explain,
    81
Science Matters. *See* Application
  of skills
Scientific notation, 134–135
Seasonal changes
  causes of, 10, 14–16
  and constellations, 8
  solstices and equinoxes, 16
  tides, 30–31
Solar eclipse, 25, 91
Solar flares, 92
Solar system, 83
  areas of, 111
  asteroids, 114
  comets, 113
  dwarf planets, 112
  elements, 83–85
  formation, 86
  geocentric and heliocentric
  models, 79–81
  inner planets, 82, 95–101
  meteoroids, 115
  in Milky Way, 153
  outer planets, 102–109
  sun, 83, 88–93
  See also Sun
Solar wind, 91, 93
Solstice, 16
Space exploration
  astronauts, 54–55, 62, 73
  conditions in space, 62–63, 73,
  82
  discoveries, 52, 56, 66, 73, 120
  history of, 46–47, 52–59, 62, 72
  measuring astronomical
  distances, 83, 122–123, 132–135
  from rockets, 46–50
  space-related technology, 42,
  46, 64–66, 72
  star classification, 137–141
  star life cycle, 142–147
  star systems and galaxies,
  148–157

INDEX

Page numbers for key terms are printed in **boldface** type.

ACKNOWLEDGMENTS

Staff Credits

The people who made up the *Interactive Science* team—representing composition services, core design digital and multimedia production services, digital product development, editorial, editorial services, manufacturing, and production—are listed below.

Jan Van Aarsen, Samah Abadir, Ernie Albanese, Zareh MacPherson Artinian, Bridget Binstock, Suzanne Biron, MJ Black, Nancy Bolsover, Stacy Boyd, Jim Brady, Katherine Bryant, Michael Burstein, Pradeep Byram, Jessica Chase, Jonathan Cheney, Arthur Ciccone, Allison Cook-Bellistri, Rebecca Cottingham, AnnMarie Coyne, Bob Craton, Chris Deliee, Paul Delsignore, Michael Di Maria, Diane Dougherty, Kristen Ellis, Theresa Eugenio, Amanda Ferguson, Jorgensen Fernandez, Kathryn Fobert, Julia Gecha, Mark Geyer, Steve Gobbell, Paula Gogan-Porter, Jeffrey Gong, Sandra Graff, Adam Groffman, Lynette Haggard, Christian Henry, Karen Holtzman, Susan Hutchinson, Sharon Inglis, Marian Jones, Sumy Joy, Sheila Kanitsch, Courtenay Kelley, Chris Kennedy, Toby Klang, Greg Lam, Russ Lappa, Margaret LaRaia, Ben Leveillee, Thea Limpus, Dotti Marshall, Kathy Martin, Robyn Matzke, John McClure, Mary Beth McDaniel, Krista McDonald, Tim McDonald, Rich McMahon, Cara McNally, Melinda Medina, Angelina Mendez, Maria Milczarek, Claudi Mimo, Mike Napieralski, Deborah Nicholls, Dave Nichols, William Oppenheimer, Jodi O'Rourke, Ameer Padshah, Lorie Park, Celio Pedrosa, Jonathan Penyack, Linda Zust Reddy, Jennifer Reichlin, Stephen Rider, Charlene Rimsa, Stephanie Rogers, Marcy Rose, Rashid Ross, Anne Rowsey, Logan Schmidt, Amanda Seldera, Laurel Smith, Nancy Smith, Ted Smykal, Emily Soltanoff, Cindy Strowman, Dee Sunday, Barry Tomack, Patricia Valencia, Ana Sofia Villaveces, Stephanie Wallace, Christine Whitney, Brad Wiatr, Heidi Wilson, Heather Wright, Rachel Youdelman

Photography

All uncredited photos copyright © 2011 Pearson Education.

Cover, Front and Back
NASA

Front Matter
Page vi, Tom Fox/Dallas Morning News/Corbis; **vii,** Corbis; **viii,** ESA/J. Clarke (Boston University)/Z. Levay (STScI)/NASA; **ix,** ESA/HEIC/Hubble Heritage Team (STScI/AURA)/NASA; **xi laptop,** iStockphoto.com; **xiii br,** JupiterImages/Getty Images; **xvi laptop,** iStockphoto.com; **xx bkgrnd,** NASA; **xx earth,** Apollo 17 Crew/NASA; **xxi l,** NASA Marshall Space Flight Center Collection; **xxi r,** ESA/CXC/JPL-CalTech/NASA.

Chapter 1
Page 1 spread, Tom Fox/Dallas Morning News/Corbis; **3 b,** Space Frontiers/Getty; **3 full moon,** John W. Bova/Photo Researchers, Inc.; **3 quarter moon,** John W. Bova/Photo Researchers, Inc.; **3 crescent moon,** John W. Bova/Photo Researchers, Inc.; **4** Sheila Terry/Science Source; **5 bkgrnd,** UVimages/Amana Images/Corbis; **5 l inset,** NASA; **5 m inset,** NASA; **5 r,** T. Rector (University of Alaska Anchorage), Z. Levay and L. Frattare (Space Telescope Science Institute) and National Optical Astronomy Observatory/Association of Universities for Research in Astronomy/National Science Foundation/Solar System Exploration/NASA; **8 bkgrnd,** Ted Spiegel/Corbis; **9,** Frank Zullo/Photo Researchers, Inc.; **10 t,** Robert Harding Picture Library Ltd/Alamy; **10 b,** John White Photos/Alamy; **13 tl,** Werner Forman/UIG/Getty Images; **13 tr,** Dea/A. Dagli Orti/Getty Images; **13 mr,** SSPL/Getty Images; **17,** Gavin Hellier/Photolibrary Group; **18–19 spread,** Blend Images/Alamy; **22 moon series,** Jeff Vanuga/Corbis; **22,** UV Images/Amana Images/Corbis; **24 l,** Eckhard Slawik/Photo Researchers, Inc.; **24 ml,** John W. Bova/Photo Researchers, Inc.; **24 m** John W. Bova/Photo Researchers, Inc.; **24 mr;** John W. Bova/Photo Researchers, Inc.; **24 r,** John W. Bova/Photo Researchers, Inc.; **25,** Space Frontiers/Getty; **26 lunar eclipse;** Fred Espenak/Photo Researchers, Inc.; **28 l and r,** Michael P. Gadomski/Science Source; **31,** Klaus Lang/All Canada Photos/Alamy; **32 m,** Omikron/Photo Researchers, Inc.; **32–33 spread,** JPL/USGS/NASA; **34 earth in chart,** NASA Langley Research Center; **34 moon in chart,** JPL/USGS/NASA; **34–35 spread,** Apollo 11 Image Library/NASA; **36 br,** Omikron/Photo Researchers, Inc.

Interchapter Feature
Page 40 ml, Andy Crawford/University Museum of Archaeology and Anthropology, Cambridge/Dorling Kindersley; **40 tl,** iStockphoto.com; **40 bl,** iStockphoto.com; **41 bl,** NASA; **41 bkgrnd,** NASA.

Chapter 2
Pages 42–43 spread, Donald Miralle/Getty Images; **45 c1,** NASA/AP Images; **45 c2,** NASA; **45 b,** StockLite/Shutterstock; **46,** Yesikka Vivancos/epa/Corbis; **47,** U.S. Civil Air Patrol/NASA; **49,** Mark Scheuern/Alamy; **52,** David Seal/NASA; **53 t,** NASA/Science Photo Library, **53 cr,** NASA, **53 cl,** Ria Novosti/Science Photo Library; **53 br,** Detlev van Ravenswaay/Science Photo Library; **53 bl,** Sovfoto/Eastfoto; **54 bl,** Hulton Archive/Getty Images; **54 tl,** RGB Ventures LLC dba SuperStock/Alamy; **54–55 footprints,** NASA; **55 b,** Corbis; **54–55 bkgrnd,** NASA; **55 tl,** Science Source; **56,** John Frassanito & Associates; **60 t,** NASA/Johns Hopkins University Applied Physics Laboratory/Southwest Research Institute/Photo Researchers, Inc.; **60 b,** Roger Arno/NASA; **61 b,** JPL/NASA; **61 tr,** David Ducros/Science Photo Library/Photo Researchers, Inc.; **62,** NASA/Science Photo Library; **63,** UPI Photo/NASA; **64 tl,** William King/Getty Images; **64 girl with cell phone,** Mark Andersen/Rubberball; **64 satellite,** Mark Evans/iStockphoto.com; **64 astronaut,** AP Photo/NASA; **64 shoes,** iStockphoto.com; **65 tr,** Terry Vine/Getty Images; **65 headphones,** StockLite/Shutterstock; **65 m,** Mehau Kulyk/Photo Researchers, Inc.; **65 shoes,** NASA Human Spaceflight Collection; **66 inset,** Joe Raedle/Getty Images; **66 b,** Kodiak Greenwood/The Image Bank/Getty Images; **67 inset b,** Steven Puetzer/Getty Images; **67 b,** Robert Nickelsberg/Getty Images; **67 2nd from top,** Colin Anderson/Blend Images/Corbis; **67 t,** John Tomaselli/Alamy; **68 t,** Mark Scheuern/Alamy; **68 m,** Roger Arno/NASA; **68 b,** Robert Nickelsberg/Getty Images.